S
M
I
STRATEGIC MISSION INTERFACE

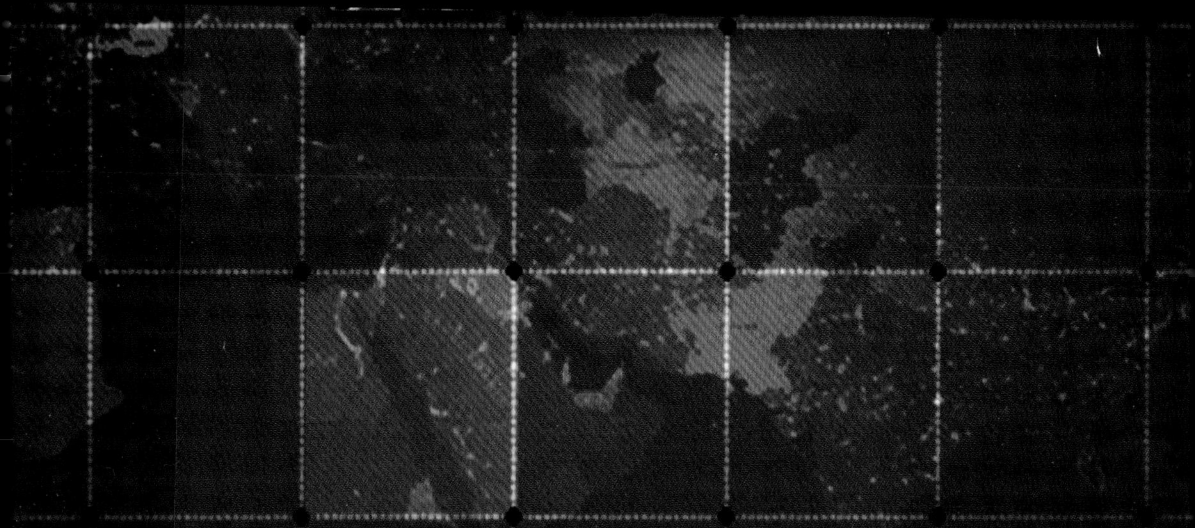

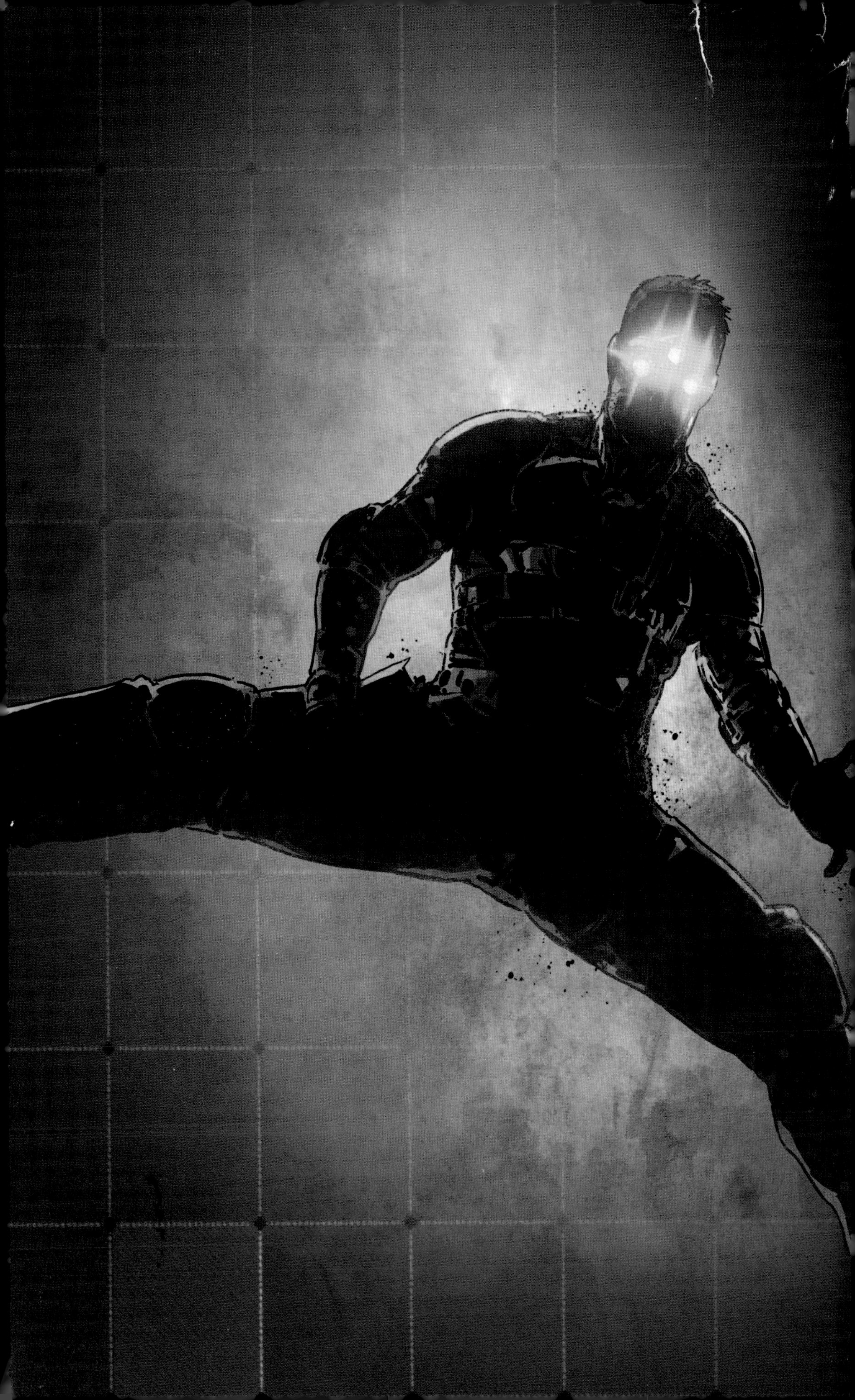

WRITTEN BY
NATHAN EDMONDSON

DRAWN BY
MARC LAMING

ADDITIONAL INKS BY
DAVE STOKES ∴ MICHEL LACOMBE ∴ SALGOOD SAM

COLOURED BY
IAN HERRING

DIRECTED BY
SERGE LAPOINTE

CREATIVE DIRECTOR
MAXIME BELAND

GAME DIRECTOR
PATRICK REDDING

ART DIRECTOR
SCOTT LEE

CENTRAL CLANCY WRITER
RICHARD DANSKY

EXECUTIVE PRODUCER
JADE RAYMOND

PRODUCER
CHRISTOPHE MARTIN

COVER ARTIST
MARC LAMING

COLLECTION DESIGNER
KATIE HIDALGO

DYNAMITE

Nick Barrucci, CEO / Publisher
Juan Collado, President / COO
Rich Young, Director Business Development
Keith Davidsen, Marketing Manager

Joe Rybandt, Senior Editor
Hannah Elder, Associate Editor
Josh Green, Traffic Coordinator
Molly Mahan, Associate Editor

Josh Johnson, Art Director
Jason Ullmeyer, Senior Graphic Designer
Katie Hidalgo, Graphic Designer
Chris Caniano, Production Assistant

Visit us online at www.DYNAMITE.com
Follow us on Twitter @dynamitecomics
Like us on Facebook /Dynamitecomics
Watch us on YouTube /Dynamitecomics

ISBN-10: 1-60690-527-9 ISBN-13: 978-1-60690-527-2 First Printing 10 9 8 7 6 5 4 3 2 1

TOM CLANCY'S SPLINTER CELL: ECHOES, VOL. 1. This volume collects material originally published in Tom Clancy's Splinter Cell: Echoes #1-4. Published by Dynamite Entertainment. 113 Gaither Dr., STE 205, Mt. Laurel, NJ 08054.

For information regarding press, media rights, foreign rights, licensing, promotions, and advertising e-mail: marketing@dynamite.com

BY

MAXIME BELAND • CREATIVE DIRECTOR
PATRICK REDDING • GAME DIRECTOR
SCOTT LEE • ART DIRECTOR
RICHARD DANSKY • CENTRAL CLANCY WRITER

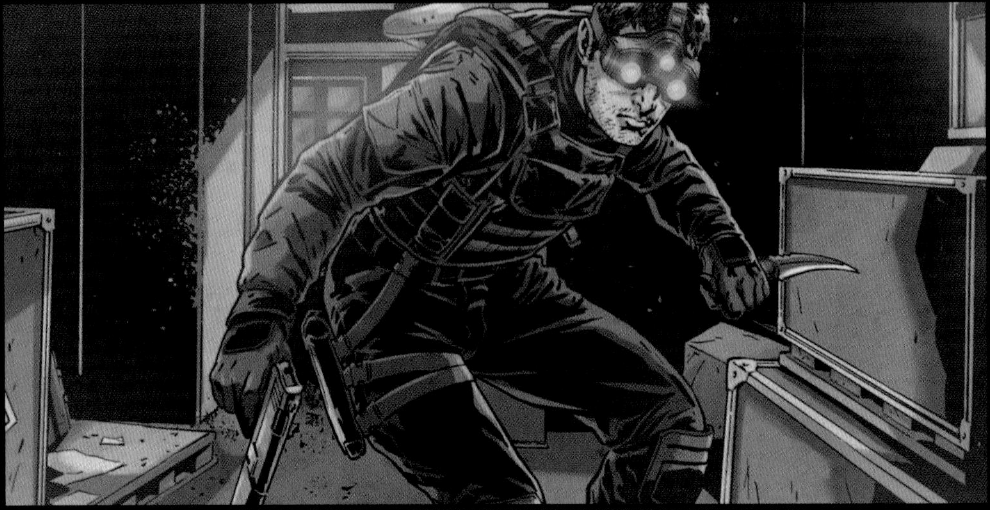

Different media tell different stories in different ways. It's a truth that we're constantly rediscovering every time a favorite comic book gets turned into a movie, every time there's a new Star Wars novel or episode of the Walking Dead game. The techniques of storytelling, and the tools that storytellers use, differ radically from medium to medium. Word balloons or lengthy descriptions, static images in frames or raw text or full motion capture animation – each of these offers different limitations, different choices and, best of all, different opportunities.

Too often, attempts to cross media fail to recognize this. We've all seen flat movie novelizations, or video game movies that replicated nothing from their source material but the carnage. But we've also seen marvelous successes, and those are inspirational. The best fictional worlds, the ones that really have lives of their own, can support stories across these media. They can inspire creators to use the tools they have, and to create works that are simultaneously of that world and yet completely unique. And once you see that happen for another fictional world, you look around and say "Why not ours?"

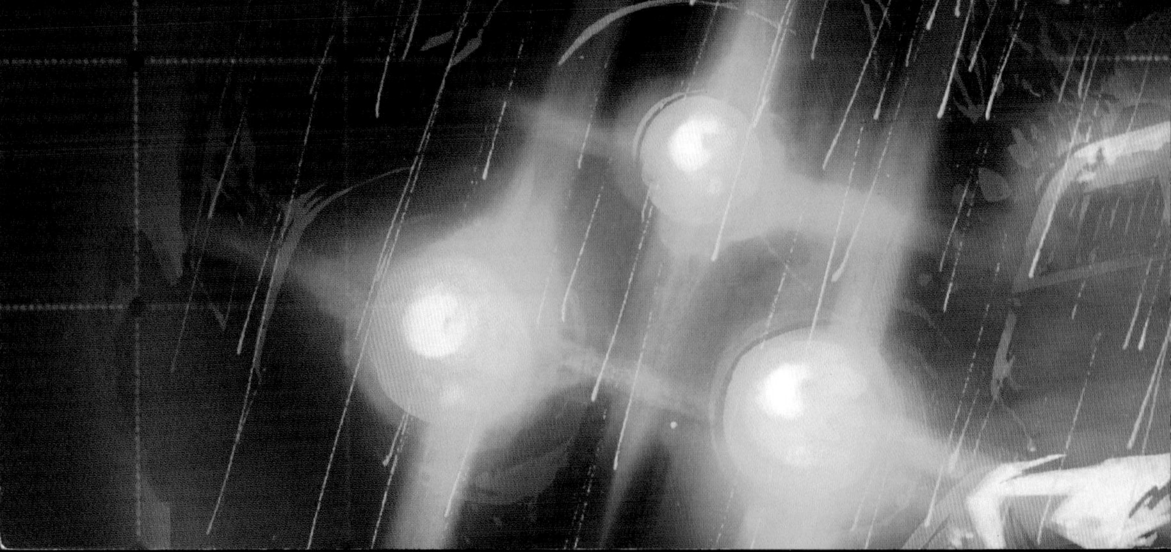

Of course, if you want someone from another medium to run with your work, you always have a "dream team" of people you want taking the shot. And with The Activity – a masterful comic with an army of fans on the SC development team – Nathan and Marc were at the top of our list. The opportunity to have their take on our world was a thrilling one, but also nerve-wracking. Would they be interested? Could Splinter Cell inspire them in their medium the way it inspires us in ours? We didn't know, but we knew we wanted to find out.

And then the magic happened. They set themselves down in the timeframe between Conviction and Blacklist and conjured up something special, a story that was indubitably a great comics story and just as much a part of our world as the games are. They understood what we were trying to do, and made it their own. Splinter Cell: Echoes is

to see two masters of their craft offer their take on something we – and many, many other people – have worked hard on over the years. Lucky enough to see Splinter Cell in a whole new way.

Now it's your turn. Enjoy.

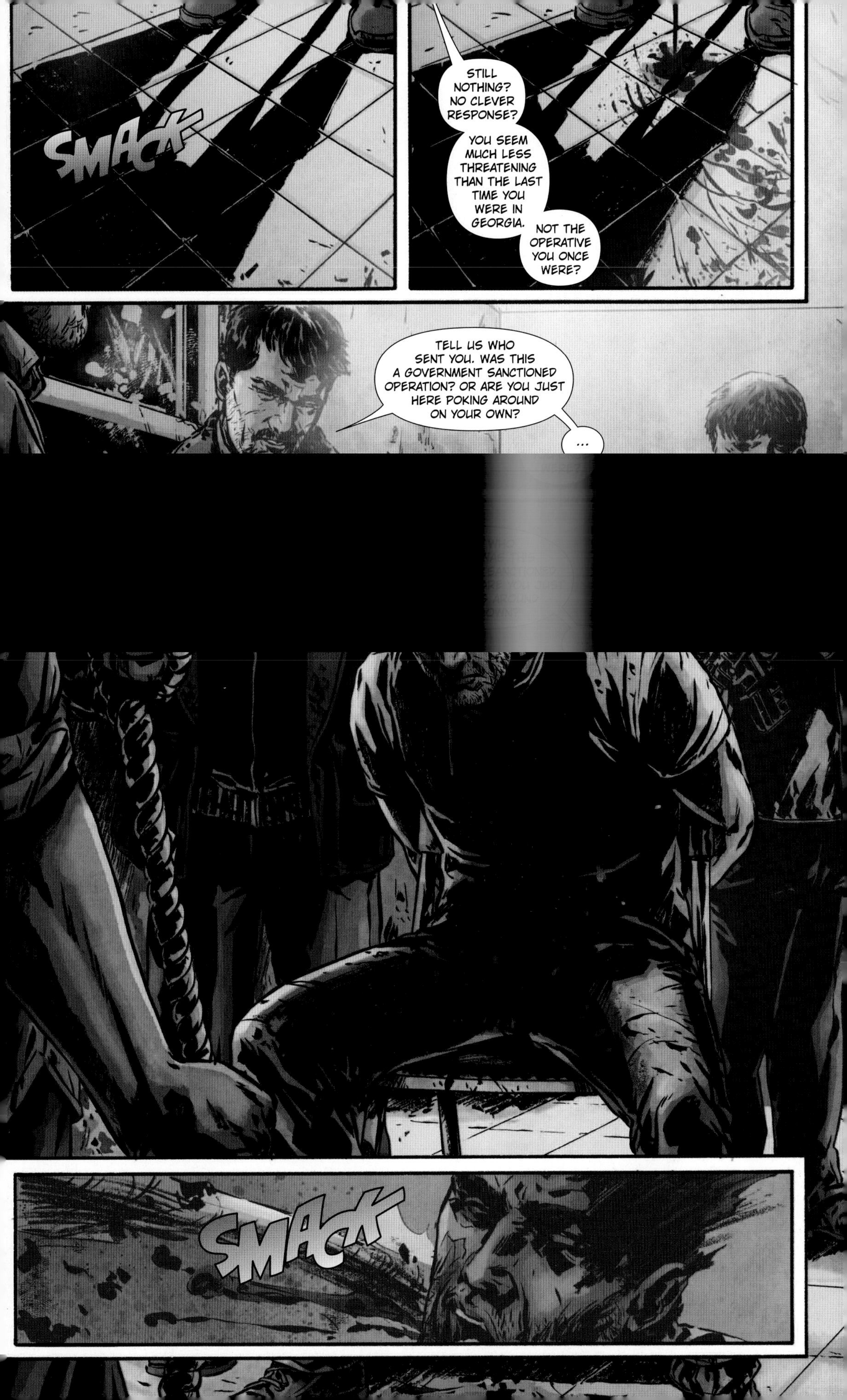
SMACK
STILL NOTHING? NO CLEVER RESPONSE?
YOU SEEM MUCH LESS THREATENING THAN THE LAST TIME YOU WERE IN GEORGIA.
NOT THE OPERATIVE YOU ONCE WERE?
TELL US WHO SENT YOU. WAS THIS A GOVERNMENT SANCTIONED OPERATION? OR ARE YOU JUST HERE POKING AROUND ON YOUR OWN?
...
SMACK

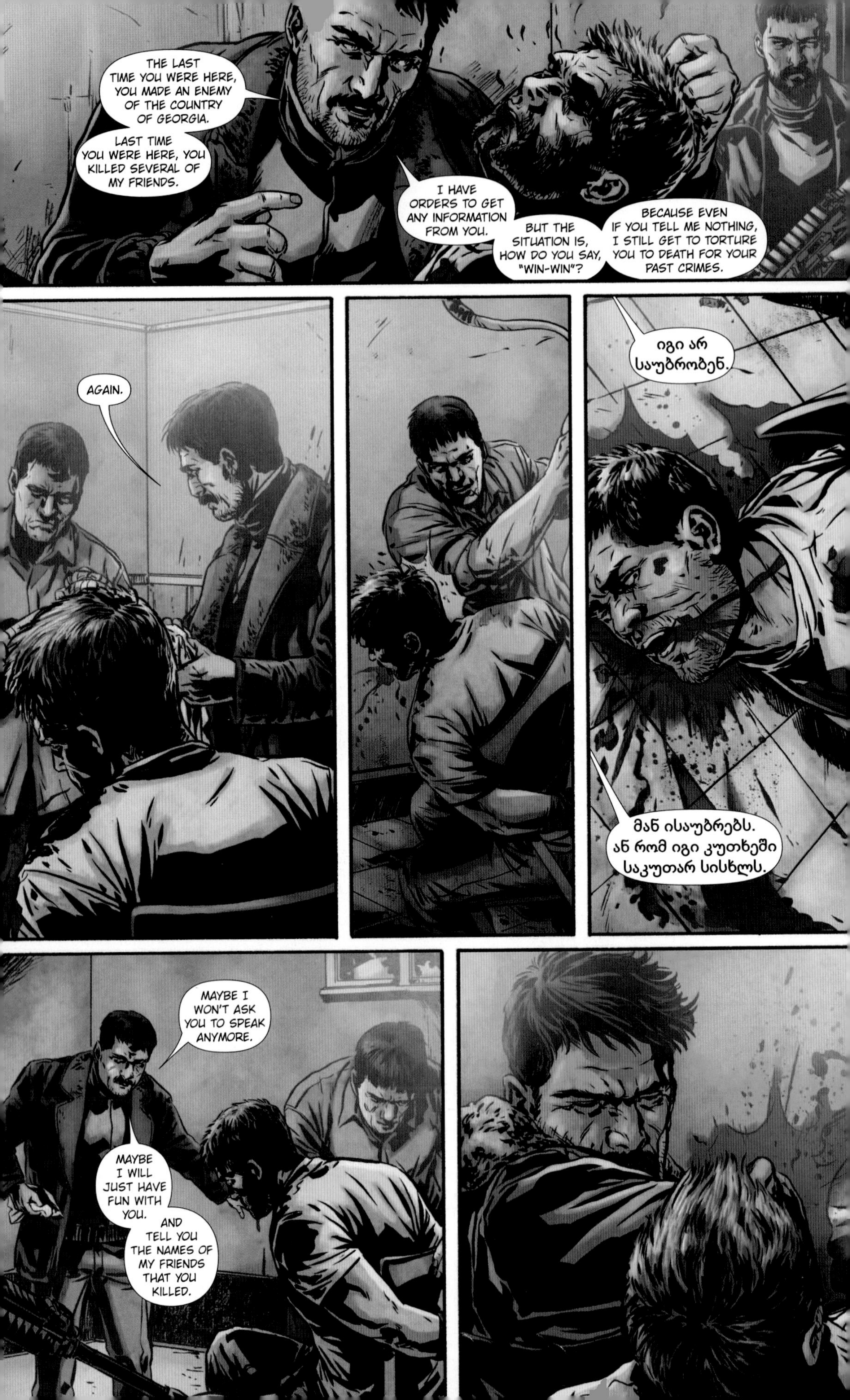
THE LAST TIME YOU WERE HERE, YOU MADE AN ENEMY OF THE COUNTRY OF GEORGIA.
LAST TIME YOU WERE HERE, YOU KILLED SEVERAL OF MY FRIENDS.
I HAVE ORDERS TO GET ANY INFORMATION FROM YOU.
BUT THE SITUATION IS, HOW DO YOU SAY, "WIN-WIN"?
BECAUSE EVEN IF YOU TELL ME NOTHING, I STILL GET TO TORTURE YOU TO DEATH FOR YOUR PAST CRIMES.
AGAIN.
იგი არ საუბრობენ.
მან ისაუბრებს. ან რომ იგი კუთხეში საკუთარ სისხლს.
MAYBE I WON'T ASK YOU TO SPEAK ANYMORE.
MAYBE I WILL JUST HAVE FUN WITH YOU.
AND TELL YOU THE NAMES OF MY FRIENDS THAT YOU KILLED.

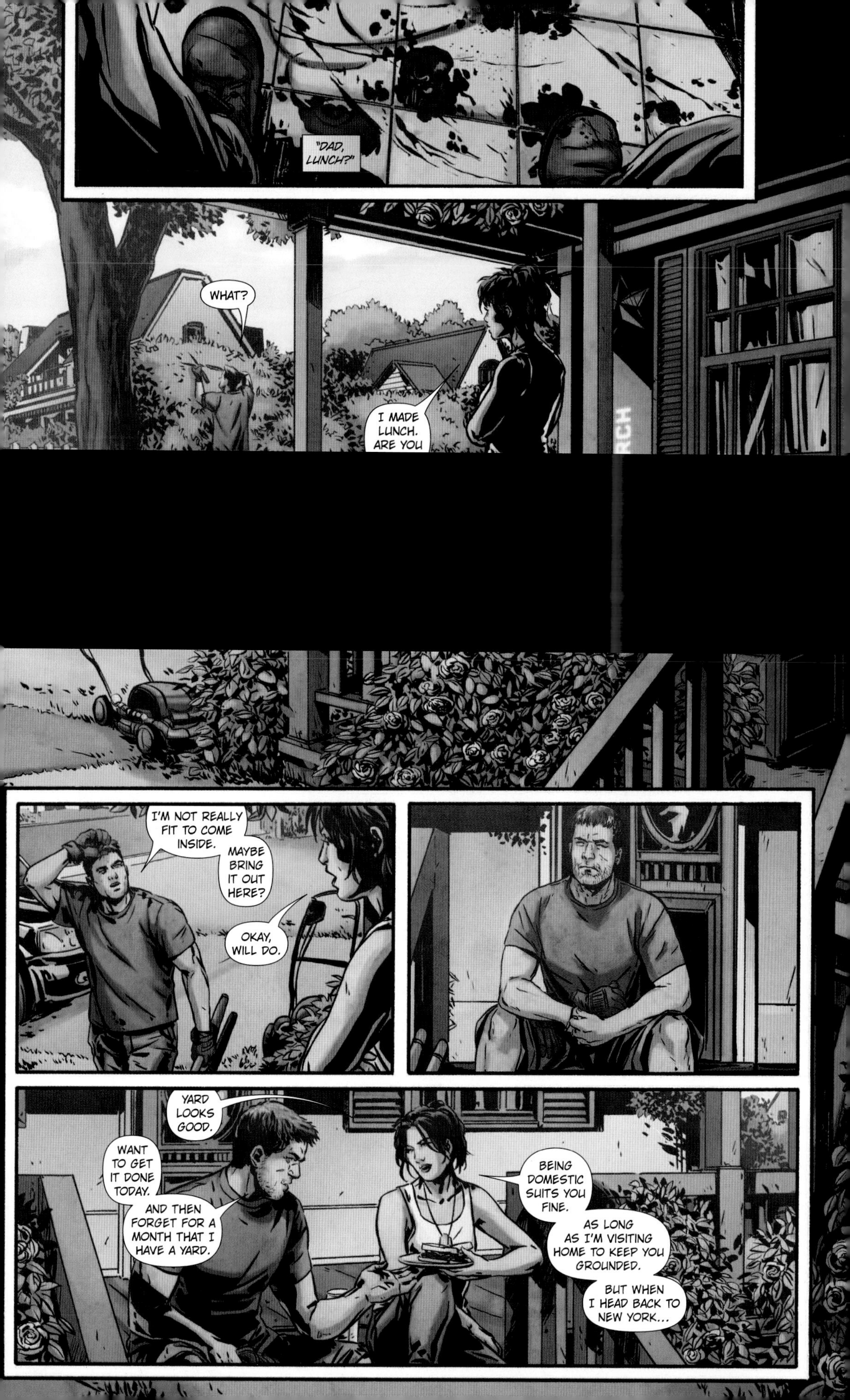
"DAD, LUNCH?"
WHAT?
I MADE LUNCH. ARE YOU [redacted]
I'M NOT REALLY FIT TO COME INSIDE.
MAYBE BRING IT OUT HERE?
OKAY, WILL DO.
YARD LOOKS GOOD.
WANT TO GET IT DONE TODAY.
AND THEN FORGET FOR A MONTH THAT I HAVE A YARD.
BEING DOMESTIC SUITS YOU FINE.
AS LONG AS I'M VISITING HOME TO KEEP YOU GROUNDED.
BUT WHEN I HEAD BACK TO NEW YORK...

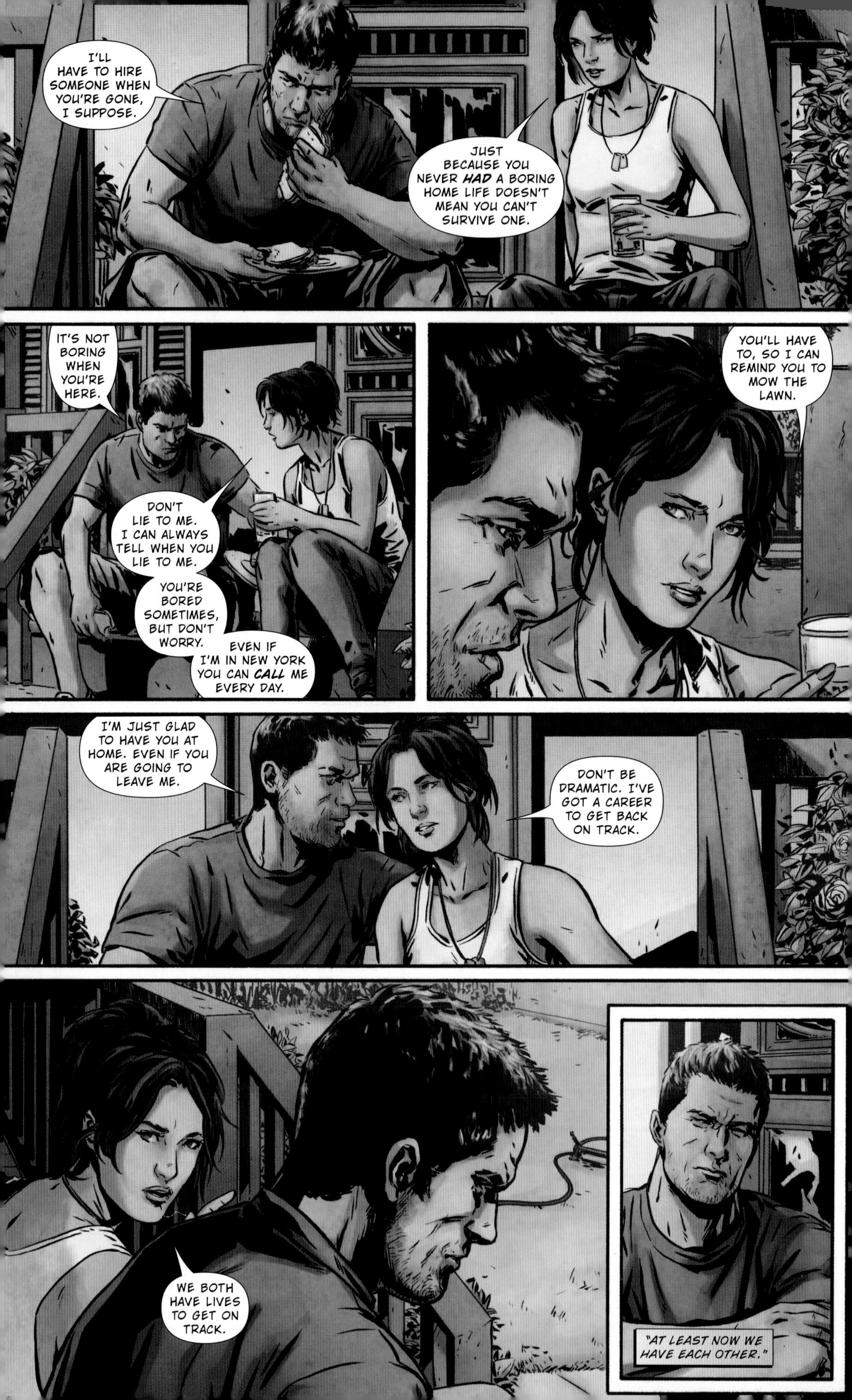
I'LL HAVE TO HIRE SOMEONE WHEN YOU'RE GONE, I SUPPOSE.
JUST BECAUSE YOU NEVER HAD A BORING HOME LIFE DOESN'T MEAN YOU CAN'T SURVIVE ONE.
IT'S NOT BORING WHEN YOU'RE HERE.
DON'T LIE TO ME. I CAN ALWAYS TELL WHEN YOU LIE TO ME.
YOU'RE BORED SOMETIMES, BUT DON'T WORRY.
EVEN IF I'M IN NEW YORK YOU CAN CALL ME EVERY DAY.
YOU'LL HAVE TO, SO I CAN REMIND YOU TO MOW THE LAWN.
I'M JUST GLAD TO HAVE YOU AT HOME. EVEN IF YOU ARE GOING TO LEAVE ME.
DON'T BE DRAMATIC. I'VE GOT A CAREER TO GET BACK ON TRACK.
WE BOTH HAVE LIVES TO GET ON TRACK.
"AT LEAST NOW WE HAVE EACH OTHER."

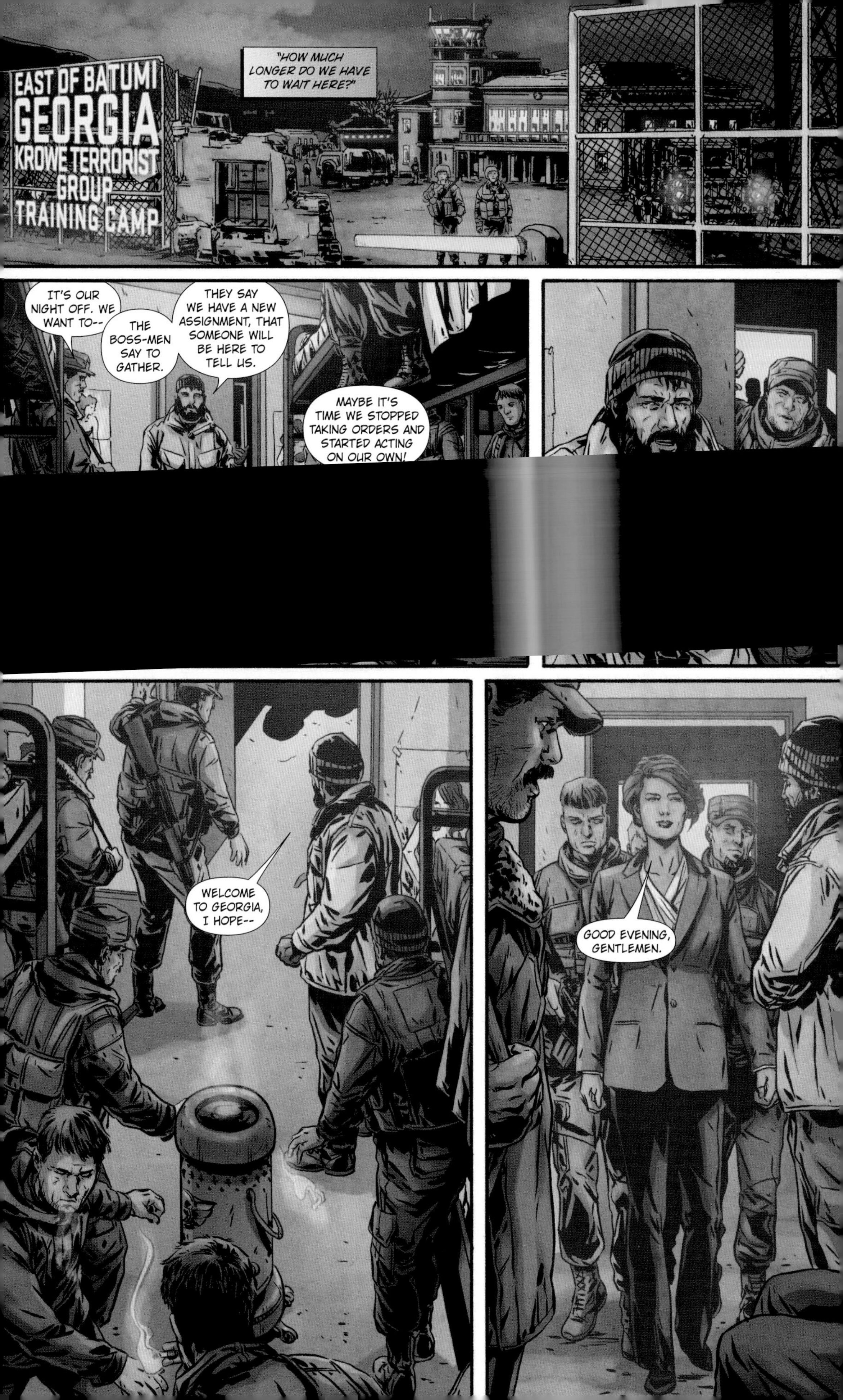
EAST OF BATUMI
GEORGIA
KROWE TERRORIST GROUP TRAINING CAMP
"HOW MUCH LONGER DO WE HAVE TO WAIT HERE?"
IT'S OUR NIGHT OFF. WE WANT TO--
THE BOSS-MEN SAY TO GATHER.
THEY SAY WE HAVE A NEW ASSIGNMENT, THAT SOMEONE WILL BE HERE TO TELL US.
MAYBE IT'S TIME WE STOPPED TAKING ORDERS AND STARTED ACTING ON OUR OWN!
WELCOME TO GEORGIA, I HOPE--
GOOD EVENING, GENTLEMEN.

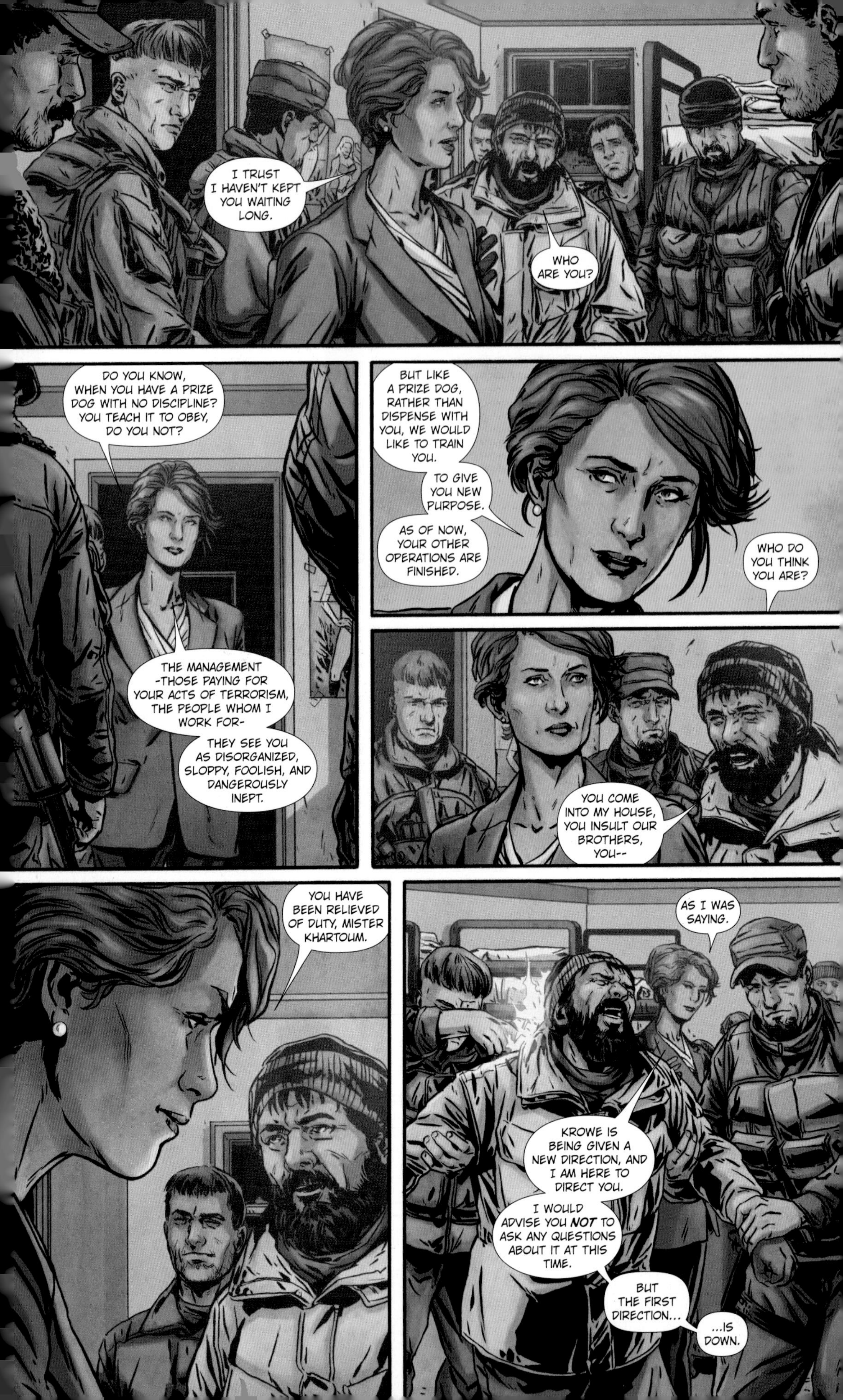
I TRUST I HAVEN'T KEPT YOU WAITING LONG.
WHO ARE YOU?
DO YOU KNOW, WHEN YOU HAVE A PRIZE DOG WITH NO DISCIPLINE? YOU TEACH IT TO OBEY, DO YOU NOT?
THE MANAGEMENT -THOSE PAYING FOR YOUR ACTS OF TERRORISM, THE PEOPLE WHOM I WORK FOR-
THEY SEE YOU AS DISORGANIZED, SLOPPY, FOOLISH, AND DANGEROUSLY INEPT.
BUT LIKE A PRIZE DOG, RATHER THAN DISPENSE WITH YOU, WE WOULD LIKE TO TRAIN YOU.
TO GIVE YOU NEW PURPOSE.
AS OF NOW, YOUR OTHER OPERATIONS ARE FINISHED.
WHO DO YOU THINK YOU ARE?
YOU COME INTO MY HOUSE, YOU INSULT OUR BROTHERS, YOU--
YOU HAVE BEEN RELIEVED OF DUTY, MISTER KHARTOUM.
AS I WAS SAYING.
KROWE IS BEING GIVEN A NEW DIRECTION, AND I AM HERE TO DIRECT YOU.
I WOULD ADVISE YOU NOT TO ASK ANY QUESTIONS ABOUT IT AT THIS TIME.
BUT THE FIRST DIRECTION...
...IS DOWN.

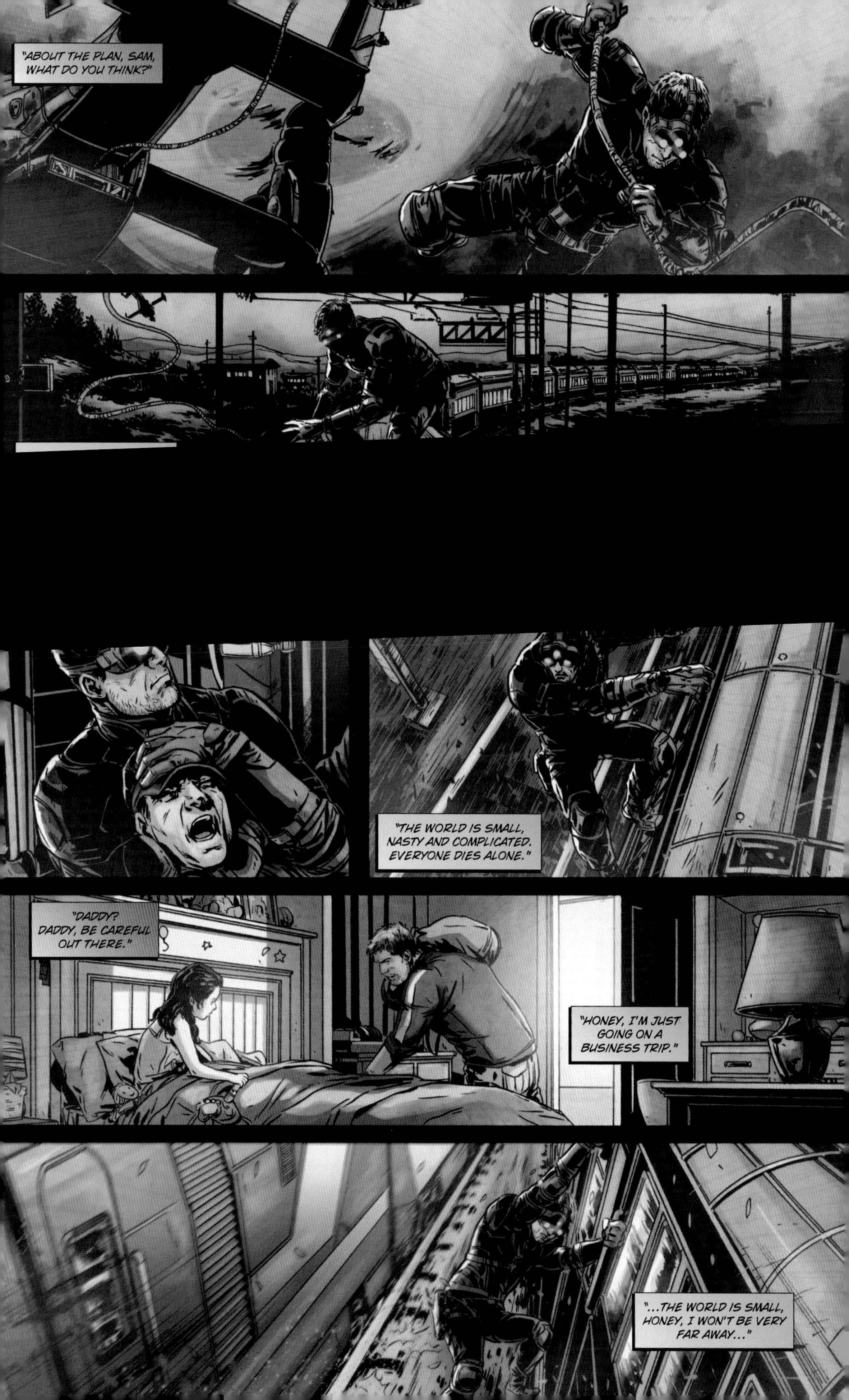
"ABOUT THE PLAN, SAM, WHAT DO YOU THINK?"
"THE WORLD IS SMALL, NASTY AND COMPLICATED. EVERYONE DIES ALONE."
"DADDY? DADDY, BE CAREFUL OUT THERE."
"HONEY, I'M JUST GOING ON A BUSINESS TRIP."
"...THE WORLD IS SMALL, HONEY, I WON'T BE VERY FAR AWAY..."

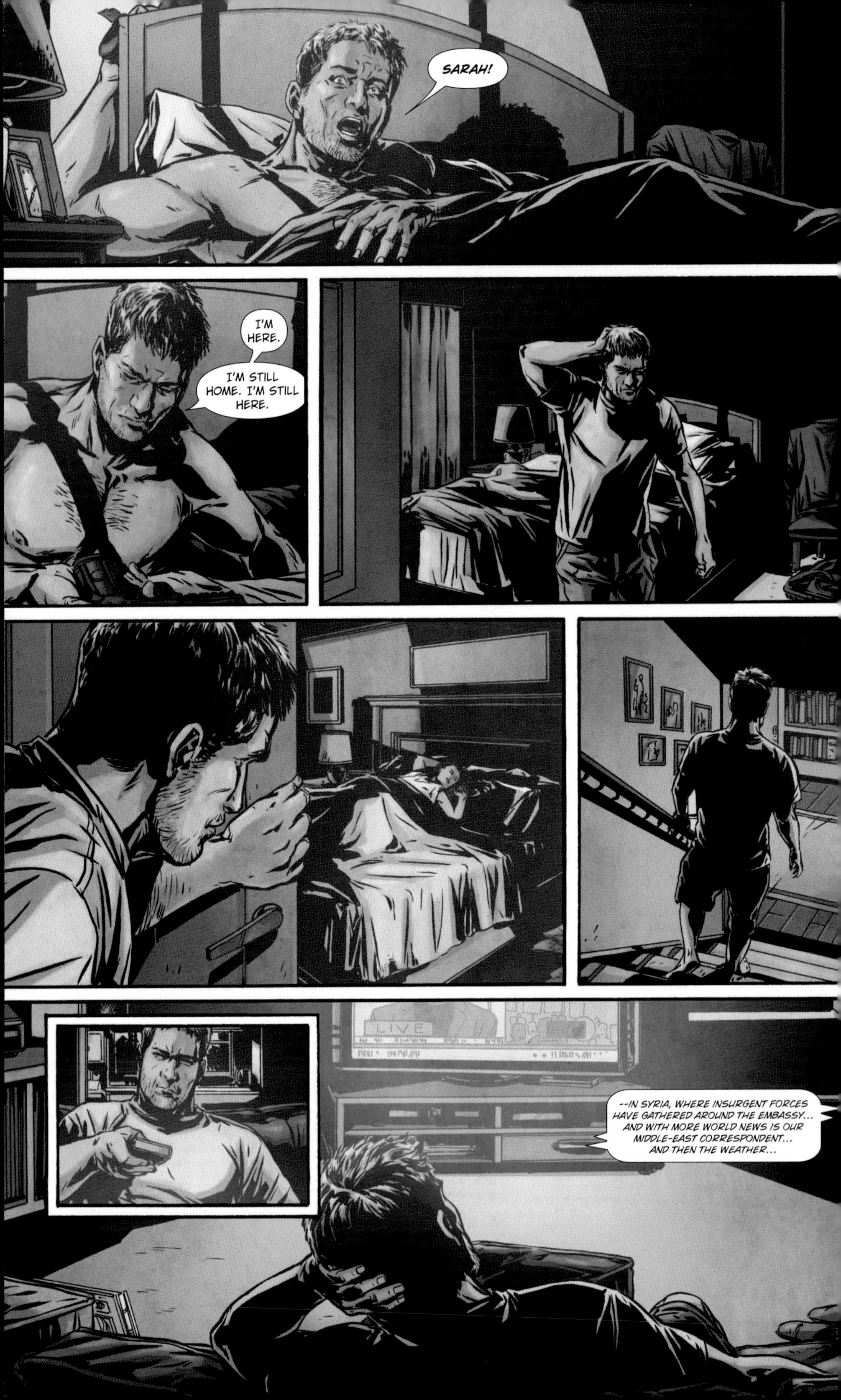
SARAH!
I'M HERE.
I'M STILL HOME. I'M STILL HERE.
LIVE
--IN SYRIA, WHERE INSURGENT FORCES HAVE GATHERED AROUND THE EMBASSY... AND WITH MORE WORLD NEWS IS OUR MIDDLE-EAST CORRESPONDENT... AND THEN THE WEATHER...

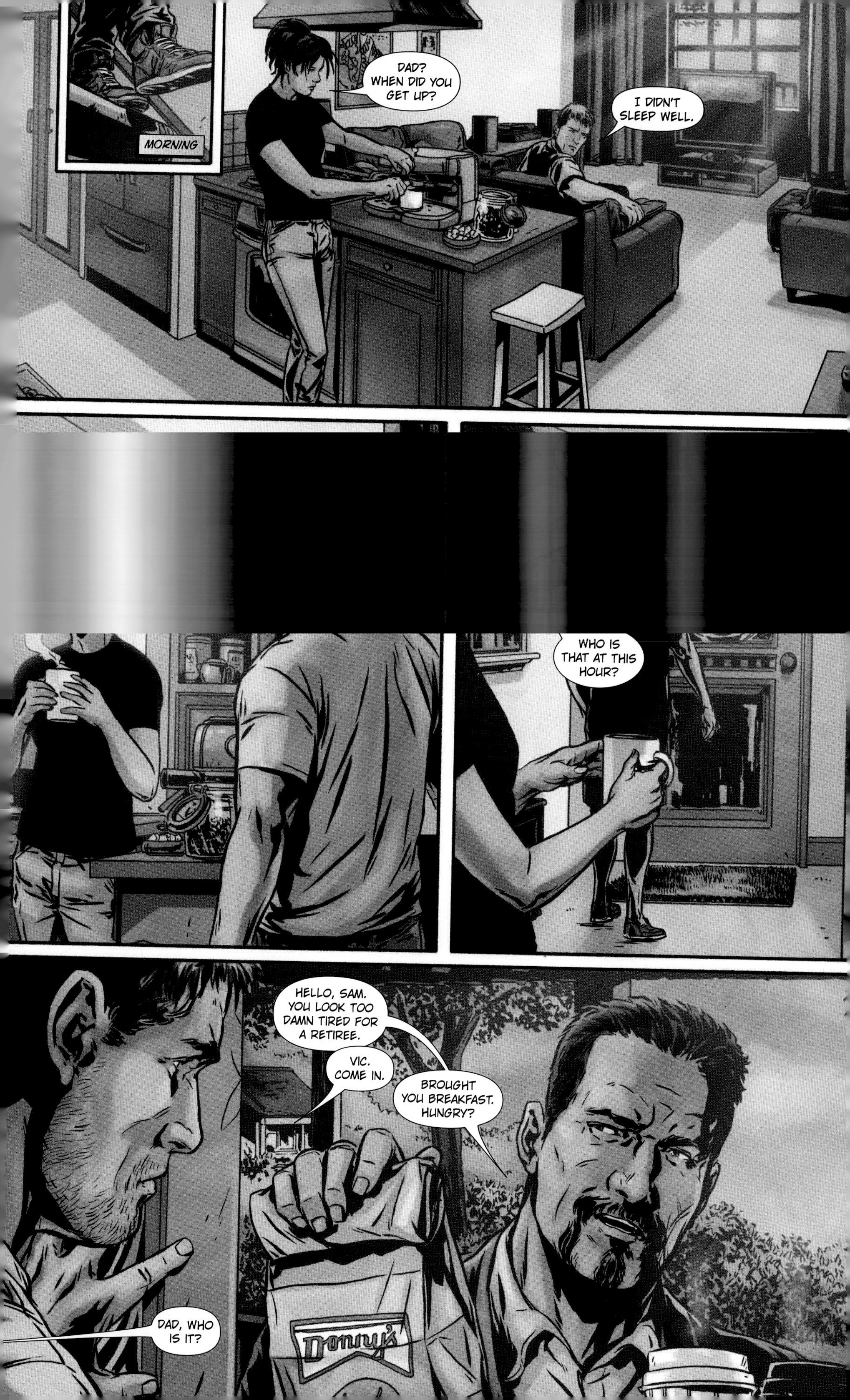
MORNING
DAD? WHEN DID YOU GET UP?
I DIDN'T SLEEP WELL.
WHO IS THAT AT THIS HOUR?
HELLO, SAM. YOU LOOK TOO DAMN TIRED FOR A RETIREE.
VIC. COME IN.
BROUGHT YOU BREAKFAST. HUNGRY?
DAD, WHO IS IT?
Donny's

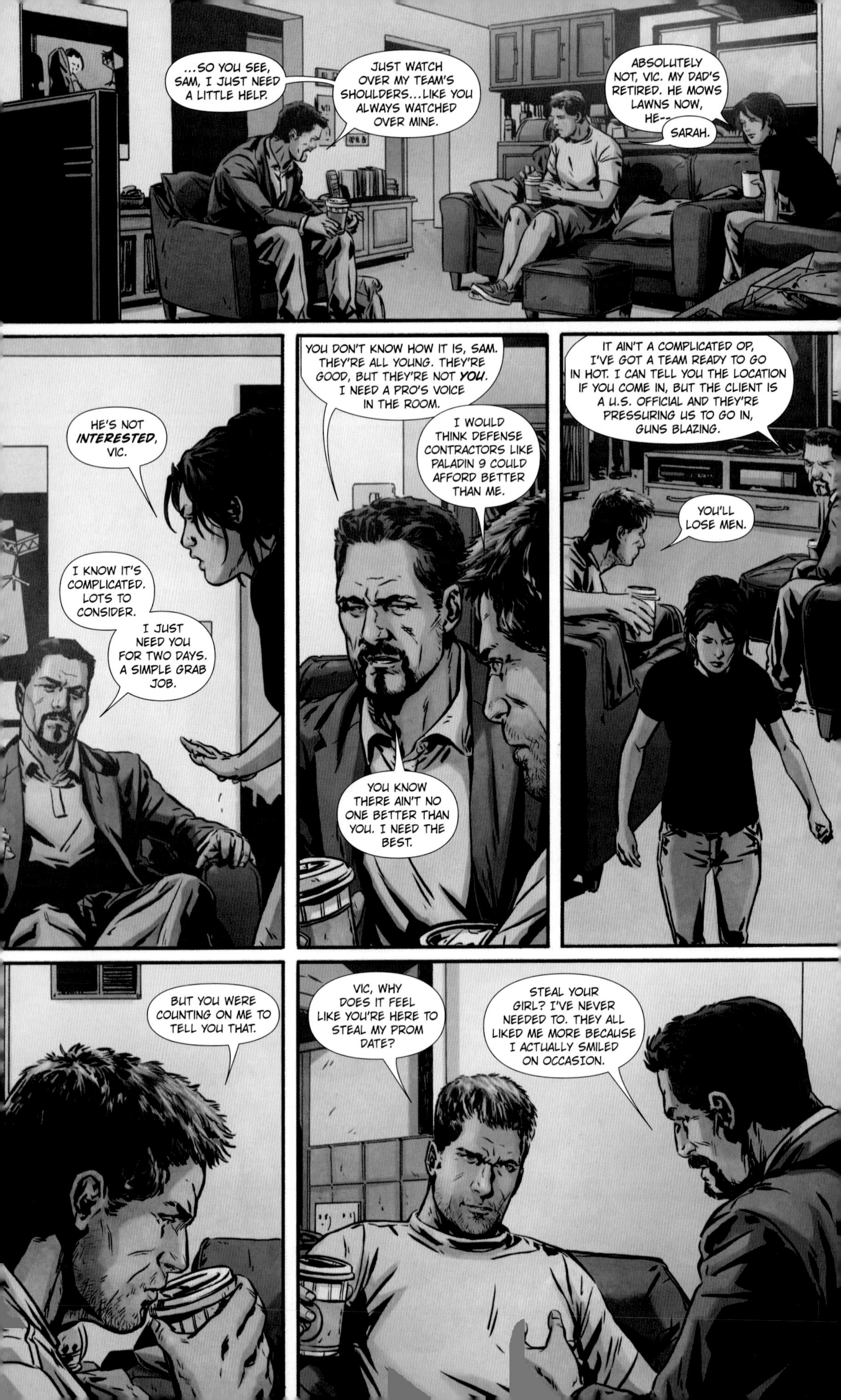
...SO YOU SEE, SAM, I JUST NEED A LITTLE HELP.
JUST WATCH OVER MY TEAM'S SHOULDERS...LIKE YOU ALWAYS WATCHED OVER MINE.
ABSOLUTELY NOT, VIC. MY DAD'S RETIRED. HE MOWS LAWNS NOW, HE--
SARAH.
HE'S NOT *INTERESTED*, VIC.
I KNOW IT'S COMPLICATED. LOTS TO CONSIDER.
I JUST NEED YOU FOR TWO DAYS. A SIMPLE GRAB JOB.
YOU DON'T KNOW HOW IT IS, SAM. THEY'RE ALL YOUNG. THEY'RE GOOD, BUT THEY'RE NOT ***YOU***. I NEED A PRO'S VOICE IN THE ROOM.
I WOULD THINK DEFENSE CONTRACTORS LIKE PALADIN 9 COULD AFFORD BETTER THAN ME.
YOU KNOW THERE AIN'T NO ONE BETTER THAN YOU. I NEED THE BEST.
IT AIN'T A COMPLICATED OP, I'VE GOT A TEAM READY TO GO IN HOT. I CAN TELL YOU THE LOCATION IF YOU COME IN, BUT THE CLIENT IS A U.S. OFFICIAL AND THEY'RE PRESSURING US TO GO IN, GUNS BLAZING.
YOU'LL LOSE MEN.
BUT YOU WERE COUNTING ON ME TO TELL YOU THAT.
VIC, WHY DOES IT FEEL LIKE YOU'RE HERE TO STEAL MY PROM DATE?
STEAL YOUR GIRL? I'VE NEVER NEEDED TO. THEY ALL LIKED ME MORE BECAUSE I ACTUALLY SMILED ON OCCASION.

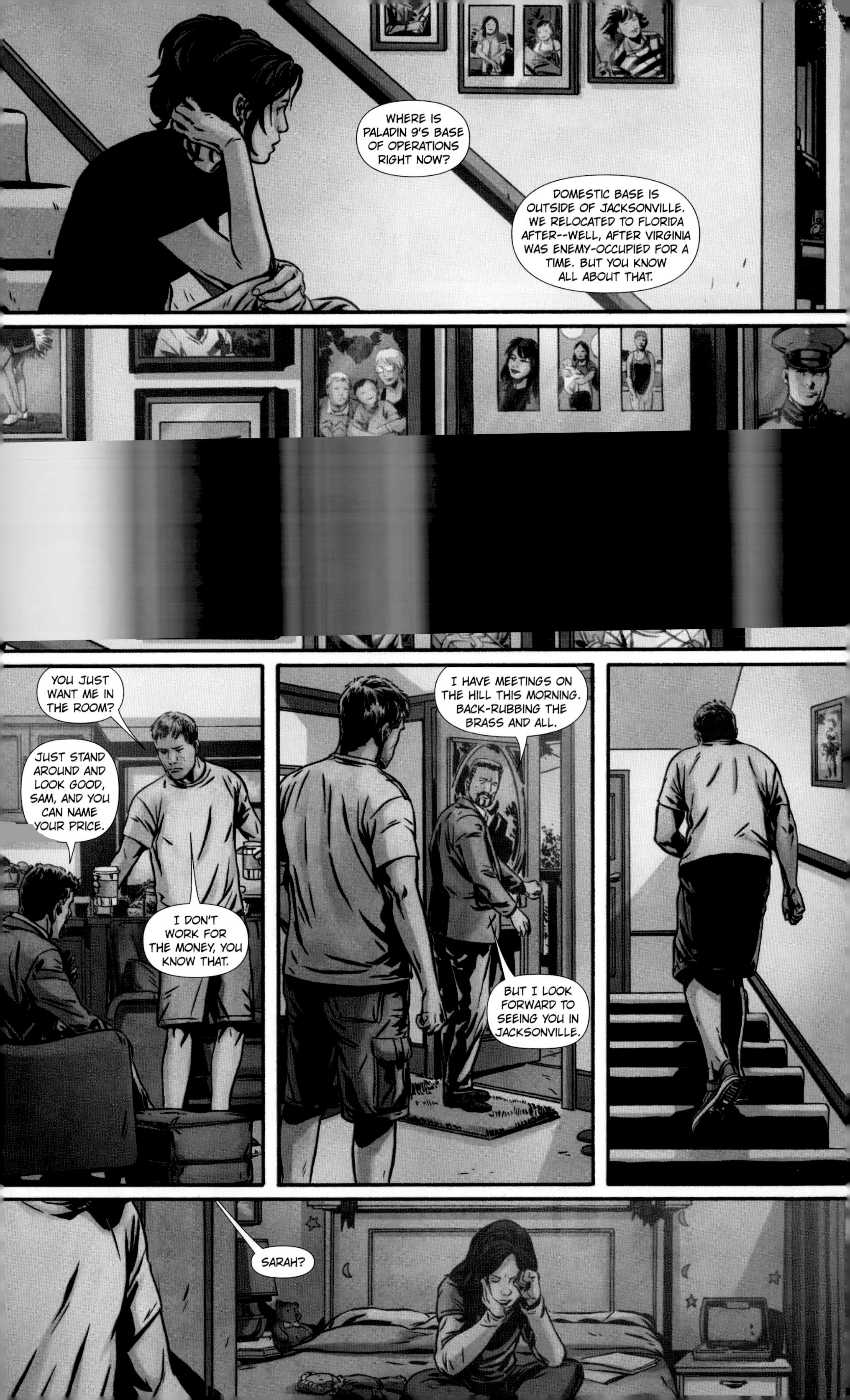
WHERE IS PALADIN 9'S BASE OF OPERATIONS RIGHT NOW?
DOMESTIC BASE IS OUTSIDE OF JACKSONVILLE. WE RELOCATED TO FLORIDA AFTER--WELL, AFTER VIRGINIA WAS ENEMY-OCCUPIED FOR A TIME. BUT YOU KNOW ALL ABOUT THAT.
YOU JUST WANT ME IN THE ROOM?
JUST STAND AROUND AND LOOK GOOD, SAM, AND YOU CAN NAME YOUR PRICE.
I DON'T WORK FOR THE MONEY, YOU KNOW THAT.
I HAVE MEETINGS ON THE HILL THIS MORNING. BACK-RUBBING THE BRASS AND ALL.
BUT I LOOK FORWARD TO SEEING YOU IN JACKSONVILLE.
SARAH?

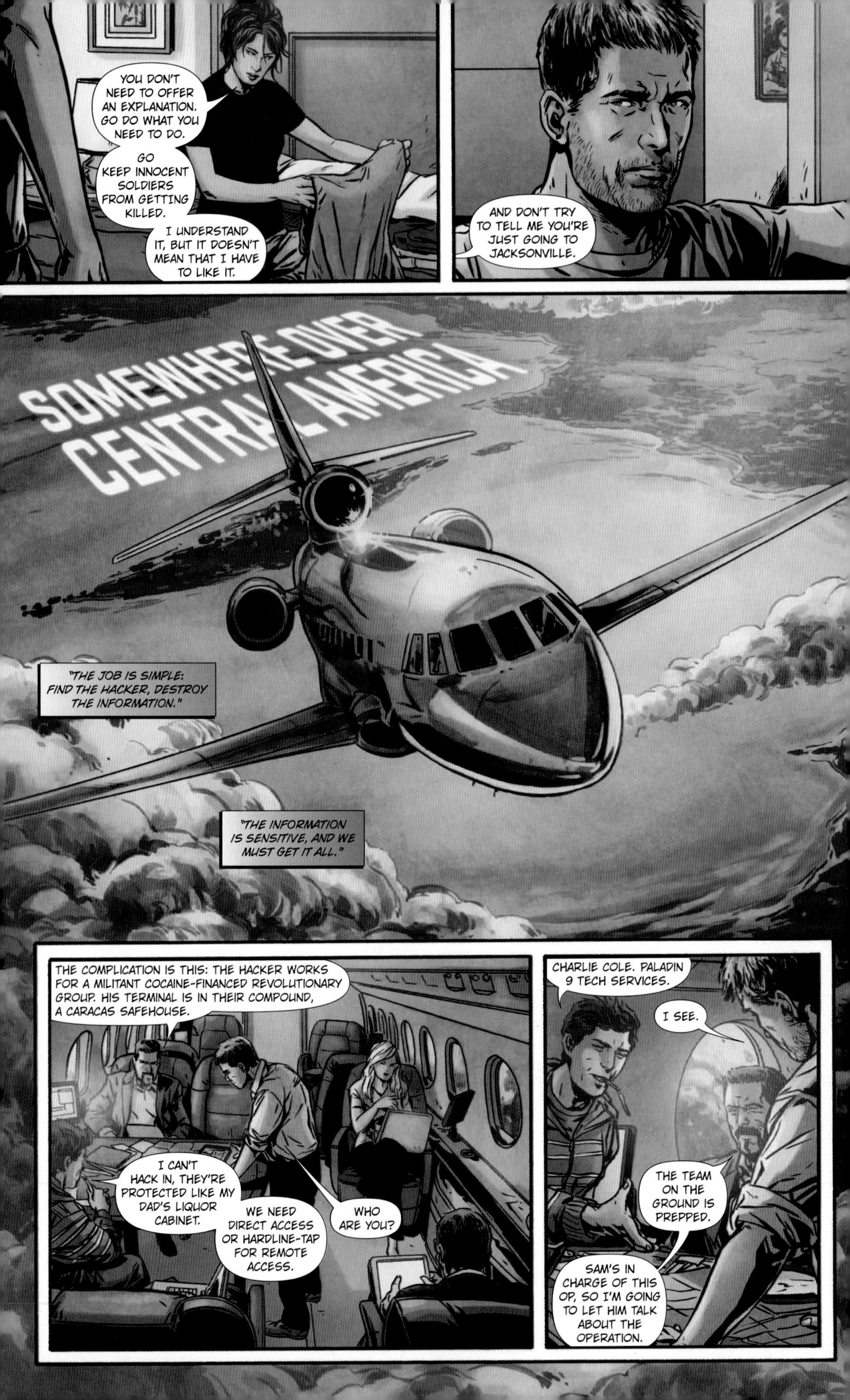
YOU DON'T NEED TO OFFER AN EXPLANATION. GO DO WHAT YOU NEED TO DO.
GO KEEP INNOCENT SOLDIERS FROM GETTING KILLED.
I UNDERSTAND IT, BUT IT DOESN'T MEAN THAT I HAVE TO LIKE IT.
AND DON'T TRY TO TELL ME YOU'RE JUST GOING TO JACKSONVILLE.
SOMEWHERE OVER CENTRAL AMERICA
"THE JOB IS SIMPLE: FIND THE HACKER, DESTROY THE INFORMATION."
"THE INFORMATION IS SENSITIVE, AND WE MUST GET IT ALL."
THE COMPLICATION IS THIS: THE HACKER WORKS FOR A MILITANT COCAINE-FINANCED REVOLUTIONARY GROUP. HIS TERMINAL IS IN THEIR COMPOUND, A CARACAS SAFEHOUSE.
I CAN'T HACK IN, THEY'RE PROTECTED LIKE MY DAD'S LIQUOR CABINET.
WE NEED DIRECT ACCESS OR HARDLINE-TAP FOR REMOTE ACCESS.
WHO ARE YOU?
CHARLIE COLE. PALADIN 9 TECH SERVICES.
I SEE.
THE TEAM ON THE GROUND IS PREPPED.
SAM'S IN CHARGE OF THIS OP, SO I'M GOING TO LET HIM TALK ABOUT THE OPERATION.

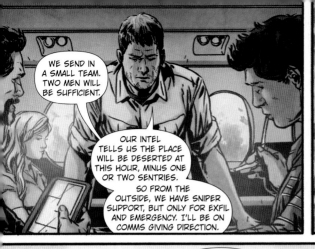

WE SEND IN A SMALL TEAM. TWO MEN WILL BE SUFFICIENT.

OUR INTEL TELLS US THE PLACE WILL BE DESERTED AT THIS HOUR, MINUS ONE OR TWO SENTRIES.
SO FROM THE OUTSIDE, WE HAVE SNIPER SUPPORT, BUT ONLY FOR EXFIL AND EMERGENCY. I'LL BE ON COMMS GIVING DIRECTION.

"NOW LET'S TALK ABOUT WHAT EACH OF US IS GOING TO DO."

GOOD PLAN. SOLID PLAN. PRICKS WON'T KNOW WHAT'S COMING.

CHARLIE, BY THE WAY. NOT SURE IF YOU CAUGHT IT EARLIER--

I DID.

I PULLED YOUR FILE. THE ONE THAT DOESN'T EXIST. YOU KNOW... THE COOL ONE.

ANYWAY. NOT TO LIKE, BUG YOU, BUT YOU'RE A BADASS.

I WANTED TO SAY IT'S A PLEASURE TO GET TO WORK WITH YOU.

YOU THINK SENDING MEN INTO HARM'S WAY IS PLEASURE?

MAYBE PLEASURE WAS THE WRONG WORD.

...THE ONLY PLEASURE IS GOING HOME.

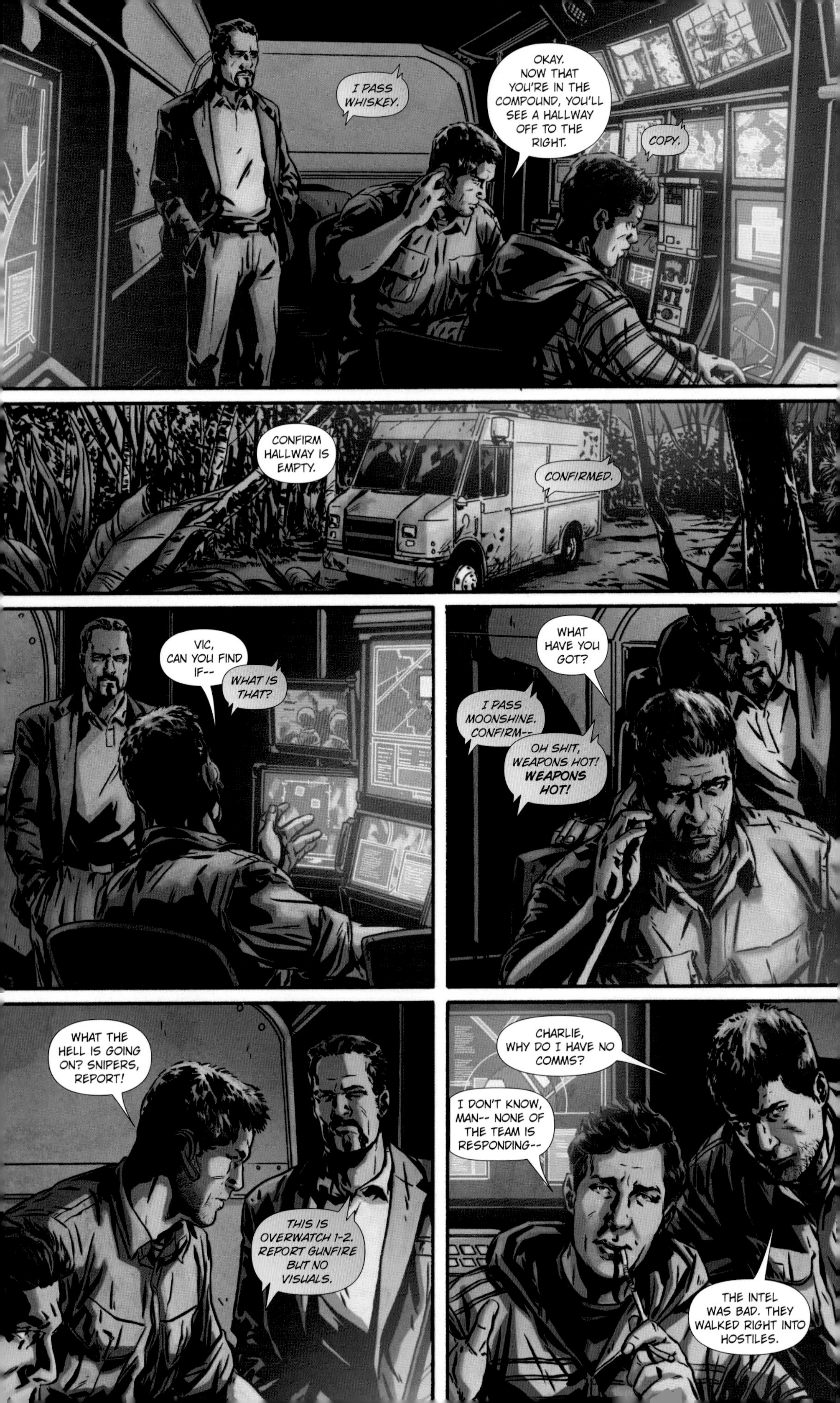
I PASS WHISKEY.
OKAY. NOW THAT YOU'RE IN THE COMPOUND, YOU'LL SEE A HALLWAY OFF TO THE RIGHT.
COPY.
CONFIRM HALLWAY IS EMPTY.
CONFIRMED.
VIC, CAN YOU FIND IF--
WHAT IS THAT?
WHAT HAVE YOU GOT?
I PASS MOONSHINE. CONFIRM--
OH SHIT, WEAPONS HOT! **WEAPONS HOT!**
WHAT THE HELL IS GOING ON? SNIPERS, REPORT!
THIS IS OVERWATCH 1-2. REPORT GUNFIRE BUT NO VISUALS.
CHARLIE, WHY DO I HAVE NO COMMS?
I DON'T KNOW, MAN-- NONE OF THE TEAM IS RESPONDING--
THE INTEL WAS BAD. THEY WALKED RIGHT INTO HOSTILES.

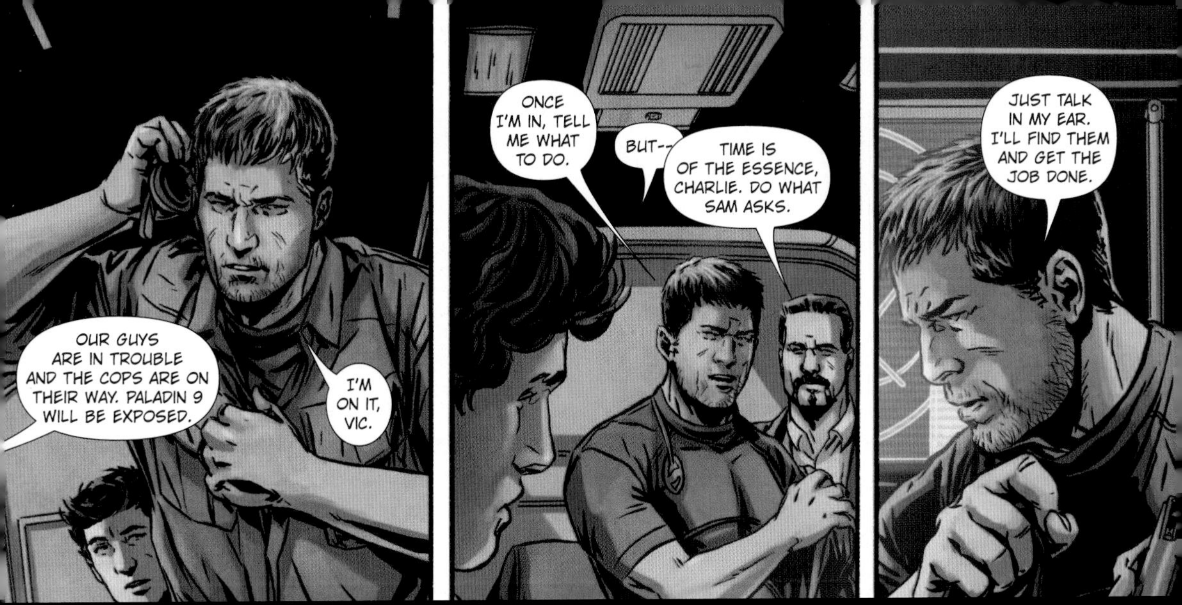
OUR GUYS ARE IN TROUBLE AND THE COPS ARE ON THEIR WAY. PALADIN 9 WILL BE EXPOSED.
I'M ON IT, VIC.
ONCE I'M IN, TELL ME WHAT TO DO.
BUT--
TIME IS OF THE ESSENCE, CHARLIE. DO WHAT SAM ASKS.
JUST TALK IN MY EAR. I'LL FIND THEM AND GET THE JOB DONE.

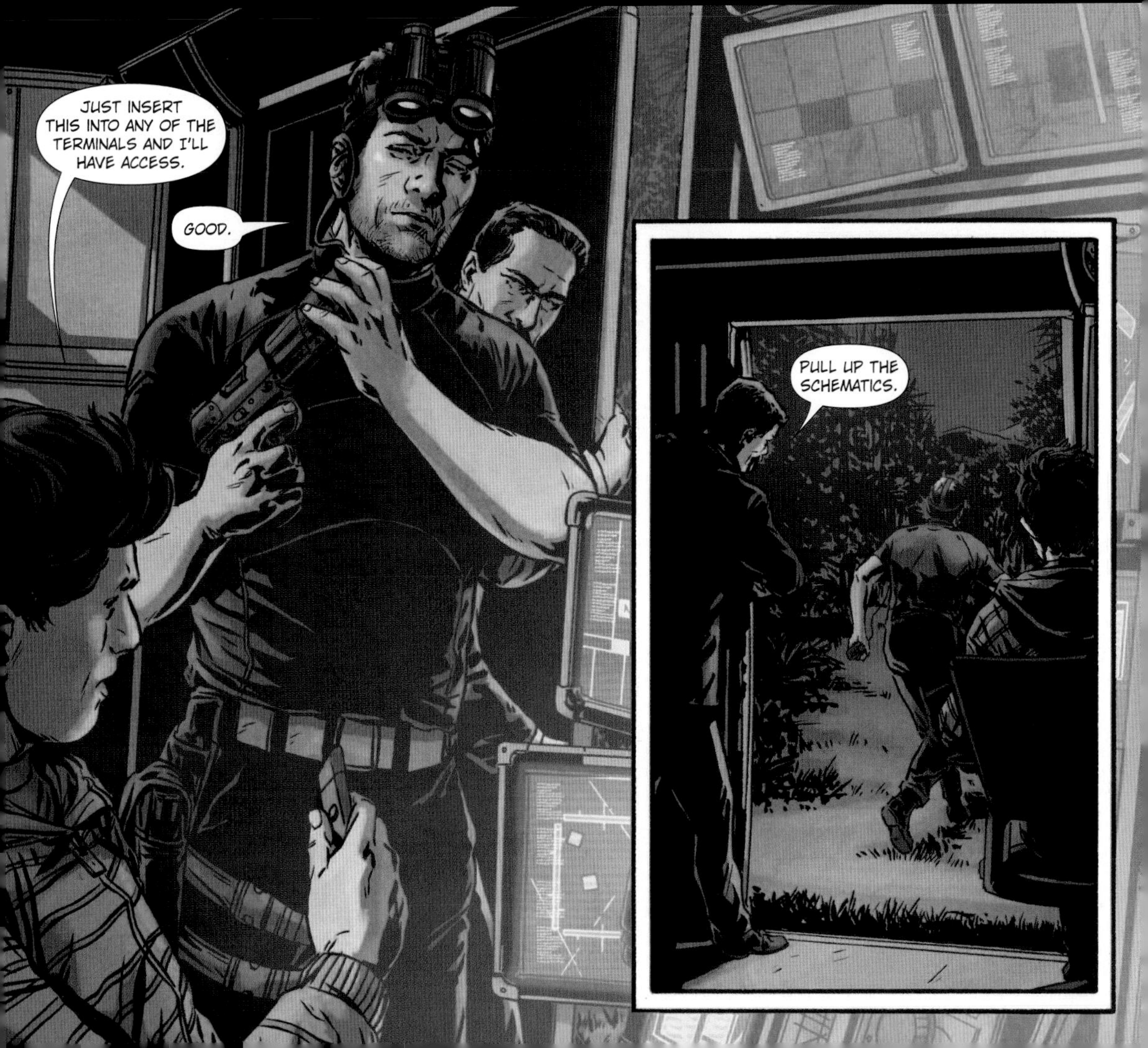
JUST INSERT THIS INTO ANY OF THE TERMINALS AND I'LL HAVE ACCESS.
GOOD.
PULL UP THE SCHEMATICS.

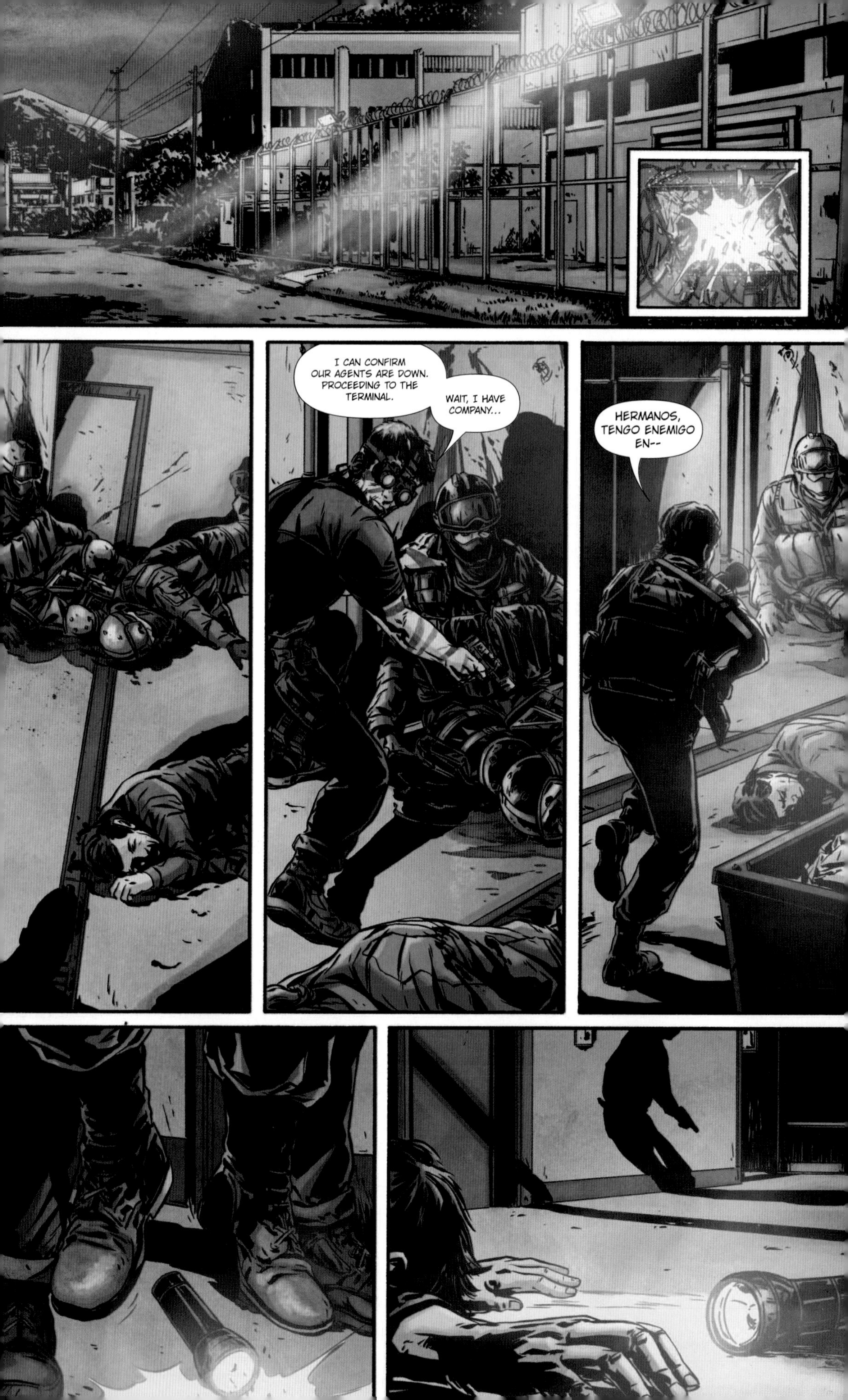
I CAN CONFIRM OUR AGENTS ARE DOWN. PROCEEDING TO THE TERMINAL.
WAIT, I HAVE COMPANY...
HERMANOS, TENGO ENEMIGO EN--

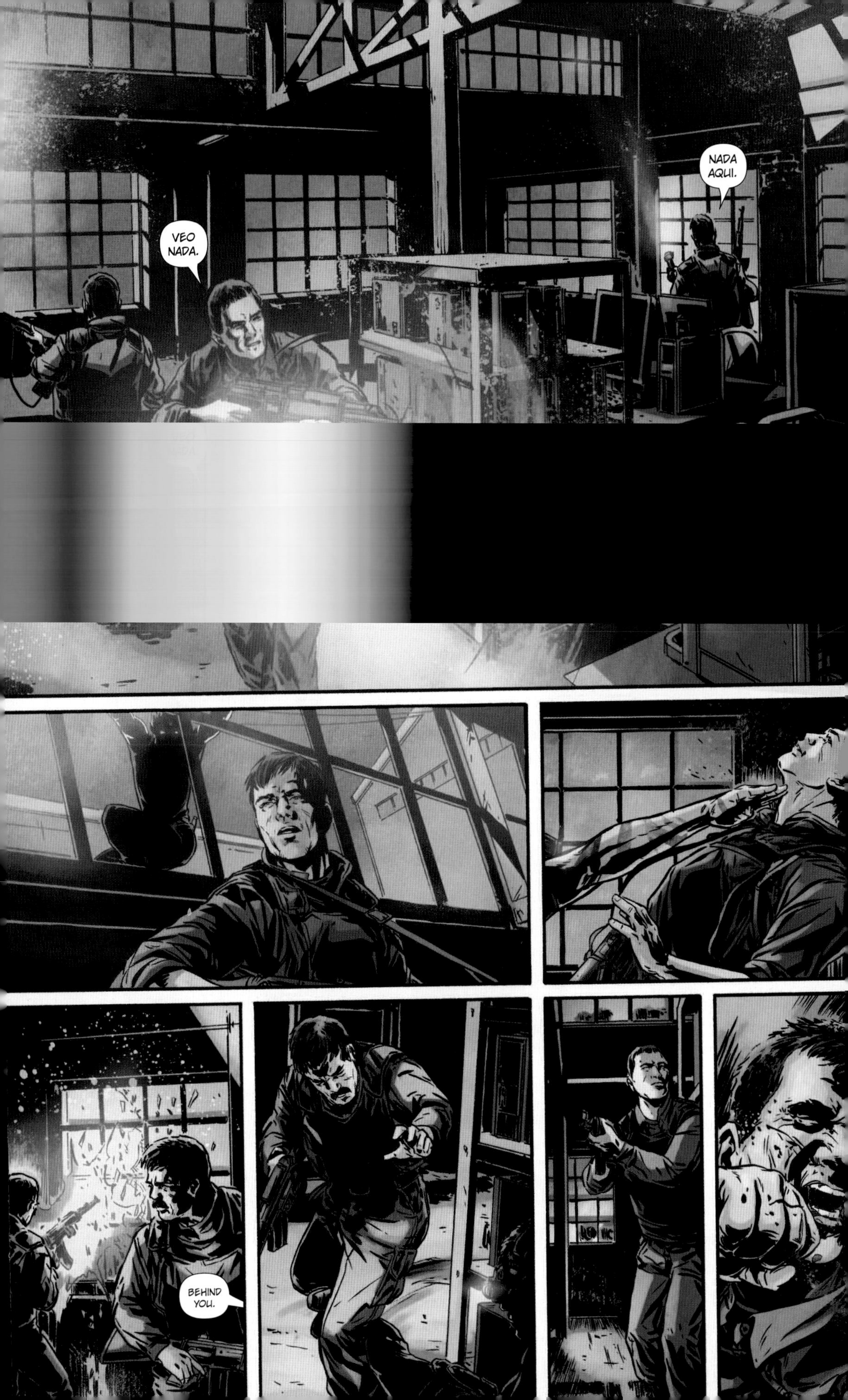
VEO NADA.
NADA AQUI.
BEHIND YOU.

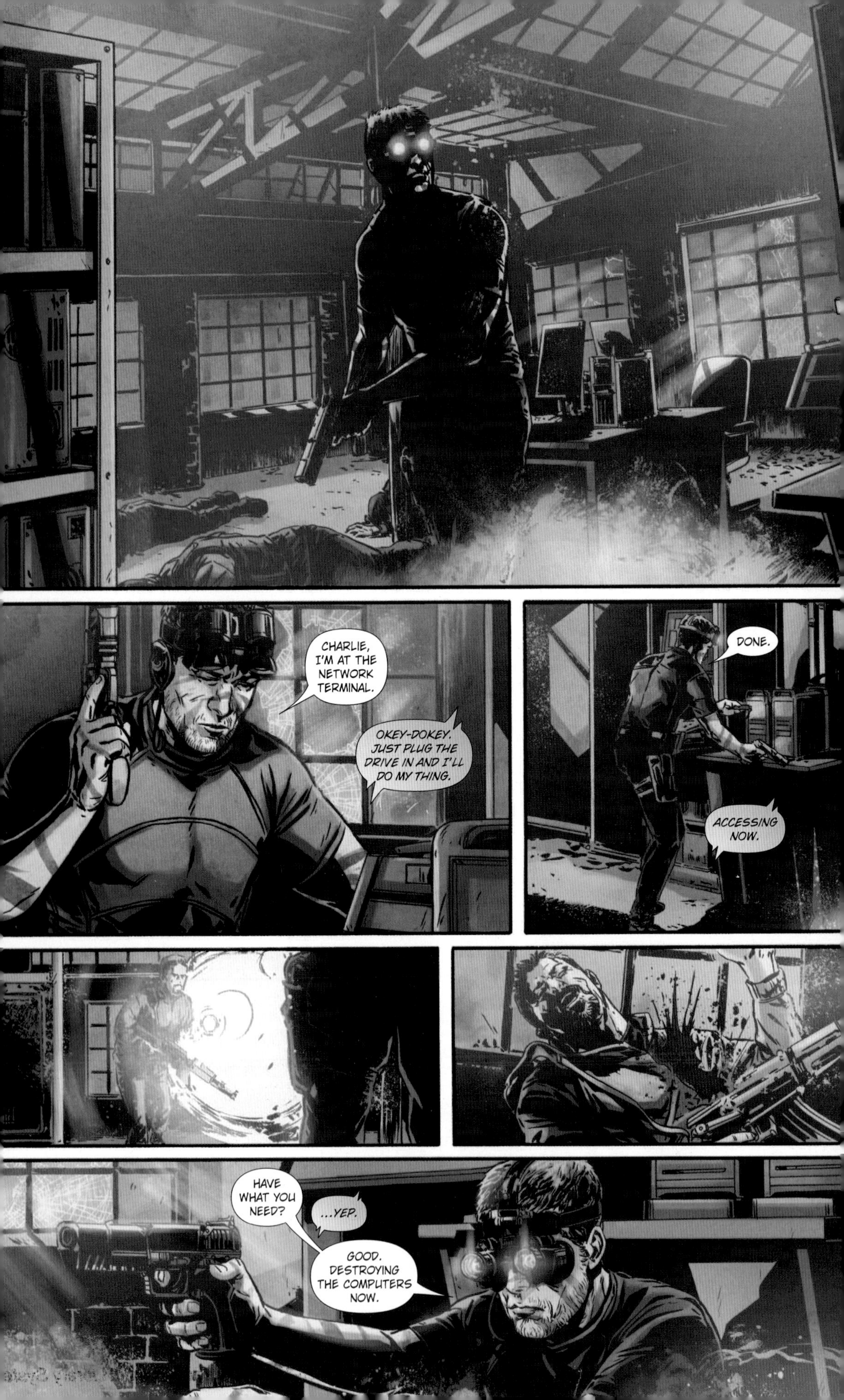
CHARLIE, I'M AT THE NETWORK TERMINAL.
OKEY-DOKEY. JUST PLUG THE DRIVE IN AND I'LL DO MY THING.
DONE.
ACCESSING NOW.
HAVE WHAT YOU NEED?
...YEP.
GOOD. DESTROYING THE COMPUTERS NOW.

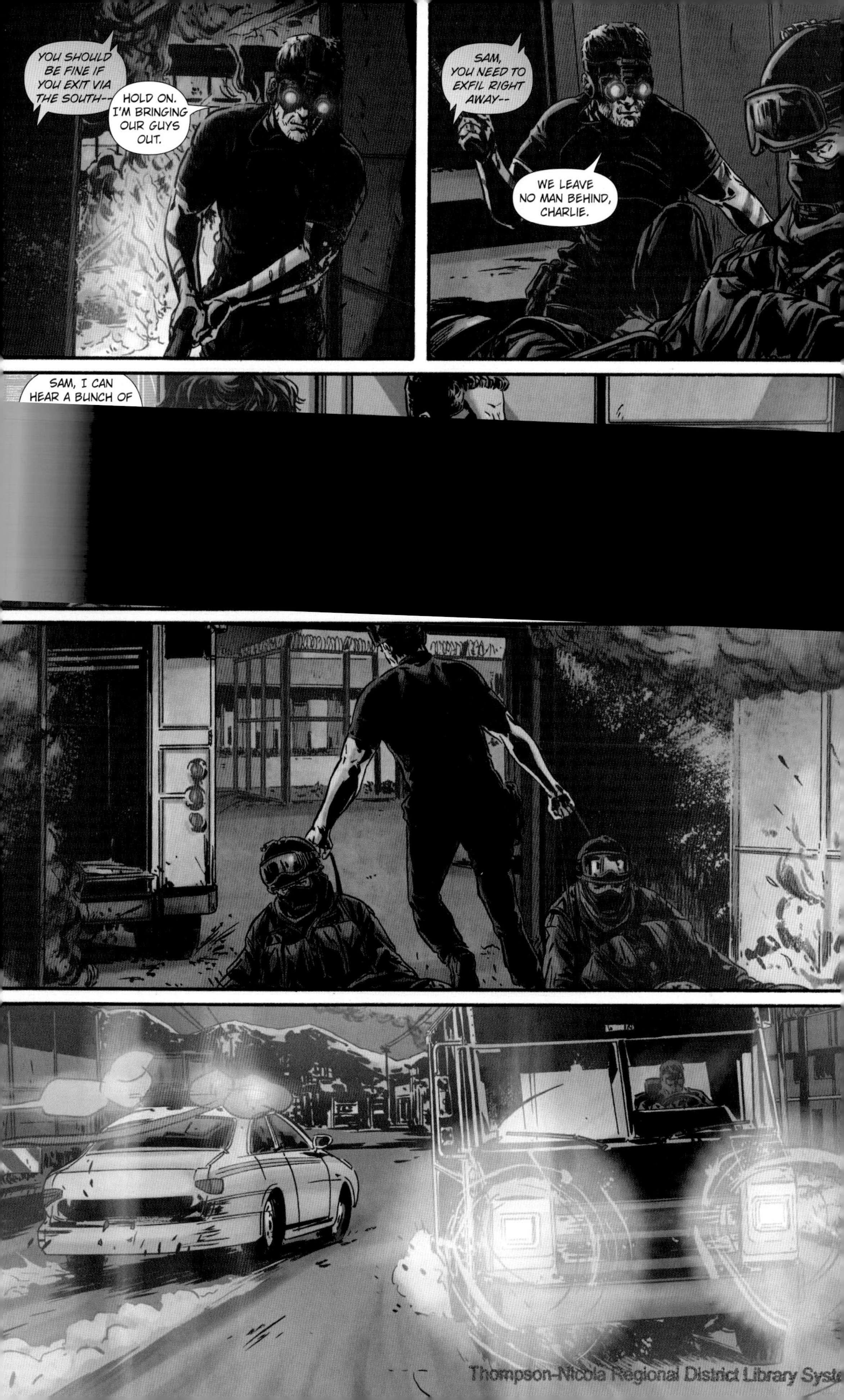
YOU SHOULD BE FINE IF YOU EXIT VIA THE SOUTH--
HOLD ON. I'M BRINGING OUR GUYS OUT.
SAM, YOU NEED TO EXFIL RIGHT AWAY--
WE LEAVE NO MAN BEHIND, CHARLIE.
SAM, I CAN HEAR A BUNCH OF [redacted]

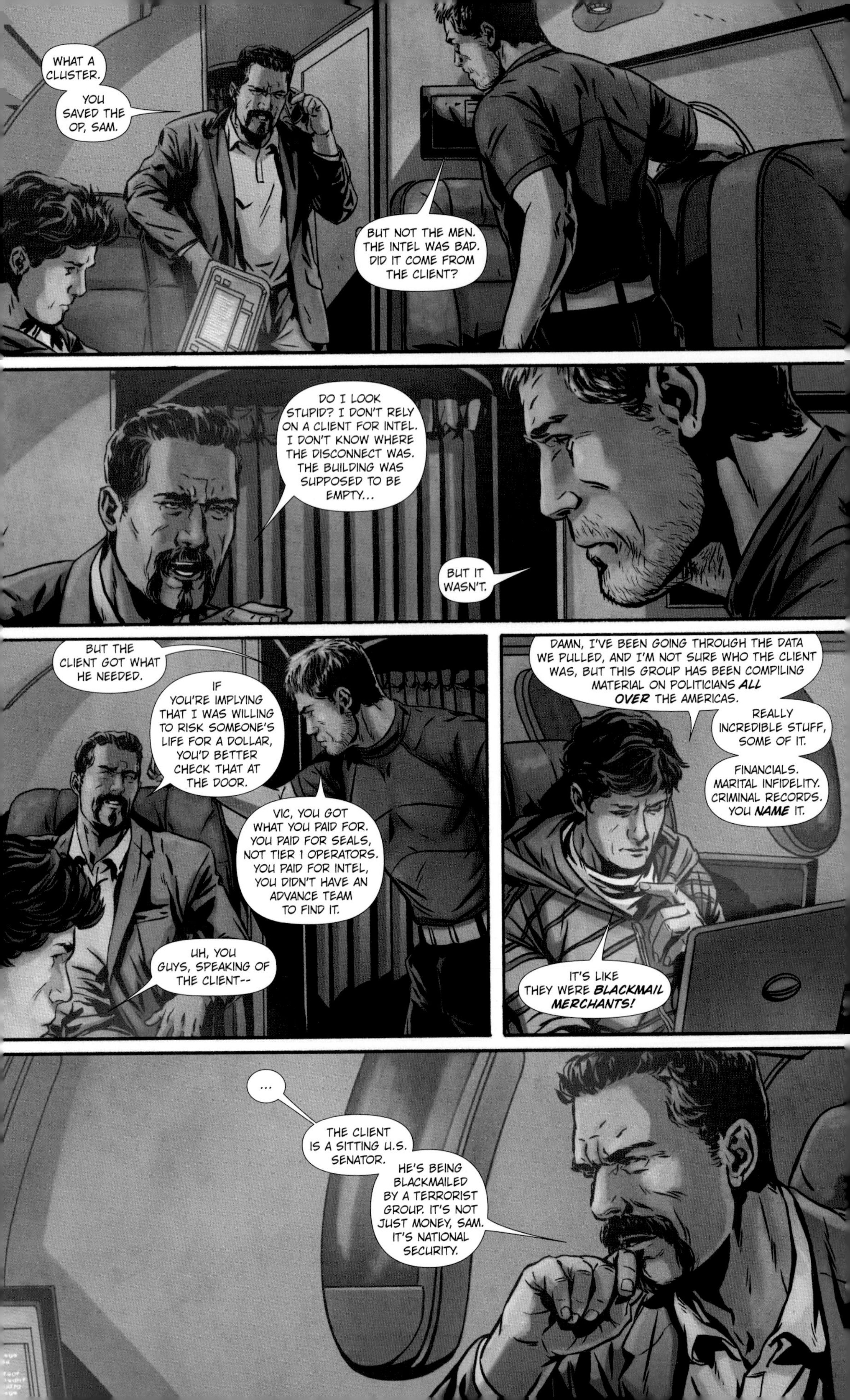
WHAT A CLUSTER.
YOU SAVED THE OP, SAM.
BUT NOT THE MEN. THE INTEL WAS BAD. DID IT COME FROM THE CLIENT?
DO I LOOK STUPID? I DON'T RELY ON A CLIENT FOR INTEL. I DON'T KNOW WHERE THE DISCONNECT WAS. THE BUILDING WAS SUPPOSED TO BE EMPTY...
BUT IT WASN'T.
BUT THE CLIENT GOT WHAT HE NEEDED.
IF YOU'RE IMPLYING THAT I WAS WILLING TO RISK SOMEONE'S LIFE FOR A DOLLAR, YOU'D BETTER CHECK THAT AT THE DOOR.
VIC, YOU GOT WHAT YOU PAID FOR. YOU PAID FOR SEALS, NOT TIER 1 OPERATORS. YOU PAID FOR INTEL, YOU DIDN'T HAVE AN ADVANCE TEAM TO FIND IT.
UH, YOU GUYS, SPEAKING OF THE CLIENT--
DAMN, I'VE BEEN GOING THROUGH THE DATA WE PULLED, AND I'M NOT SURE WHO THE CLIENT WAS, BUT THIS GROUP HAS BEEN COMPILING MATERIAL ON POLITICIANS **ALL OVER** THE AMERICAS.
REALLY INCREDIBLE STUFF, SOME OF IT.
FINANCIALS. MARITAL INFIDELITY. CRIMINAL RECORDS. YOU **NAME** IT.
IT'S LIKE THEY WERE **BLACKMAIL MERCHANTS!**
...
THE CLIENT IS A SITTING U.S. SENATOR.
HE'S BEING BLACKMAILED BY A TERRORIST GROUP. IT'S NOT JUST MONEY, SAM. IT'S NATIONAL SECURITY.

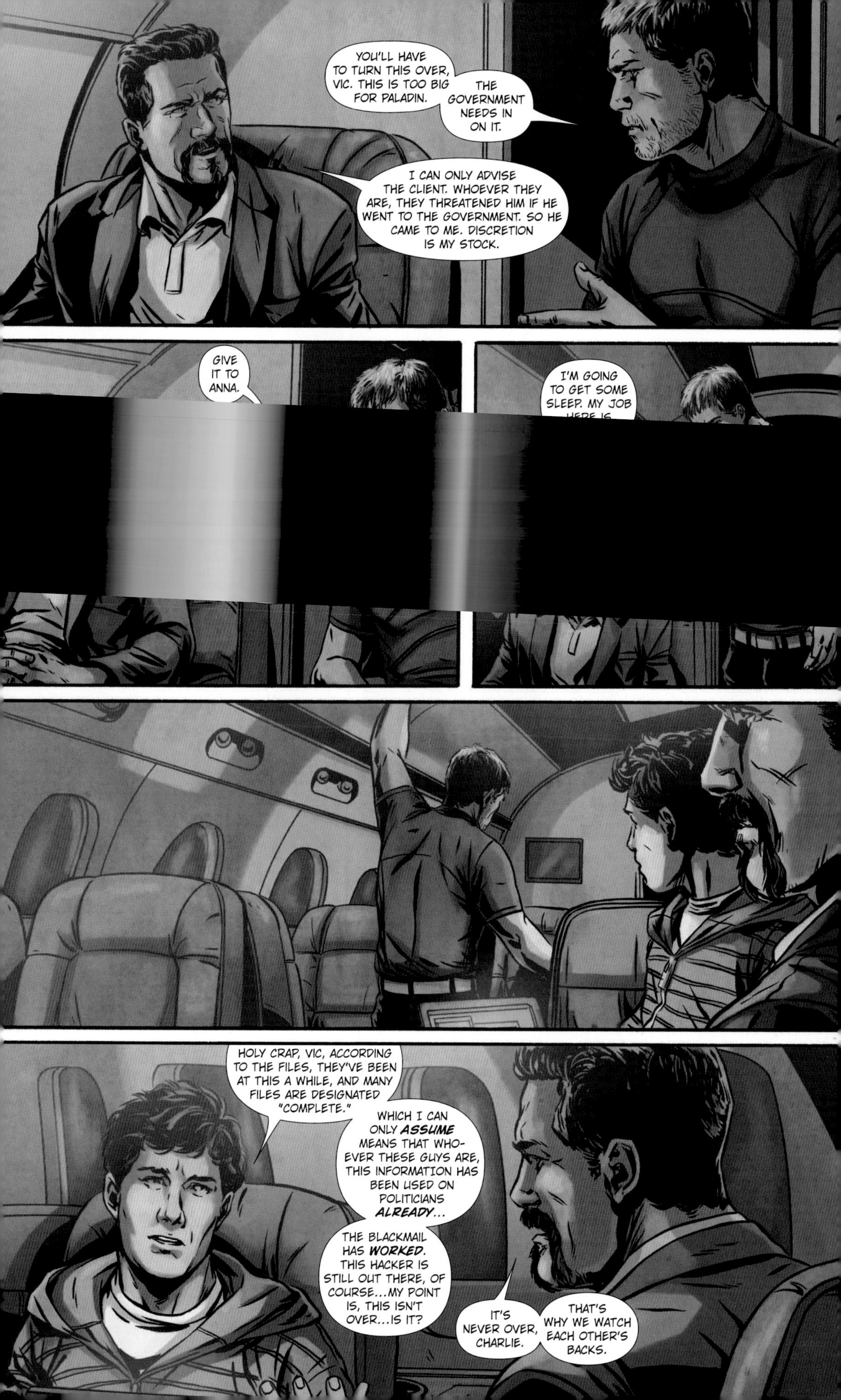
YOU'LL HAVE TO TURN THIS OVER, VIC. THIS IS TOO BIG FOR PALADIN.
THE GOVERNMENT NEEDS IN ON IT.
I CAN ONLY ADVISE THE CLIENT. WHOEVER THEY ARE, THEY THREATENED HIM IF HE WENT TO THE GOVERNMENT. SO HE CAME TO ME. DISCRETION IS MY STOCK.
GIVE IT TO ANNA.
I'M GOING TO GET SOME SLEEP. MY JOB
HOLY CRAP, VIC, ACCORDING TO THE FILES, THEY'VE BEEN AT THIS A WHILE, AND MANY FILES ARE DESIGNATED "COMPLETE."
WHICH I CAN ONLY ***ASSUME*** MEANS THAT WHO-EVER THESE GUYS ARE, THIS INFORMATION HAS BEEN USED ON POLITICIANS ***ALREADY***...
THE BLACKMAIL HAS ***WORKED***. THIS HACKER IS STILL OUT THERE, OF COURSE...MY POINT IS, THIS ISN'T OVER...IS IT?
IT'S NEVER OVER, CHARLIE.
THAT'S WHY WE WATCH EACH OTHER'S BACKS.

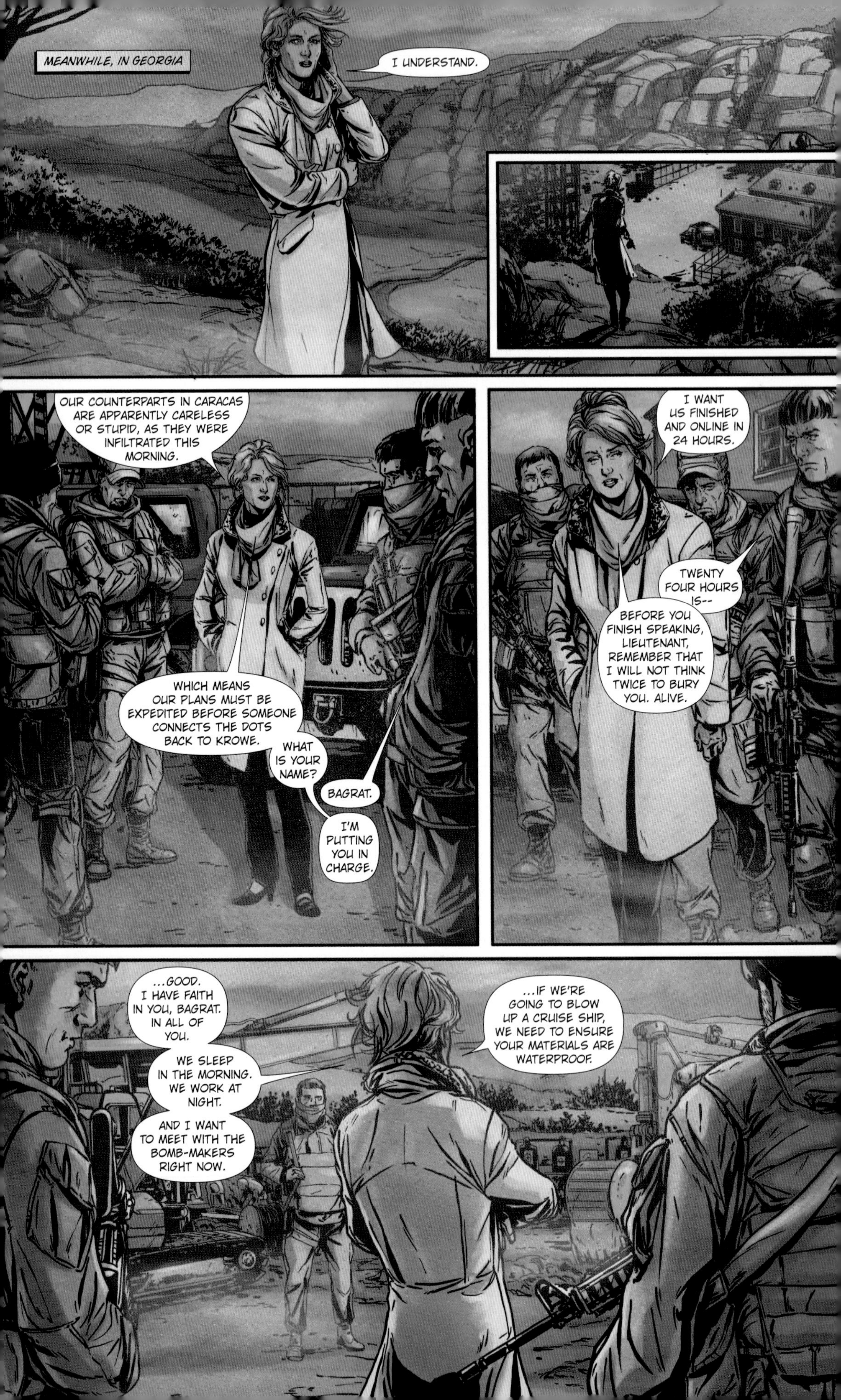
MEANWHILE, IN GEORGIA
I UNDERSTAND.
OUR COUNTERPARTS IN CARACAS ARE APPARENTLY CARELESS OR STUPID, AS THEY WERE INFILTRATED THIS MORNING.
WHICH MEANS OUR PLANS MUST BE EXPEDITED BEFORE SOMEONE CONNECTS THE DOTS BACK TO KROWE.
WHAT IS YOUR NAME?
BAGRAT.
I'M PUTTING YOU IN CHARGE.
I WANT US FINISHED AND ONLINE IN 24 HOURS.
TWENTY FOUR HOURS IS--
BEFORE YOU FINISH SPEAKING, LIEUTENANT, REMEMBER THAT I WILL NOT THINK TWICE TO BURY YOU. ALIVE.
...GOOD. I HAVE FAITH IN YOU, BAGRAT. IN ALL OF YOU.
WE SLEEP IN THE MORNING. WE WORK AT NIGHT.
AND I WANT TO MEET WITH THE BOMB-MAKERS RIGHT NOW.
...IF WE'RE GOING TO BLOW UP A CRUISE SHIP, WE NEED TO ENSURE YOUR MATERIALS ARE WATERPROOF.

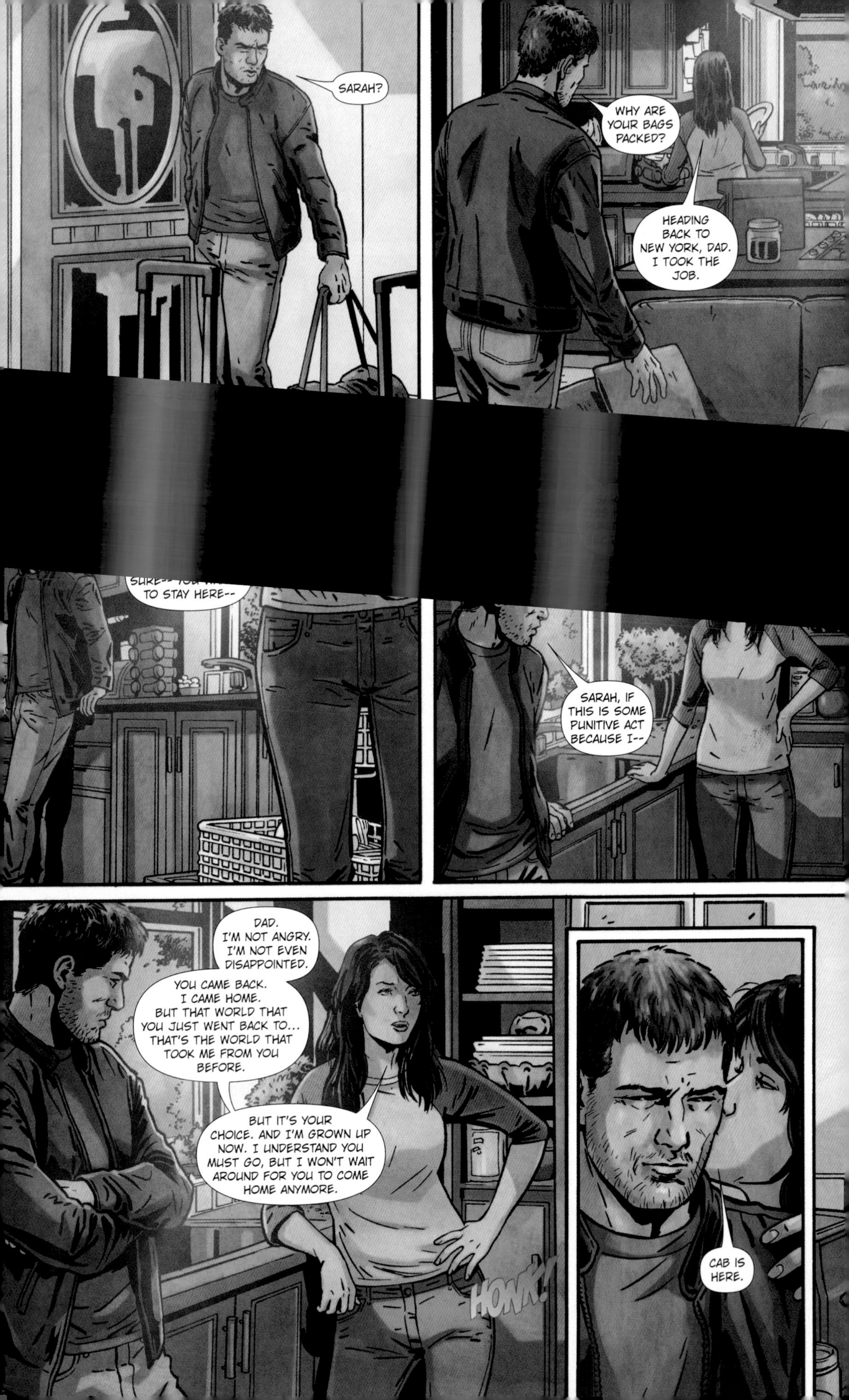
SARAH?
WHY ARE YOUR BAGS PACKED?
HEADING BACK TO NEW YORK, DAD. I TOOK THE JOB.
TO STAY HERE--
SARAH, IF THIS IS SOME PUNITIVE ACT BECAUSE I--
DAD. I'M NOT ANGRY. I'M NOT EVEN DISAPPOINTED.
YOU CAME BACK. I CAME HOME. BUT THAT WORLD THAT YOU JUST WENT BACK TO... THAT'S THE WORLD THAT TOOK ME FROM YOU BEFORE.
BUT IT'S YOUR CHOICE. AND I'M GROWN UP NOW. I UNDERSTAND YOU MUST GO, BUT I WON'T WAIT AROUND FOR YOU TO COME HOME ANYMORE.
HONK!
CAB IS HERE.

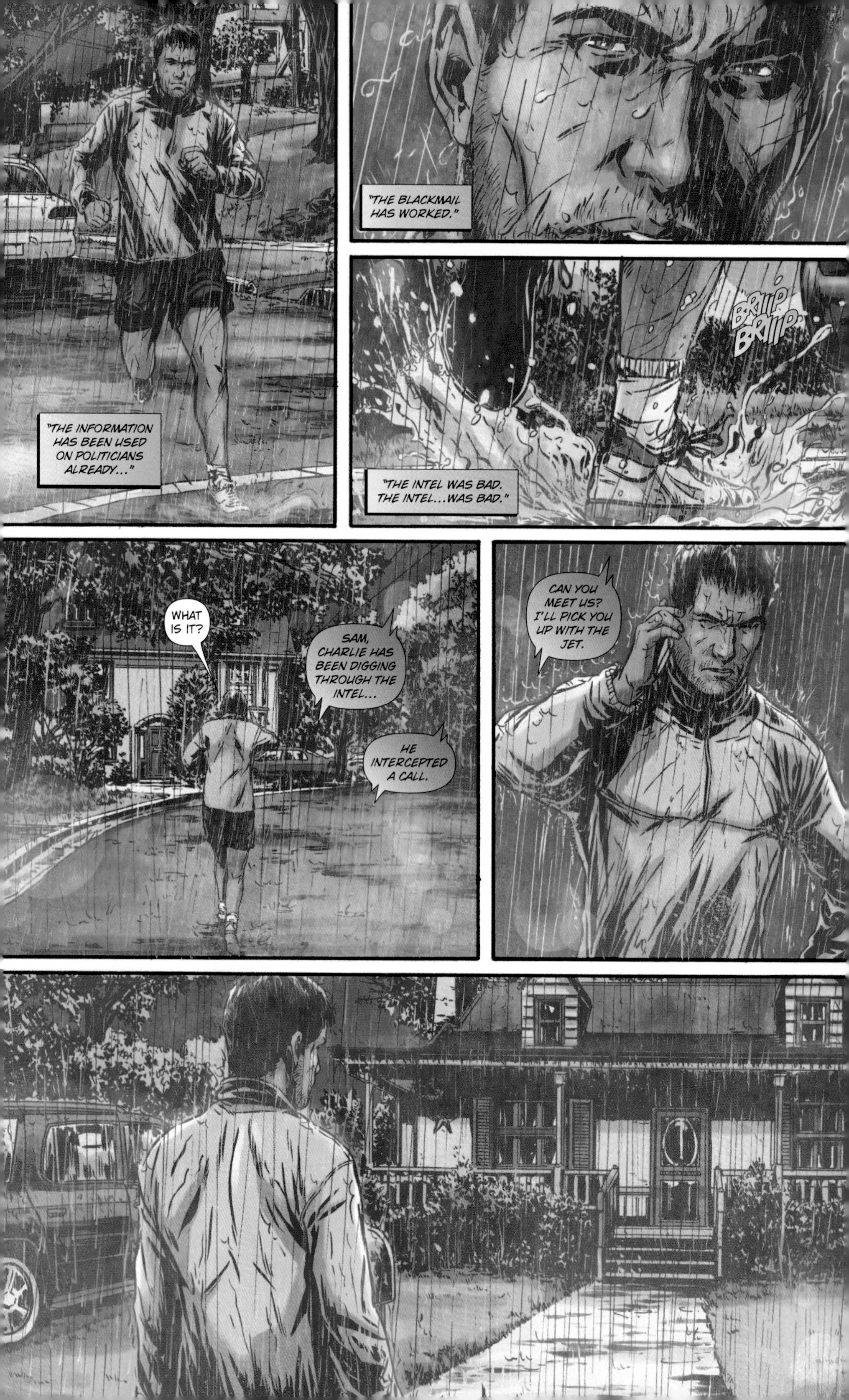
"THE INFORMATION HAS BEEN USED ON POLITICIANS ALREADY..."
"THE BLACKMAIL HAS WORKED."
BRIIIP BRIIIP
"THE INTEL WAS BAD. THE INTEL...WAS BAD."
WHAT IS IT?
SAM, CHARLIE HAS BEEN DIGGING THROUGH THE INTEL...
HE INTERCEPTED A CALL.
CAN YOU MEET US? I'LL PICK YOU UP WITH THE JET.

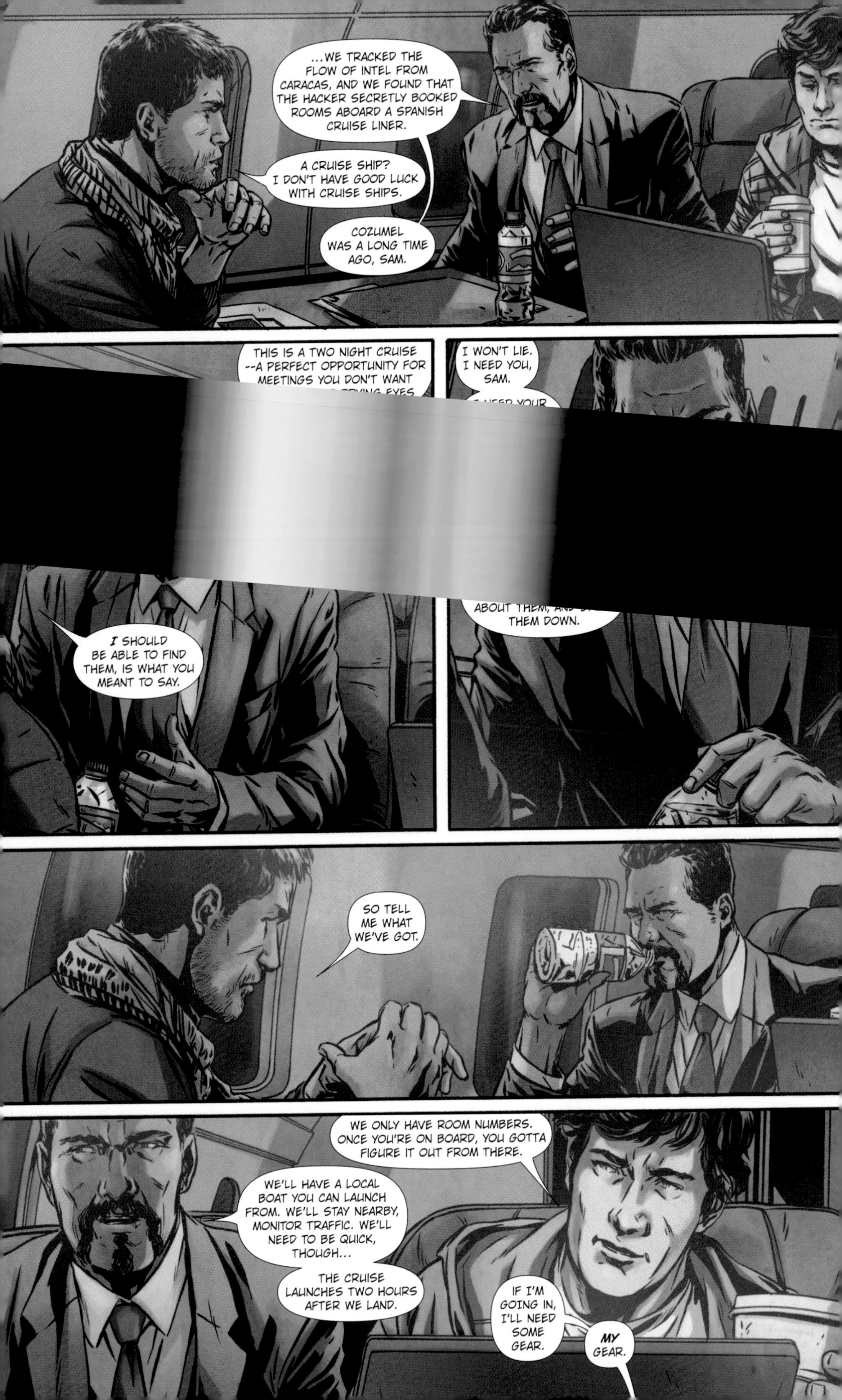
...WE TRACKED THE FLOW OF INTEL FROM CARACAS, AND WE FOUND THAT THE HACKER SECRETLY BOOKED ROOMS ABOARD A SPANISH CRUISE LINER.
A CRUISE SHIP? I DON'T HAVE GOOD LUCK WITH CRUISE SHIPS.
COZUMEL WAS A LONG TIME AGO, SAM.
THIS IS A TWO NIGHT CRUISE --A PERFECT OPPORTUNITY FOR MEETINGS YOU DON'T WANT
I WON'T LIE. I NEED YOU, SAM.
THEM DOWN.
I SHOULD BE ABLE TO FIND THEM, IS WHAT YOU MEANT TO SAY.
SO TELL ME WHAT WE'VE GOT.
WE ONLY HAVE ROOM NUMBERS. ONCE YOU'RE ON BOARD, YOU GOTTA FIGURE IT OUT FROM THERE.
WE'LL HAVE A LOCAL BOAT YOU CAN LAUNCH FROM. WE'LL STAY NEARBY, MONITOR TRAFFIC. WE'LL NEED TO BE QUICK, THOUGH...
THE CRUISE LAUNCHES TWO HOURS AFTER WE LAND.
IF I'M GOING IN, I'LL NEED SOME GEAR.
MY GEAR.

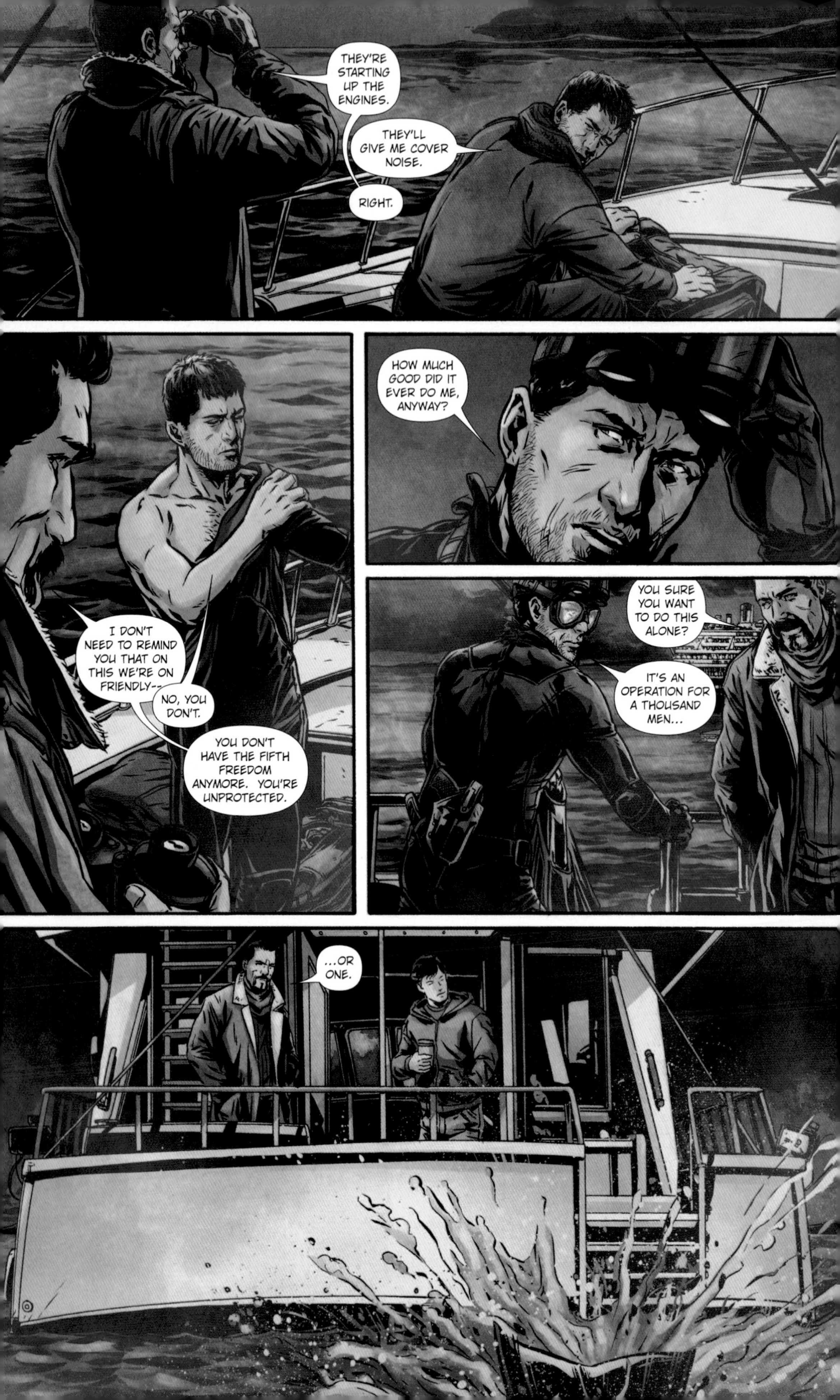
THEY'RE STARTING UP THE ENGINES.
THEY'LL GIVE ME COVER NOISE.
RIGHT.
I DON'T NEED TO REMIND YOU THAT ON THIS WE'RE ON FRIENDLY--
NO, YOU DON'T.
YOU DON'T HAVE THE FIFTH FREEDOM ANYMORE. YOU'RE UNPROTECTED.
HOW MUCH GOOD DID IT EVER DO ME, ANYWAY?
YOU SURE YOU WANT TO DO THIS ALONE?
IT'S AN OPERATION FOR A THOUSAND MEN...
...OR ONE.

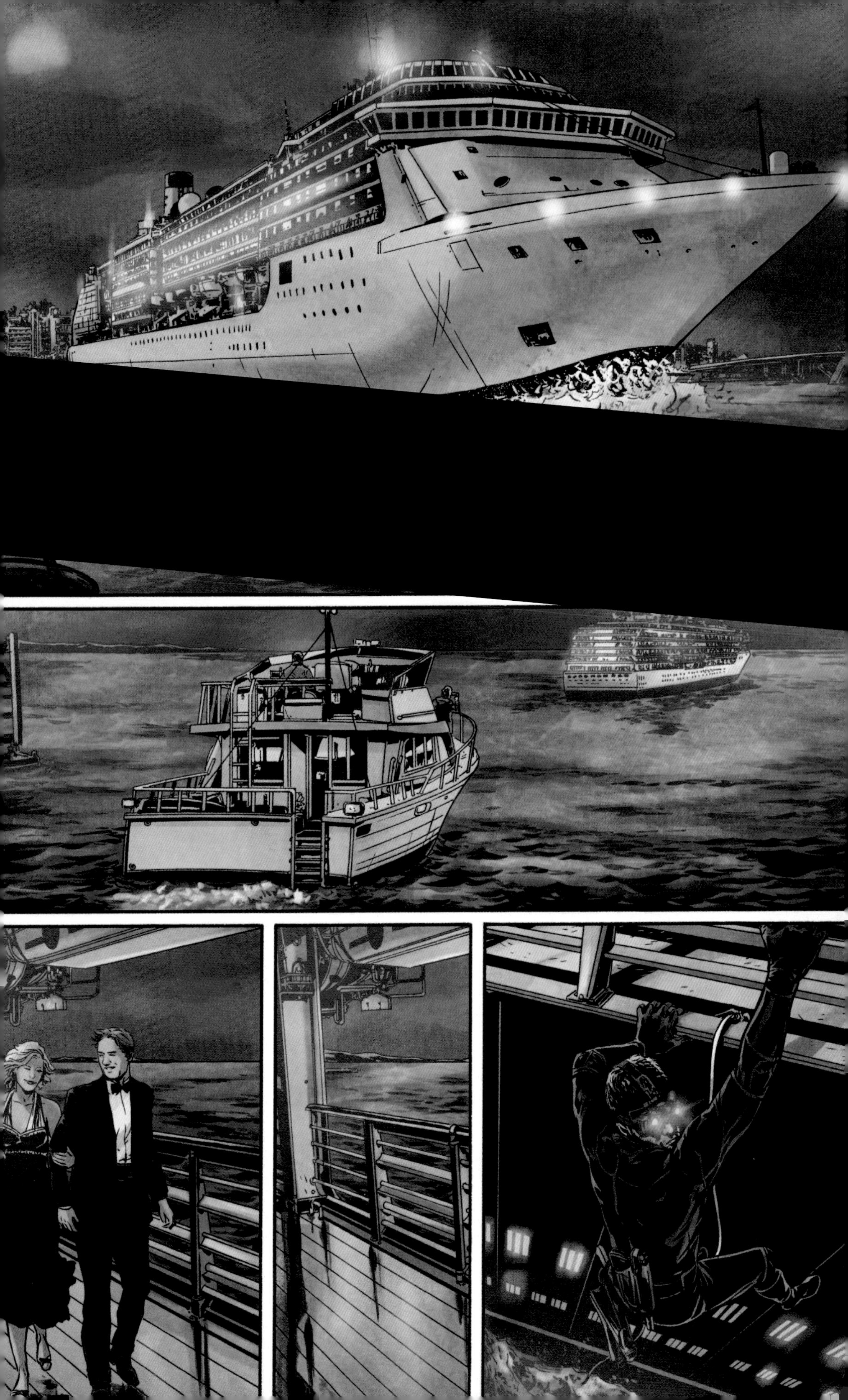

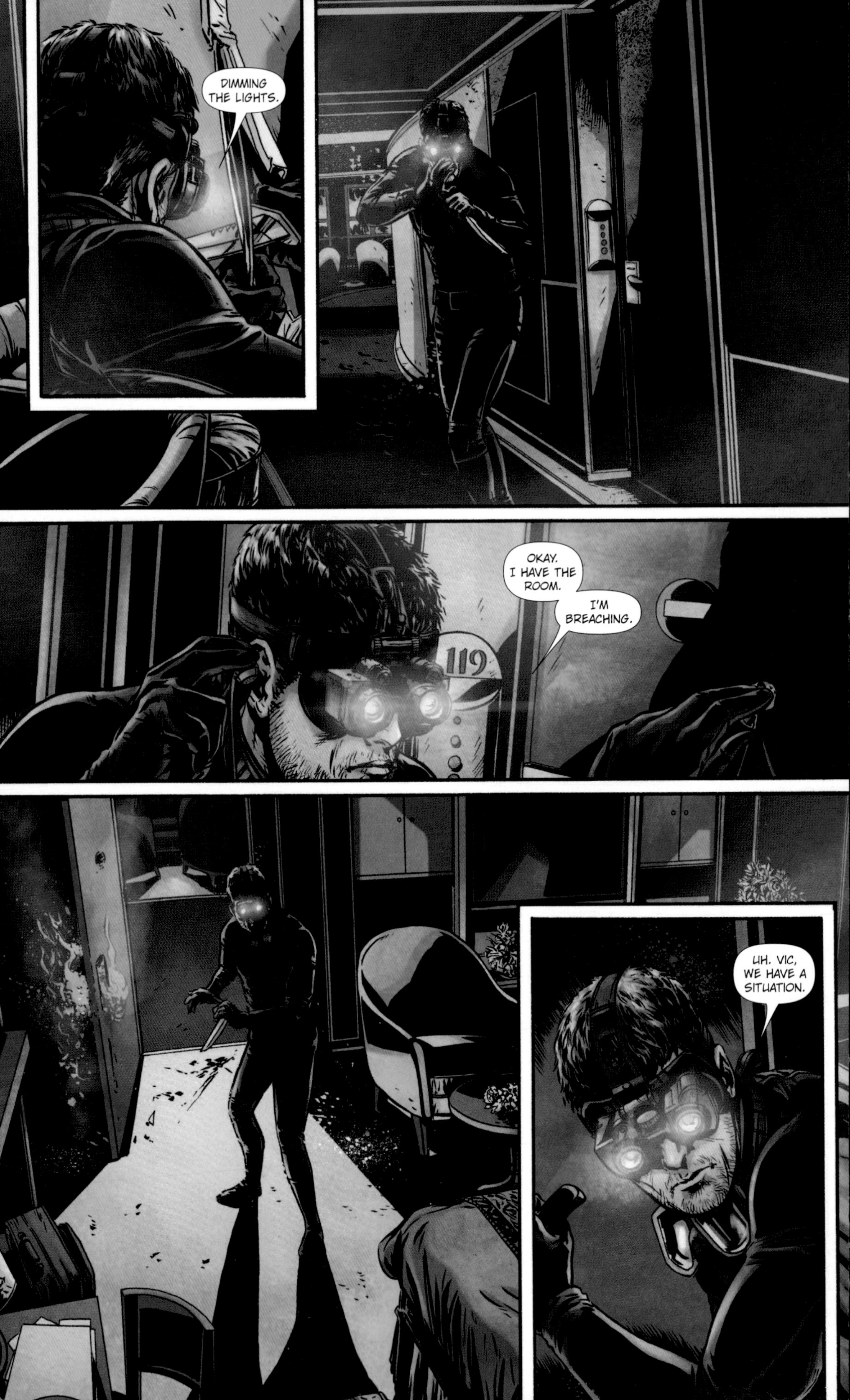
DIMMING THE LIGHTS.
OKAY. I HAVE THE ROOM.
I'M BREACHING.
119
UH. VIC, WE HAVE A SITUATION.

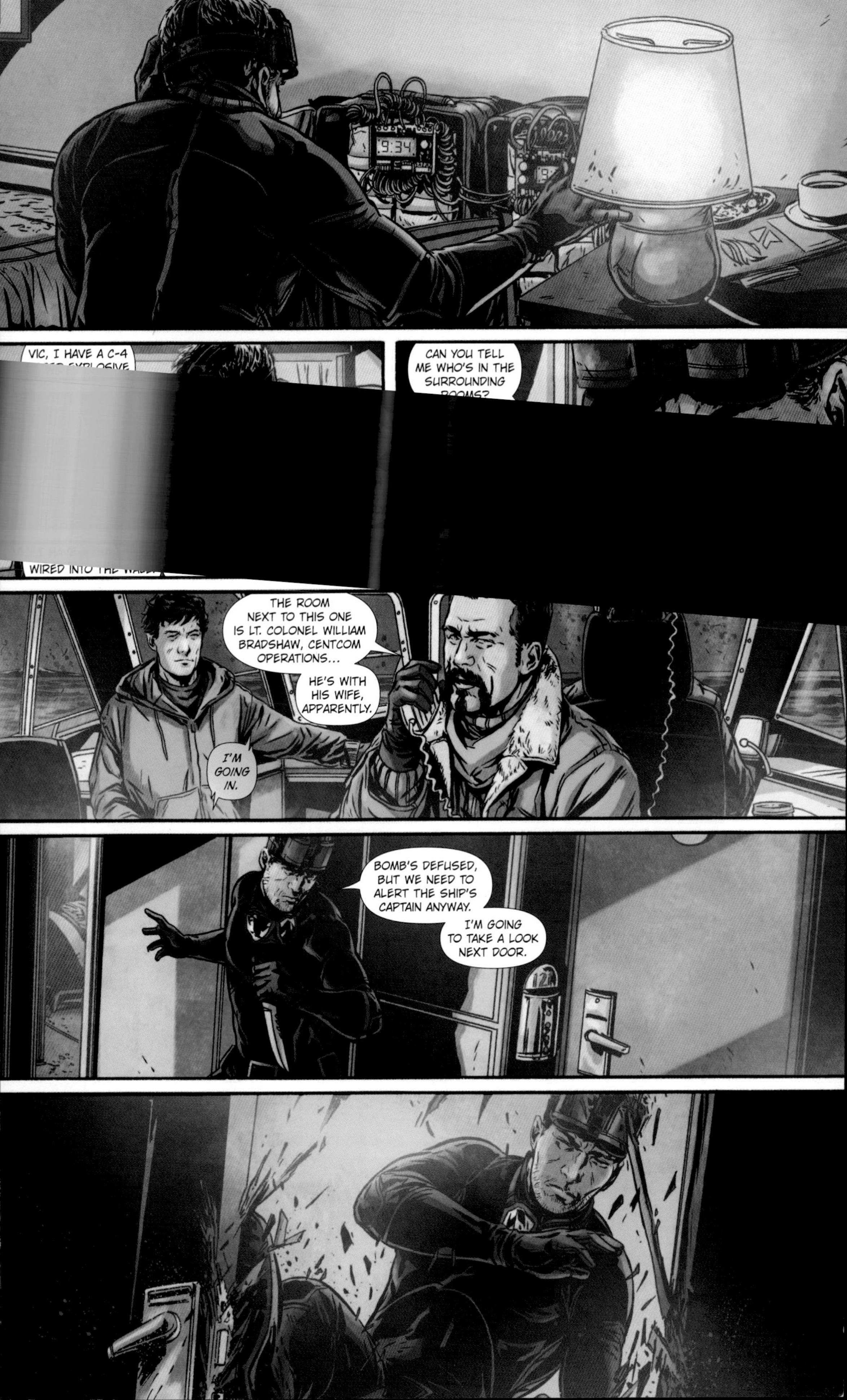
VIC, I HAVE A C-4 [redacted]
CAN YOU TELL ME WHO'S IN THE SURROUNDING [redacted]
THE ROOM NEXT TO THIS ONE IS LT. COLONEL WILLIAM BRADSHAW, CENTCOM OPERATIONS...
HE'S WITH HIS WIFE, APPARENTLY.
I'M GOING IN.
BOMB'S DEFUSED, BUT WE NEED TO ALERT THE SHIP'S CAPTAIN ANYWAY.
I'M GOING TO TAKE A LOOK NEXT DOOR.

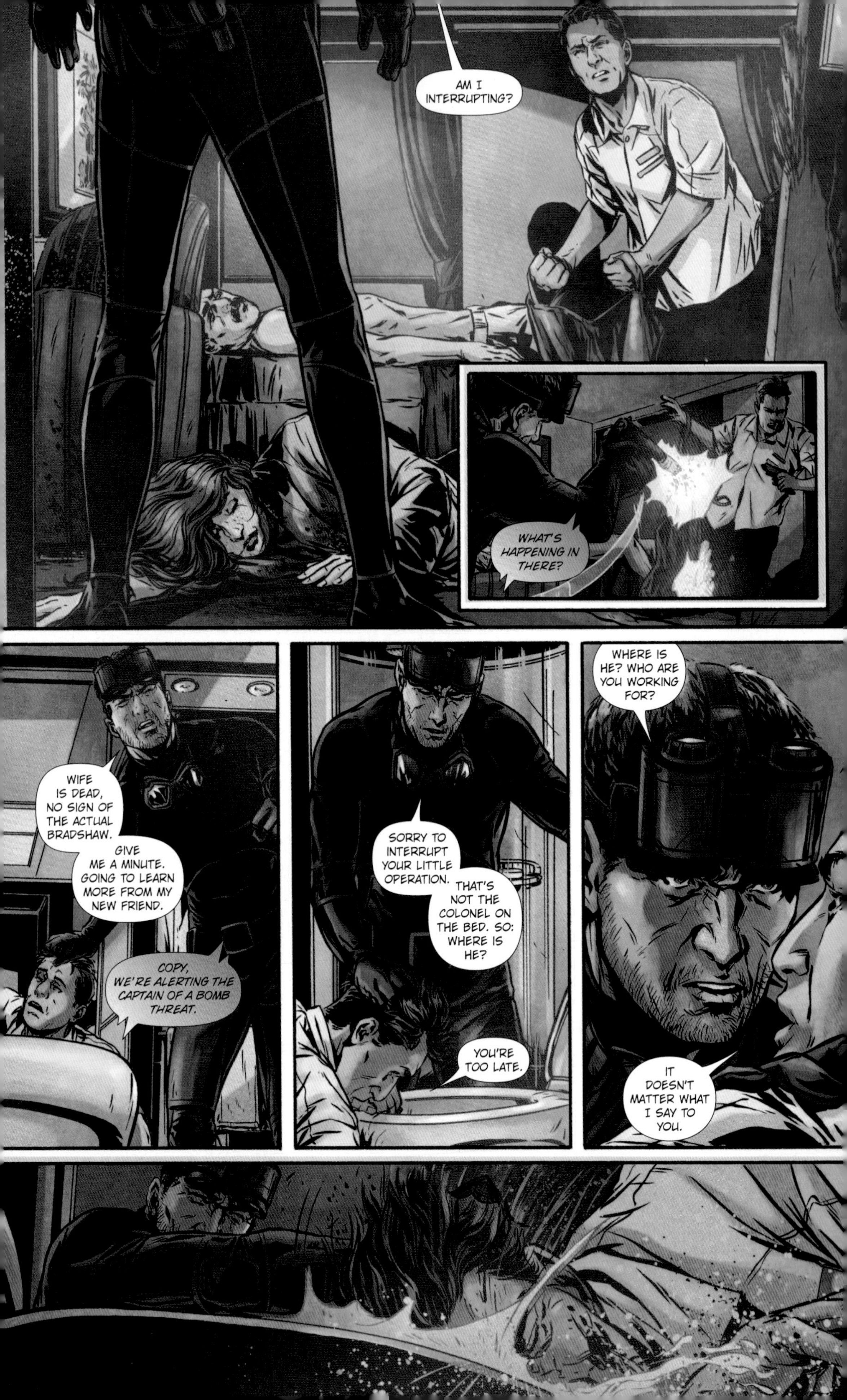
AM I INTERRUPTING?
WHAT'S HAPPENING IN THERE?
WIFE IS DEAD, NO SIGN OF THE ACTUAL BRADSHAW.
GIVE ME A MINUTE. GOING TO LEARN MORE FROM MY NEW FRIEND.
COPY, WE'RE ALERTING THE CAPTAIN OF A BOMB THREAT.
SORRY TO INTERRUPT YOUR LITTLE OPERATION.
THAT'S NOT THE COLONEL ON THE BED. SO: WHERE IS HE?
YOU'RE TOO LATE.
WHERE IS HE? WHO ARE YOU WORKING FOR?
IT DOESN'T MATTER WHAT I SAY TO YOU.

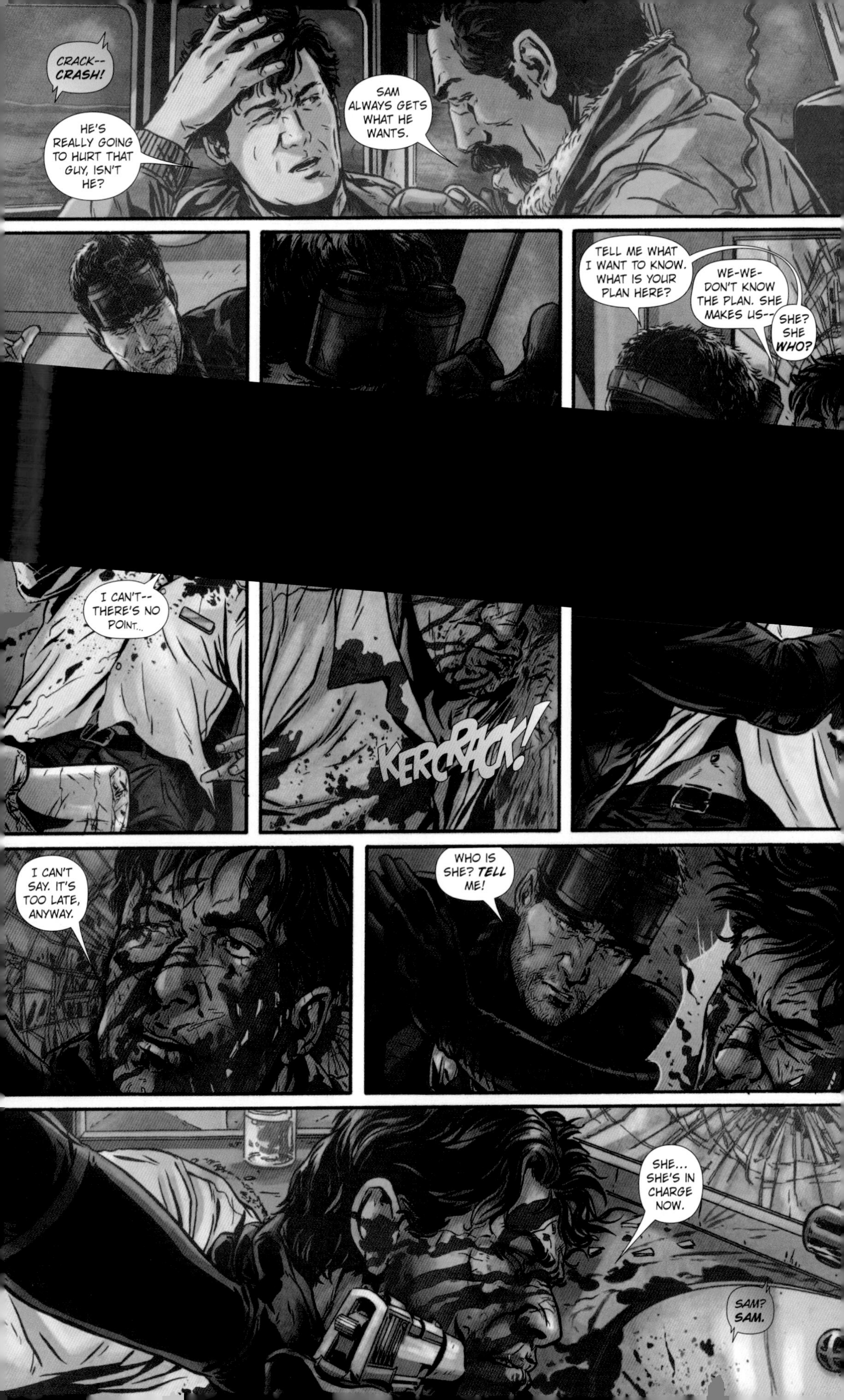
CRACK-- CRASH!
HE'S REALLY GOING TO HURT THAT GUY, ISN'T HE?
SAM ALWAYS GETS WHAT HE WANTS.
TELL ME WHAT I WANT TO KNOW. WHAT IS YOUR PLAN HERE?
WE-WE- DON'T KNOW THE PLAN. SHE MAKES US--
SHE? SHE WHO?
[redacted]
I CAN'T-- THERE'S NO POINT...
KERCRACK!
I CAN'T SAY. IT'S TOO LATE, ANYWAY.
WHO IS SHE? TELL ME!
SHE... SHE'S IN CHARGE NOW.
SAM? SAM.

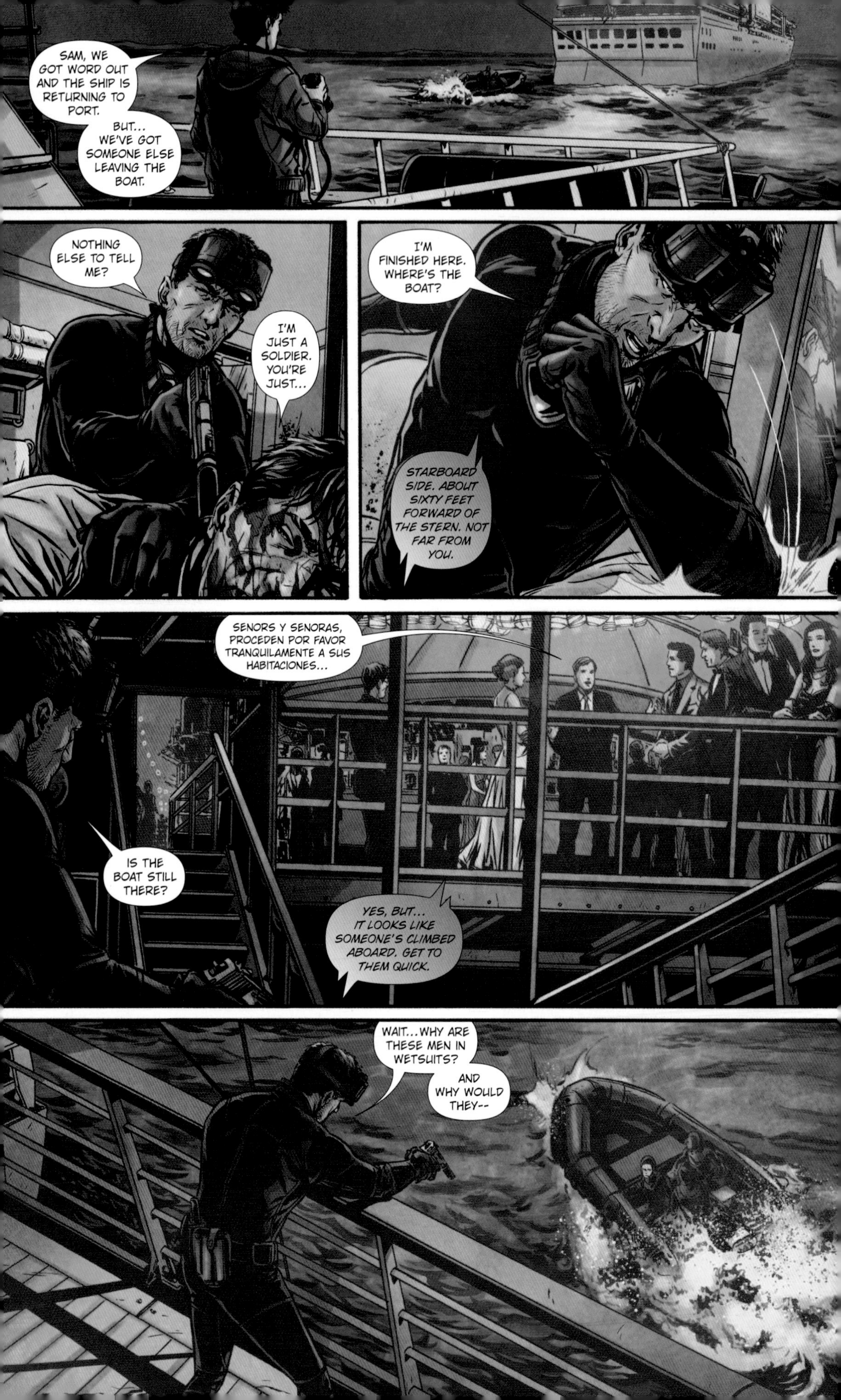
SAM, WE GOT WORD OUT AND THE SHIP IS RETURNING TO PORT.
BUT... WE'VE GOT SOMEONE ELSE LEAVING THE BOAT.
NOTHING ELSE TO TELL ME?
I'M JUST A SOLDIER. YOU'RE JUST...
I'M FINISHED HERE. WHERE'S THE BOAT?
STARBOARD SIDE. ABOUT SIXTY FEET FORWARD OF THE STERN. NOT FAR FROM YOU.
SENORS Y SENORAS, PROCEDEN POR FAVOR TRANQUILAMENTE A SUS HABITACIONES...
IS THE BOAT STILL THERE?
YES, BUT... IT LOOKS LIKE SOMEONE'S CLIMBED ABOARD. GET TO THEM QUICK.
WAIT...WHY ARE THESE MEN IN WETSUITS?
AND WHY WOULD THEY--

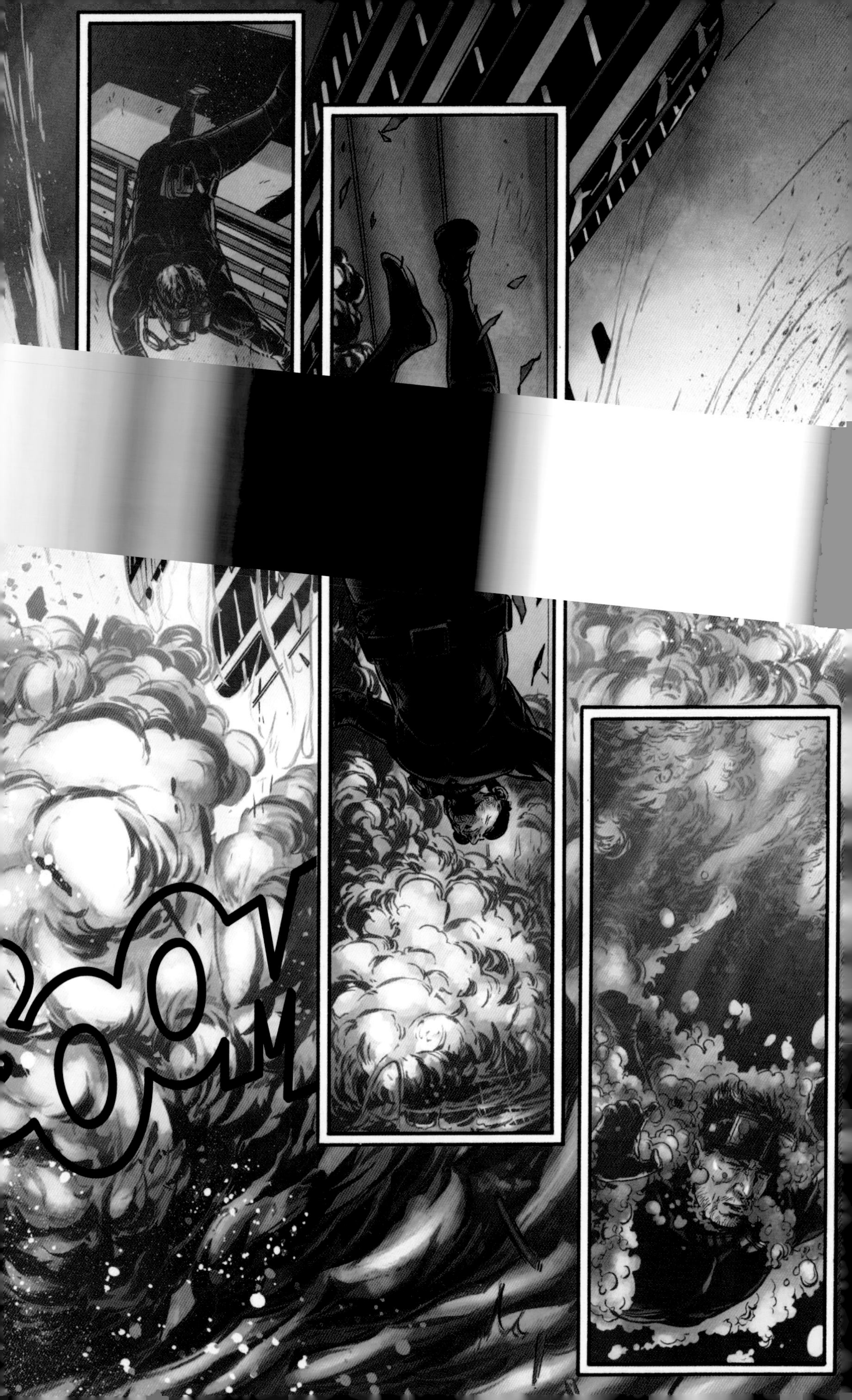

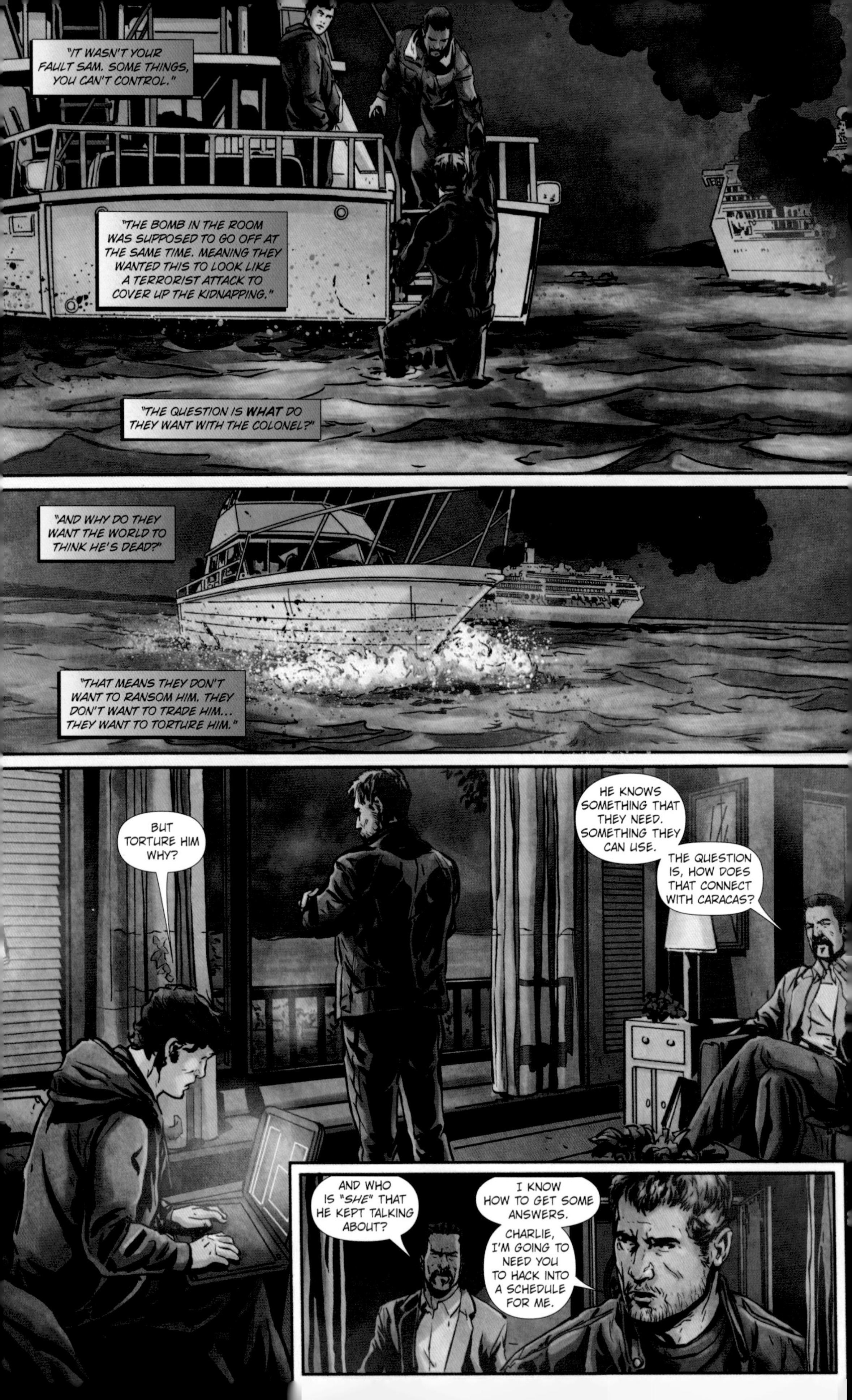
"IT WASN'T YOUR FAULT SAM. SOME THINGS, YOU CAN'T CONTROL."
"THE BOMB IN THE ROOM WAS SUPPOSED TO GO OFF AT THE SAME TIME. MEANING THEY WANTED THIS TO LOOK LIKE A TERRORIST ATTACK TO COVER UP THE KIDNAPPING."
"THE QUESTION IS WHAT DO THEY WANT WITH THE COLONEL?"
"AND WHY DO THEY WANT THE WORLD TO THINK HE'S DEAD?"
"THAT MEANS THEY DON'T WANT TO RANSOM HIM. THEY DON'T WANT TO TRADE HIM... THEY WANT TO TORTURE HIM."
BUT TORTURE HIM WHY?
HE KNOWS SOMETHING THAT THEY NEED. SOMETHING THEY CAN USE.
THE QUESTION IS, HOW DOES THAT CONNECT WITH CARACAS?
AND WHO IS "SHE" THAT HE KEPT TALKING ABOUT?
I KNOW HOW TO GET SOME ANSWERS.
CHARLIE, I'M GOING TO NEED YOU TO HACK INTO A SCHEDULE FOR ME.

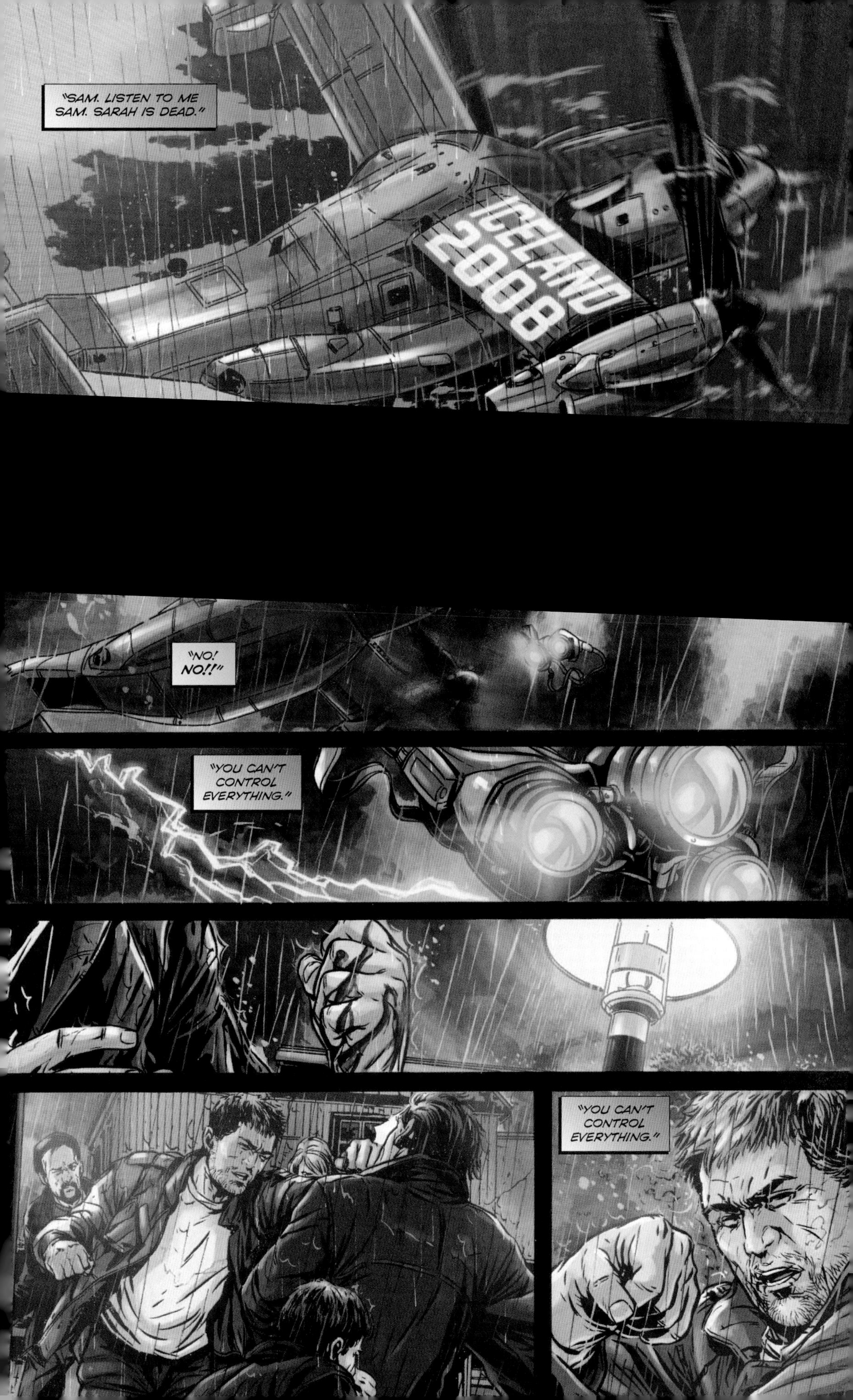
"SAM. LISTEN TO ME SAM. SARAH IS DEAD."
ICELAND 2008
"NO! NO!!"
"YOU CAN'T CONTROL EVERYTHING."
"YOU CAN'T CONTROL EVERYTHING."

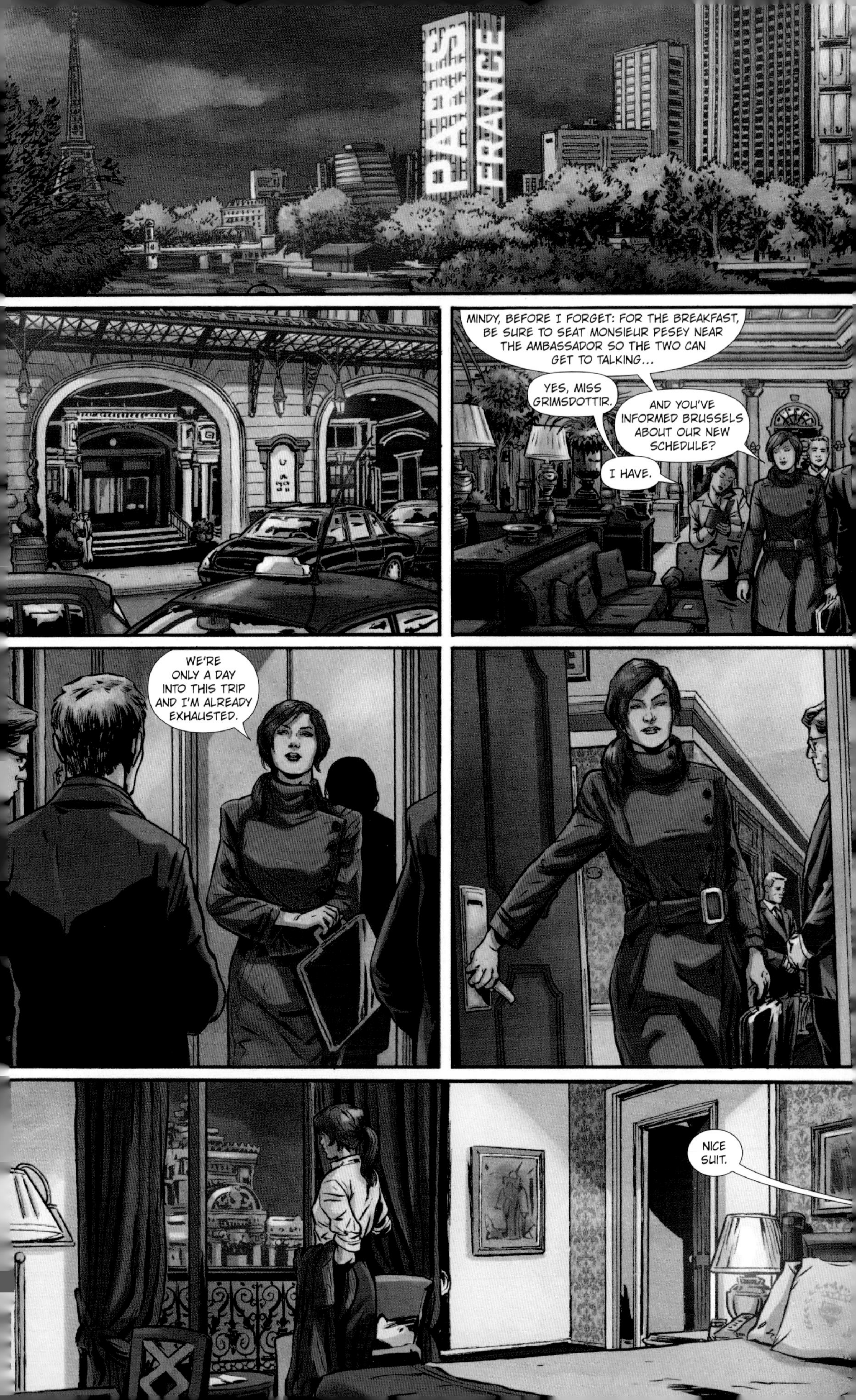
PARIS
FRANCE
MINDY, BEFORE I FORGET: FOR THE BREAKFAST, BE SURE TO SEAT MONSIEUR PESEY NEAR THE AMBASSADOR SO THE TWO CAN GET TO TALKING...
YES, MISS GRIMSDOTTIR.
AND YOU'VE INFORMED BRUSSELS ABOUT OUR NEW SCHEDULE?
I HAVE.
WE'RE ONLY A DAY INTO THIS TRIP AND I'M ALREADY EXHAUSTED.
NICE SUIT.

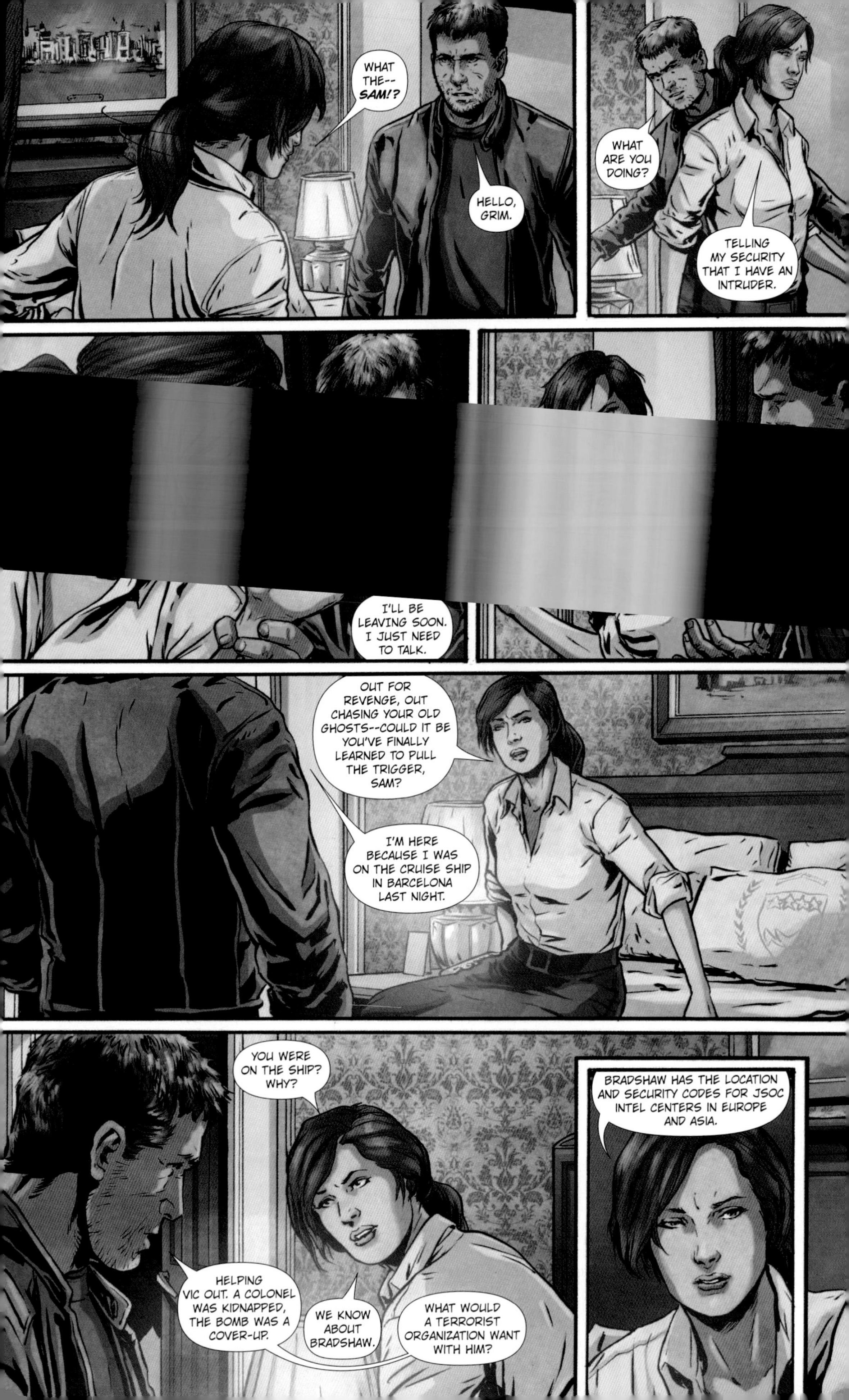
WHAT THE-- SAM!?
HELLO, GRIM.
WHAT ARE YOU DOING?
TELLING MY SECURITY THAT I HAVE AN INTRUDER.
I'LL BE LEAVING SOON. I JUST NEED TO TALK.
OUT FOR REVENGE, OUT CHASING YOUR OLD GHOSTS--COULD IT BE YOU'VE FINALLY LEARNED TO PULL THE TRIGGER, SAM?
I'M HERE BECAUSE I WAS ON THE CRUISE SHIP IN BARCELONA LAST NIGHT.
YOU WERE ON THE SHIP? WHY?
HELPING VIC OUT. A COLONEL WAS KIDNAPPED, THE BOMB WAS A COVER-UP.
WE KNOW ABOUT BRADSHAW.
WHAT WOULD A TERRORIST ORGANIZATION WANT WITH HIM?
BRADSHAW HAS THE LOCATION AND SECURITY CODES FOR JSOC INTEL CENTERS IN EUROPE AND ASIA.

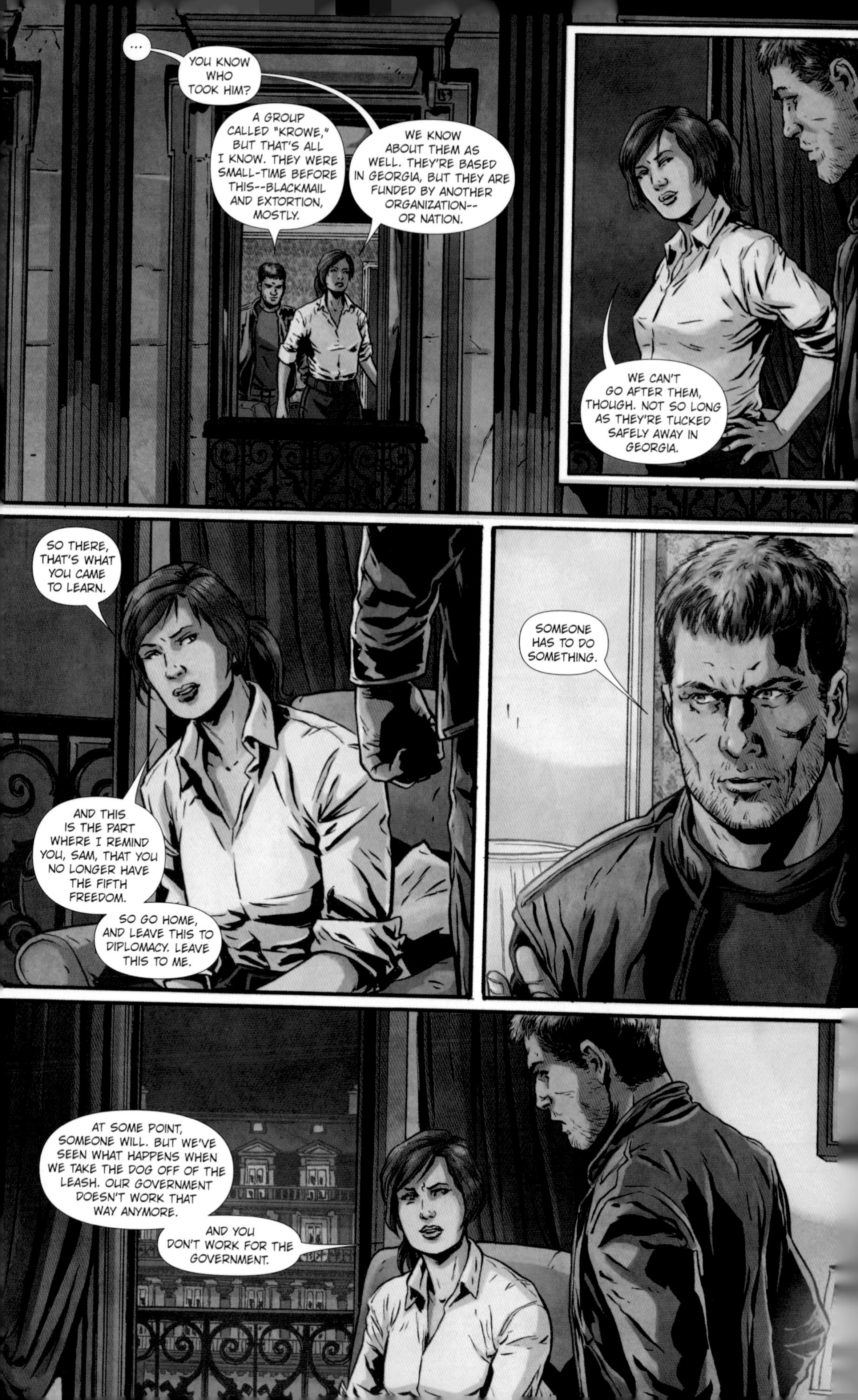
...
YOU KNOW WHO TOOK HIM?
A GROUP CALLED "KROWE," BUT THAT'S ALL I KNOW. THEY WERE SMALL-TIME BEFORE THIS--BLACKMAIL AND EXTORTION, MOSTLY.
WE KNOW ABOUT THEM AS WELL. THEY'RE BASED IN GEORGIA, BUT THEY ARE FUNDED BY ANOTHER ORGANIZATION-- OR NATION.
WE CAN'T GO AFTER THEM, THOUGH. NOT SO LONG AS THEY'RE TUCKED SAFELY AWAY IN GEORGIA.
SO THERE, THAT'S WHAT YOU CAME TO LEARN.
AND THIS IS THE PART WHERE I REMIND YOU, SAM, THAT YOU NO LONGER HAVE THE FIFTH FREEDOM.
SO GO HOME, AND LEAVE THIS TO DIPLOMACY. LEAVE THIS TO ME.
SOMEONE HAS TO DO SOMETHING.
AT SOME POINT, SOMEONE WILL. BUT WE'VE SEEN WHAT HAPPENS WHEN WE TAKE THE DOG OFF OF THE LEASH. OUR GOVERNMENT DOESN'T WORK THAT WAY ANYMORE.
AND YOU DON'T WORK FOR THE GOVERNMENT.

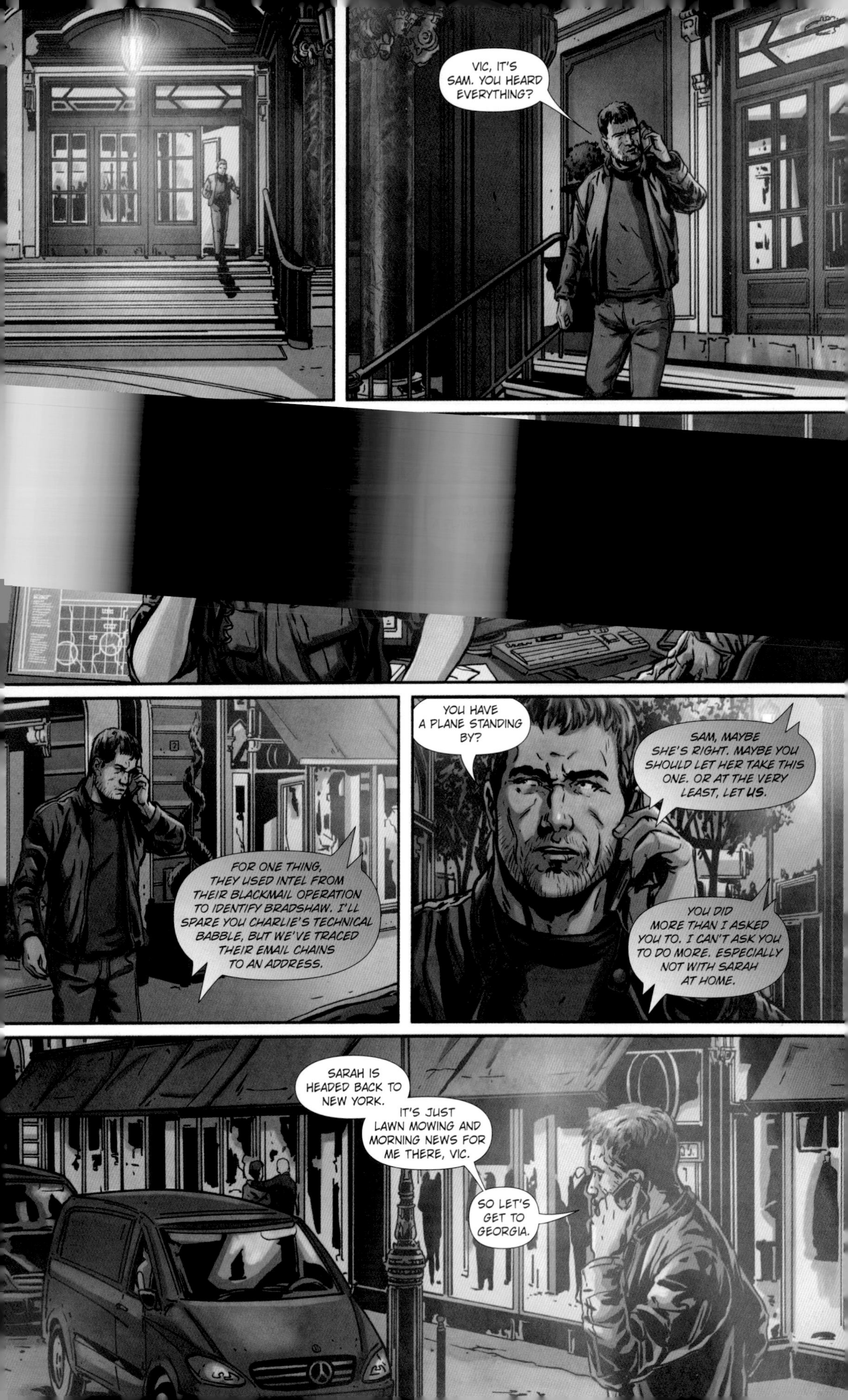
VIC, IT'S SAM. YOU HEARD EVERYTHING?
FOR ONE THING, THEY USED INTEL FROM THEIR BLACKMAIL OPERATION TO IDENTIFY BRADSHAW. I'LL SPARE YOU CHARLIE'S TECHNICAL BABBLE, BUT WE'VE TRACED THEIR EMAIL CHAINS TO AN ADDRESS.
YOU HAVE A PLANE STANDING BY?
SAM, MAYBE SHE'S RIGHT. MAYBE YOU SHOULD LET HER TAKE THIS ONE. OR AT THE VERY LEAST, LET US.
YOU DID MORE THAN I ASKED YOU TO. I CAN'T ASK YOU TO DO MORE. ESPECIALLY NOT WITH SARAH AT HOME.
SARAH IS HEADED BACK TO NEW YORK.
IT'S JUST LAWN MOWING AND MORNING NEWS FOR ME THERE, VIC.
SO LET'S GET TO GEORGIA.

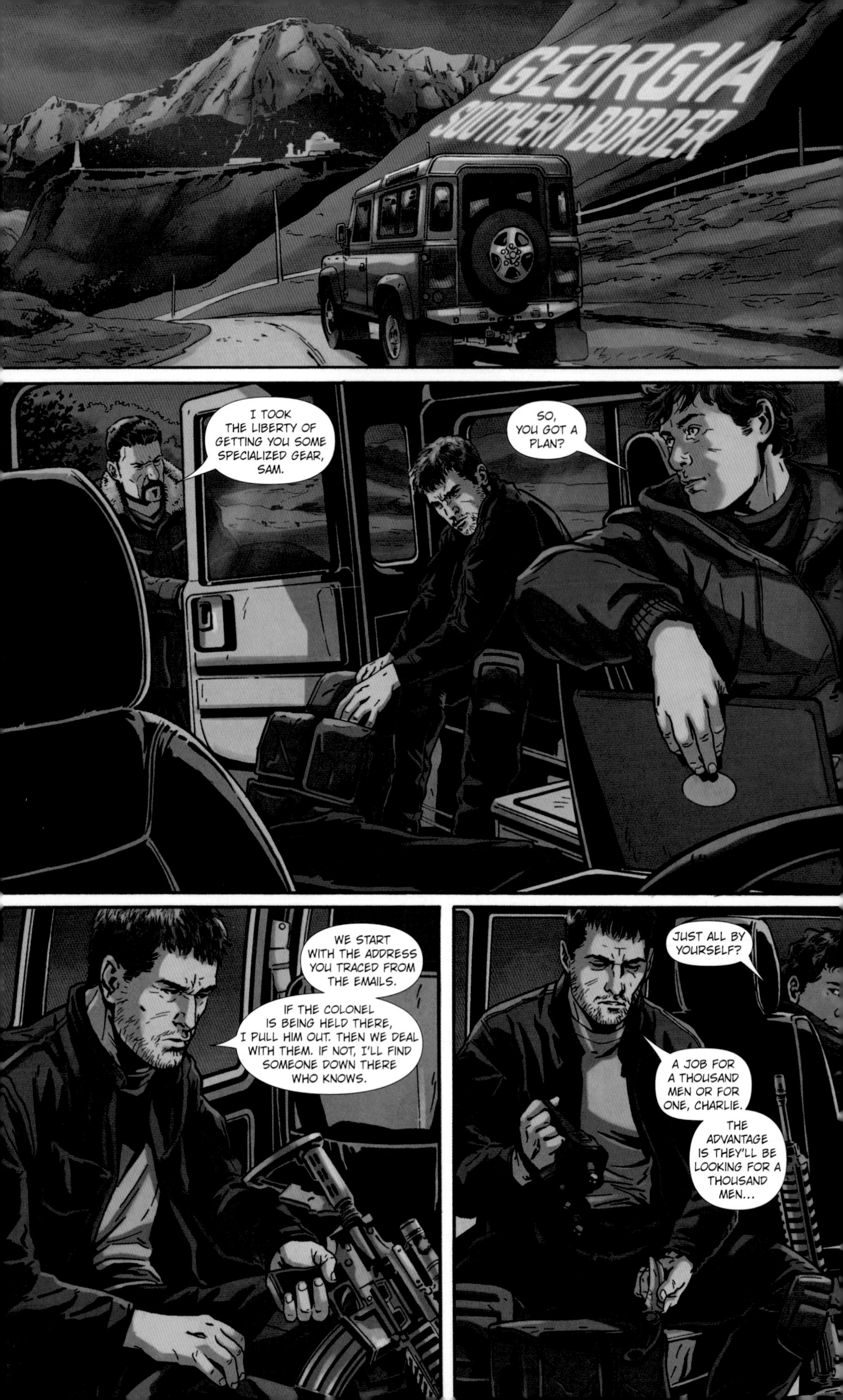
GEORGIA
SOUTHERN BORDER
I TOOK THE LIBERTY OF GETTING YOU SOME SPECIALIZED GEAR, SAM.
SO, YOU GOT A PLAN?
WE START WITH THE ADDRESS YOU TRACED FROM THE EMAILS.
IF THE COLONEL IS BEING HELD THERE, I PULL HIM OUT. THEN WE DEAL WITH THEM. IF NOT, I'LL FIND SOMEONE DOWN THERE WHO KNOWS.
JUST ALL BY YOURSELF?
A JOB FOR A THOUSAND MEN OR FOR ONE, CHARLIE.
THE ADVANTAGE IS THEY'LL BE LOOKING FOR A THOUSAND MEN...

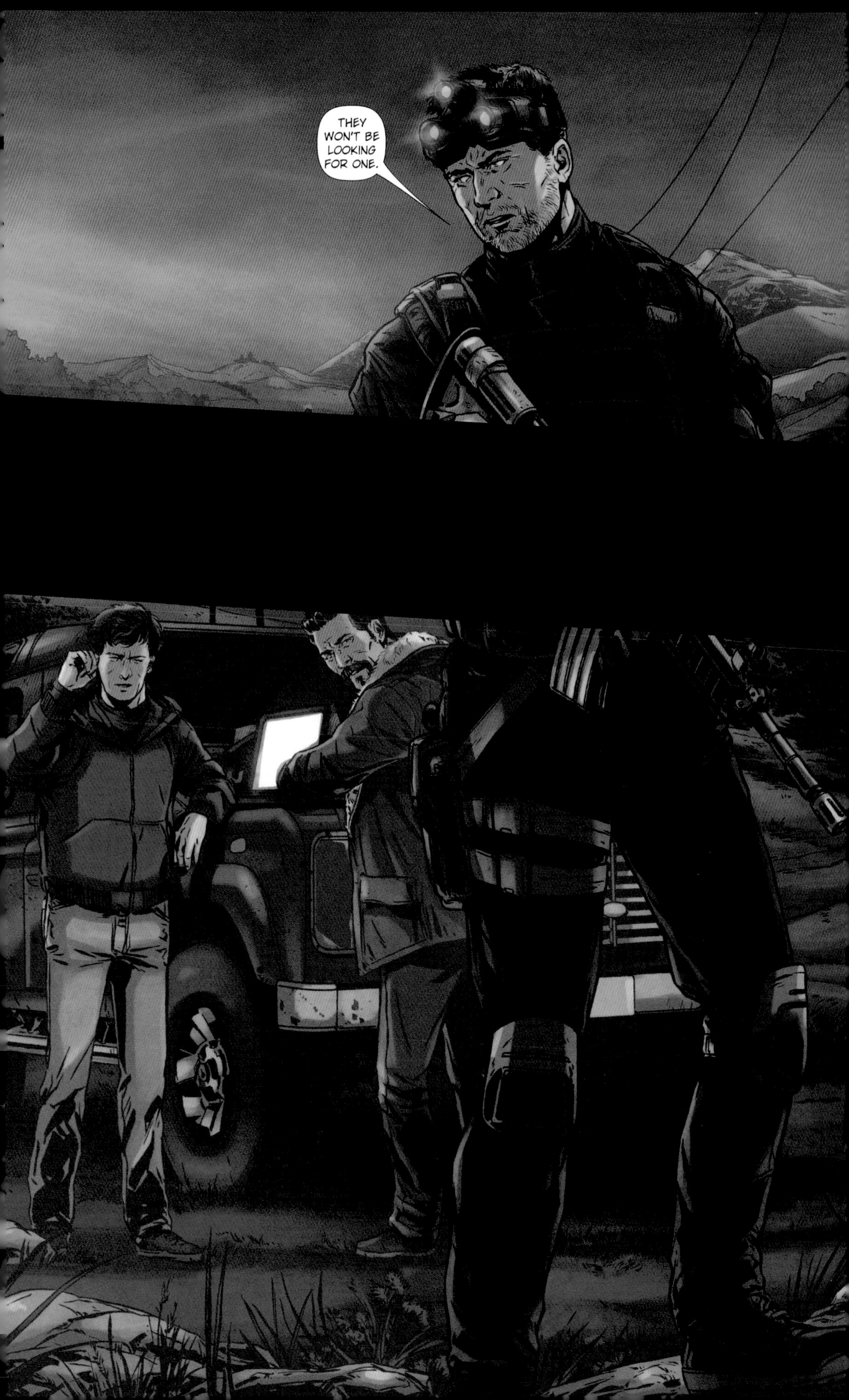
THEY WON'T BE LOOKING FOR ONE.

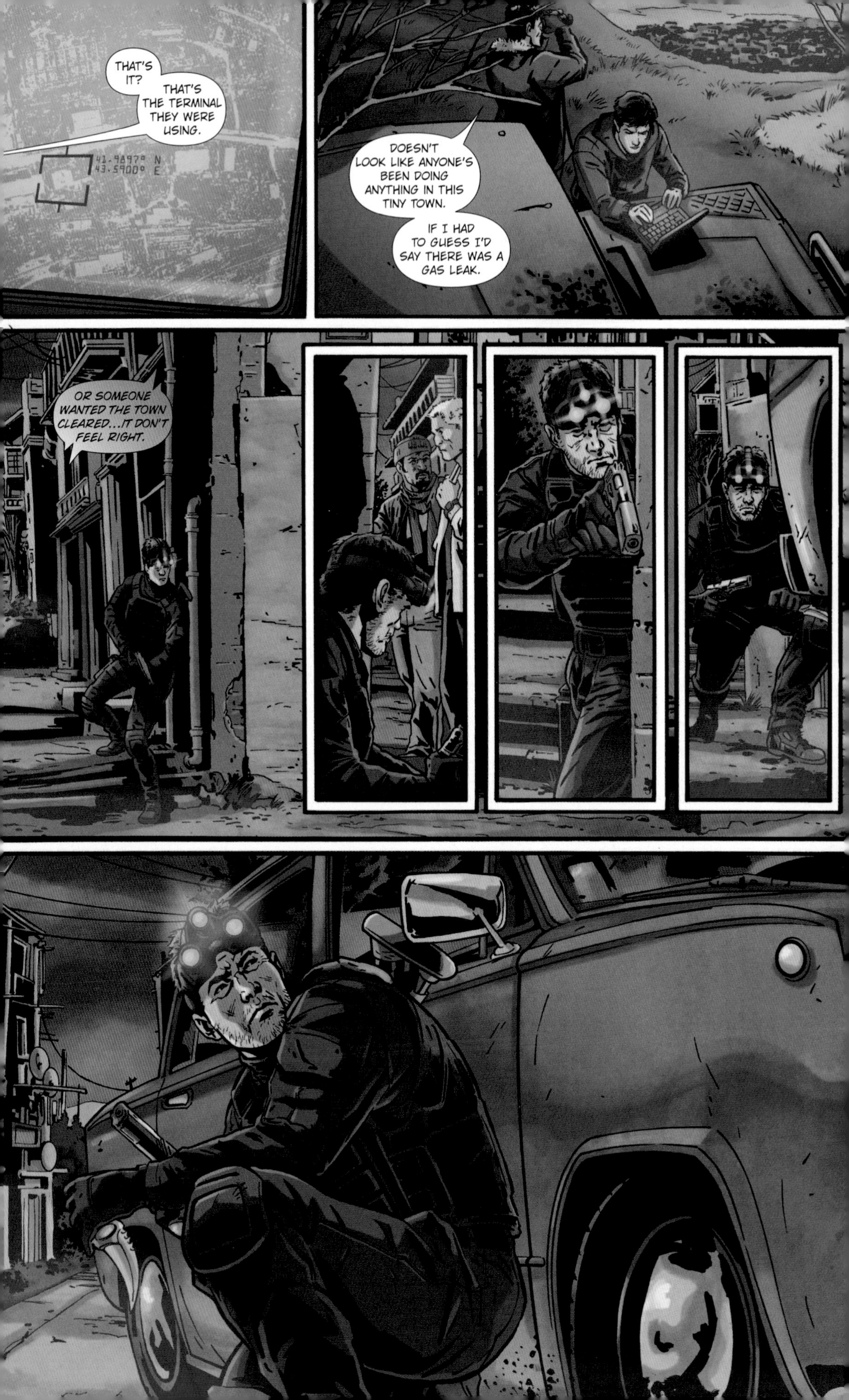
THAT'S IT?
THAT'S THE TERMINAL THEY WERE USING.
41.9897° N
43.5900° E
DOESN'T LOOK LIKE ANYONE'S BEEN DOING ANYTHING IN THIS TINY TOWN.
IF I HAD TO GUESS I'D SAY THERE WAS A GAS LEAK.
OR SOMEONE WANTED THE TOWN CLEARED...IT DON'T FEEL RIGHT.

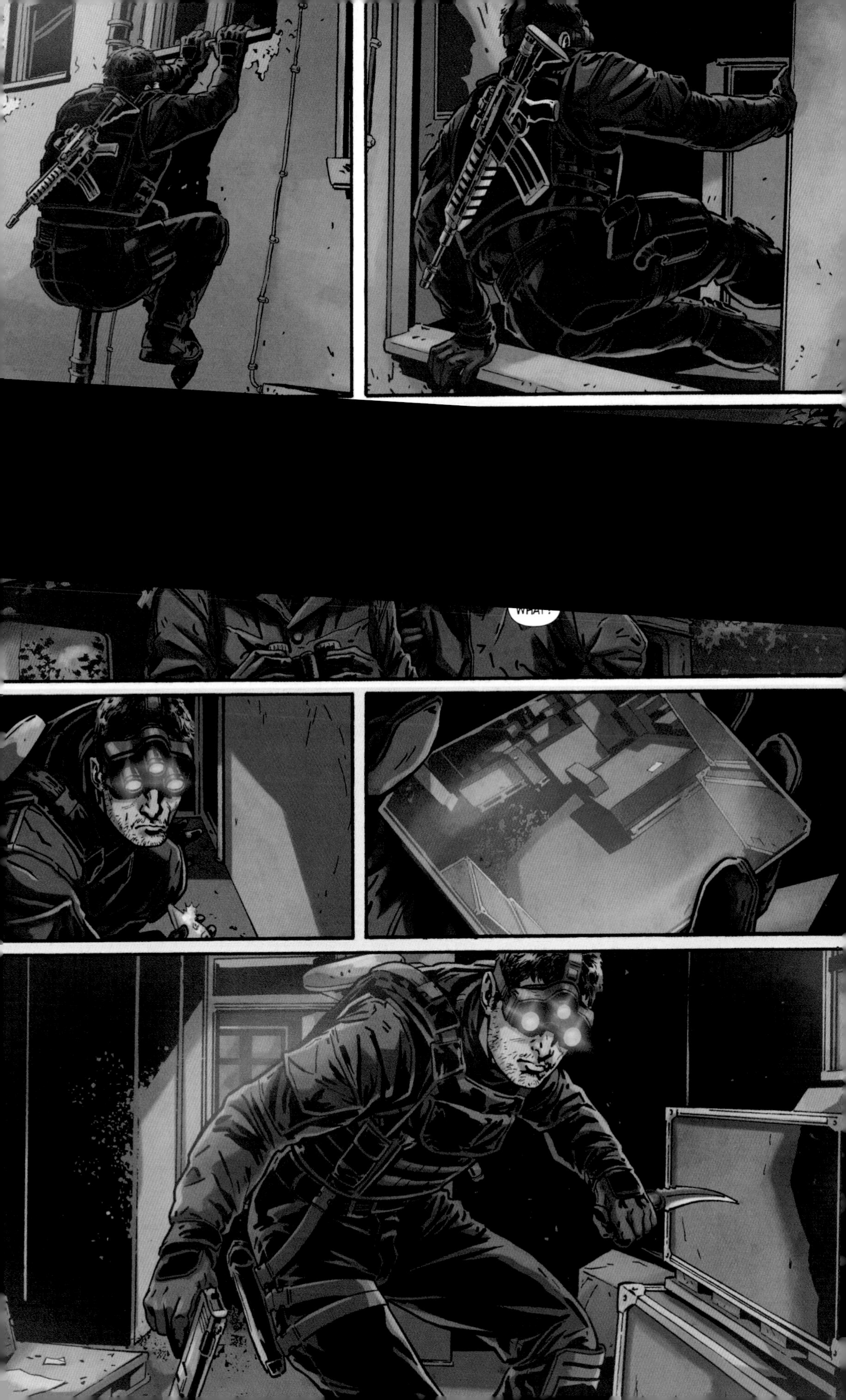
[redacted]

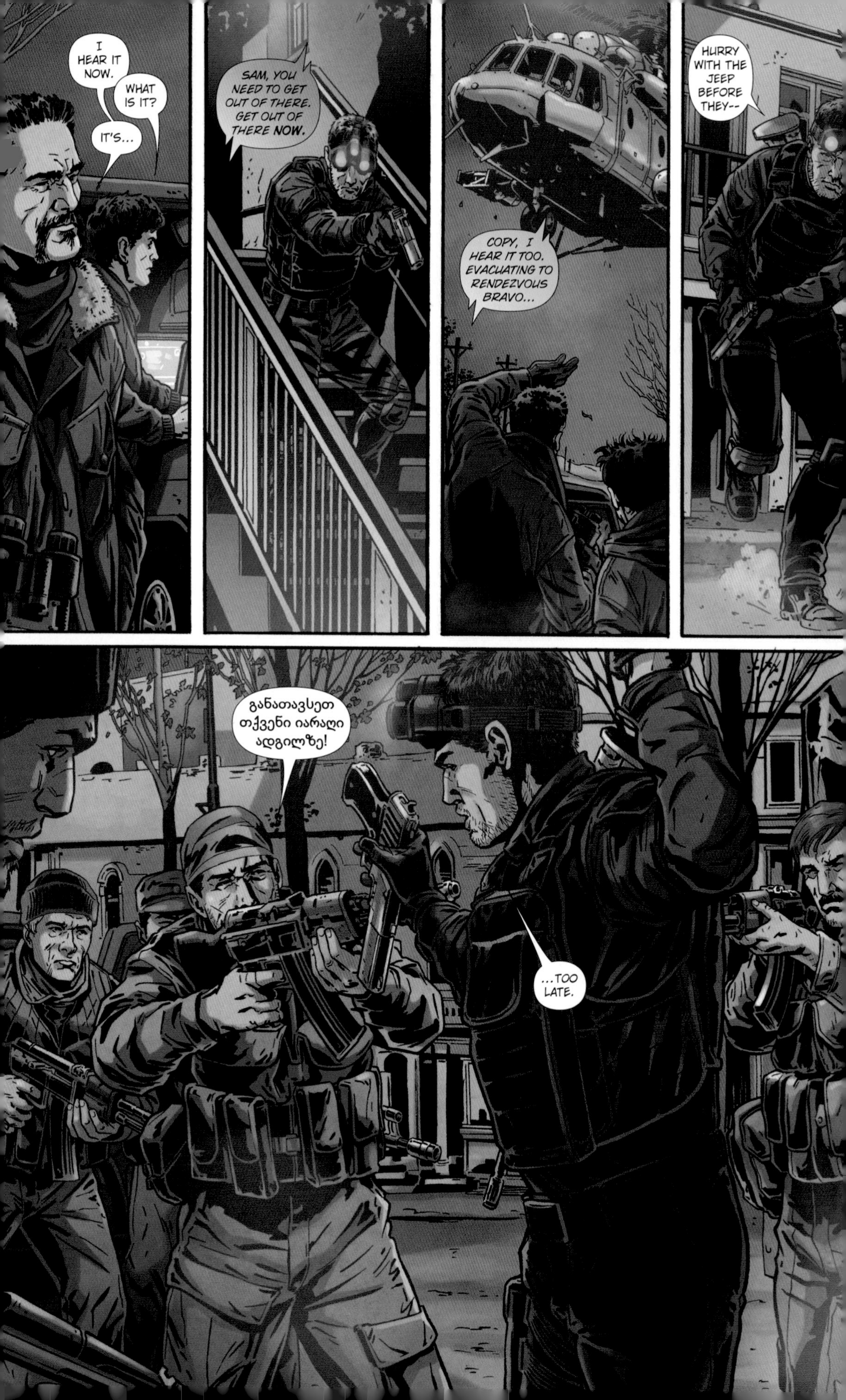
I HEAR IT NOW.
WHAT IS IT?
IT'S...
SAM, YOU NEED TO GET OUT OF THERE. GET OUT OF THERE NOW.
COPY, I HEAR IT TOO. EVACUATING TO RENDEZVOUS BRAVO...
HURRY WITH THE JEEP BEFORE THEY--
განათავსეთ თქვენი იარაღი ადგილზე!
...TOO LATE.

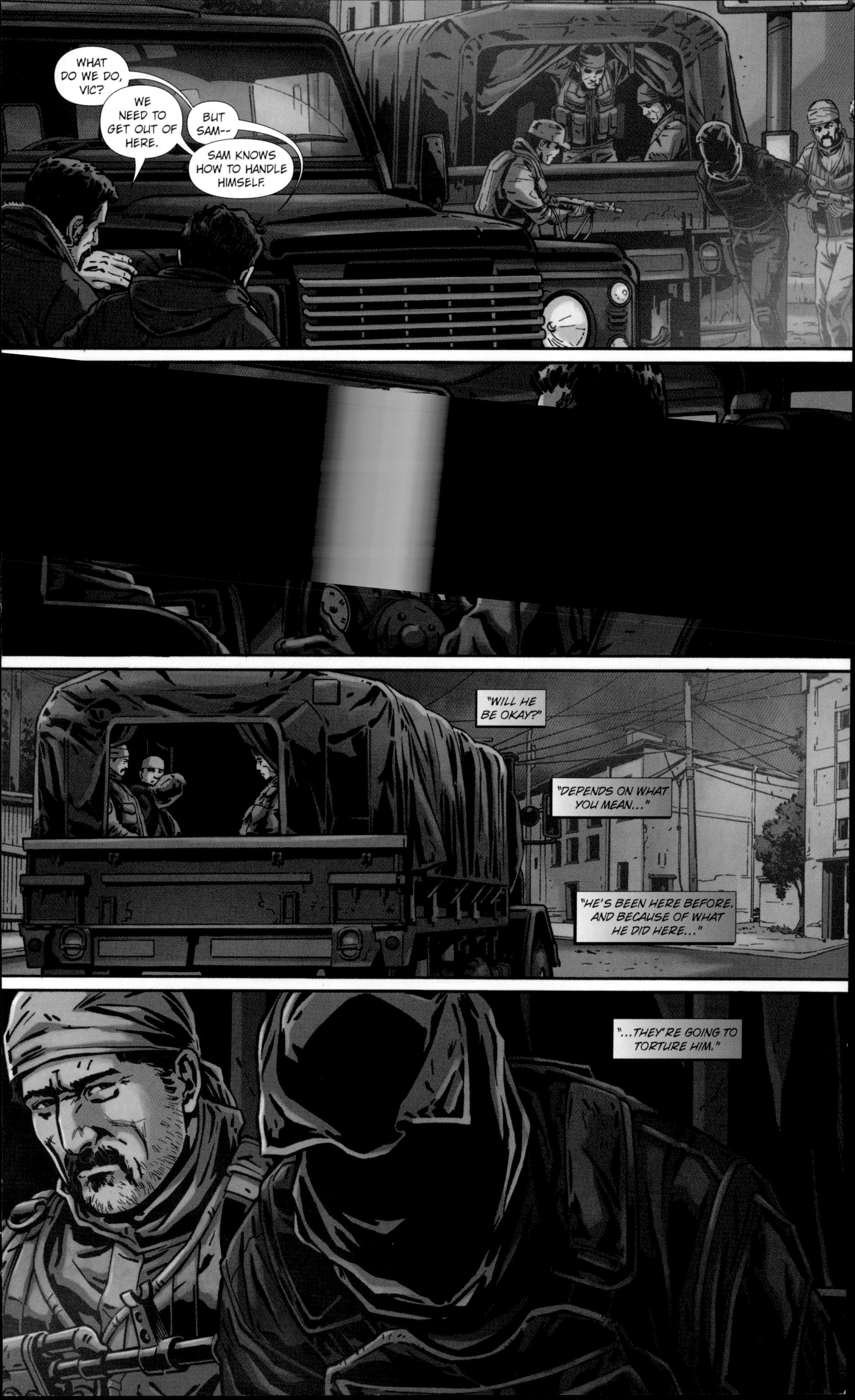
WHAT DO WE DO, VIC?
WE NEED TO GET OUT OF HERE.
BUT SAM--
SAM KNOWS HOW TO HANDLE HIMSELF.
"WILL HE BE OKAY?"
"DEPENDS ON WHAT YOU MEAN..."
"HE'S BEEN HERE BEFORE. AND BECAUSE OF WHAT HE DID HERE..."
"...THEY'RE GOING TO TORTURE HIM."

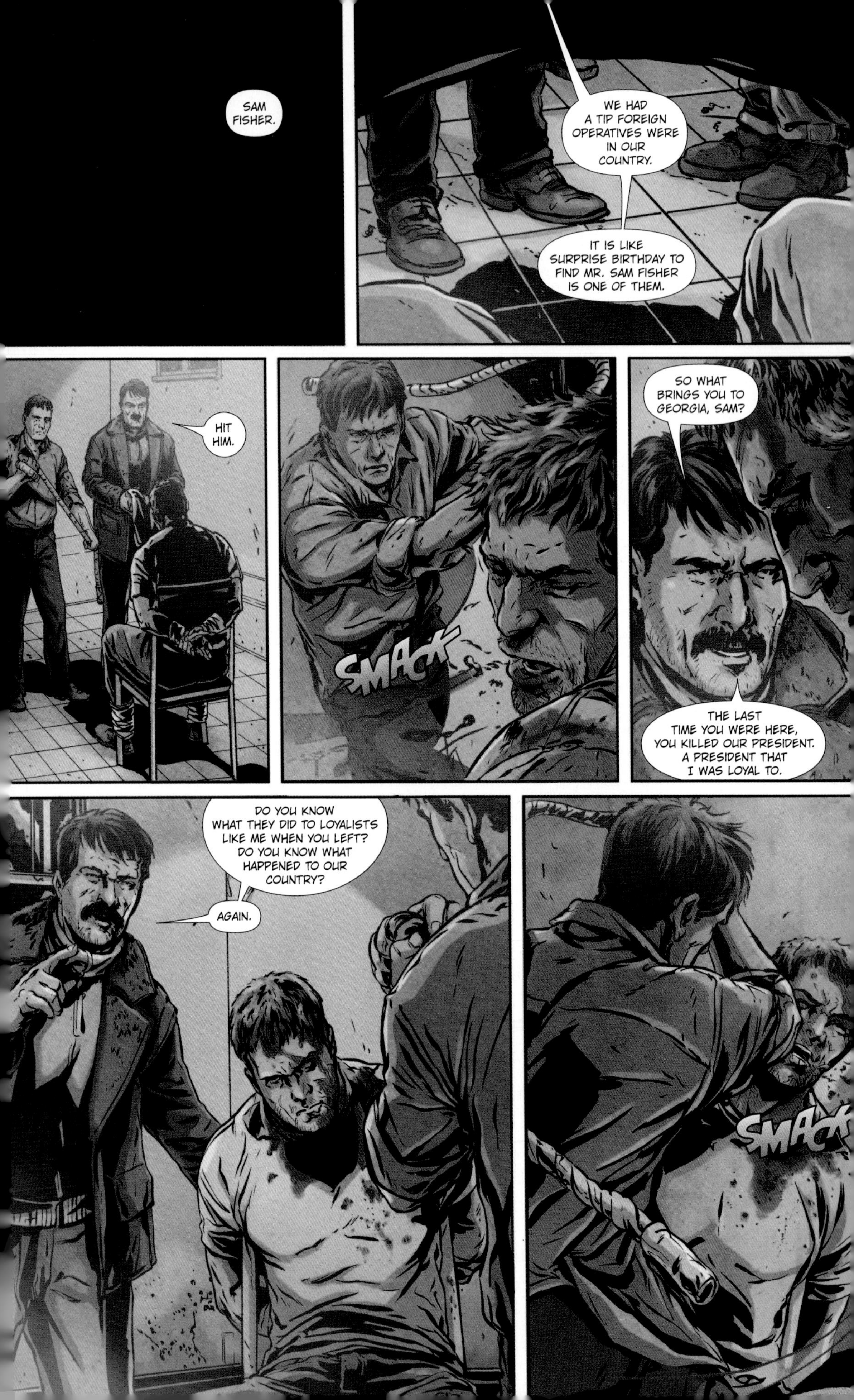
SAM FISHER.
WE HAD A TIP FOREIGN OPERATIVES WERE IN OUR COUNTRY.
IT IS LIKE SURPRISE BIRTHDAY TO FIND MR. SAM FISHER IS ONE OF THEM.
HIT HIM.
SMACK
SO WHAT BRINGS YOU TO GEORGIA, SAM?
THE LAST TIME YOU WERE HERE, YOU KILLED OUR PRESIDENT. A PRESIDENT THAT I WAS LOYAL TO.
DO YOU KNOW WHAT THEY DID TO LOYALISTS LIKE ME WHEN YOU LEFT? DO YOU KNOW WHAT HAPPENED TO OUR COUNTRY?
AGAIN.
SMACK

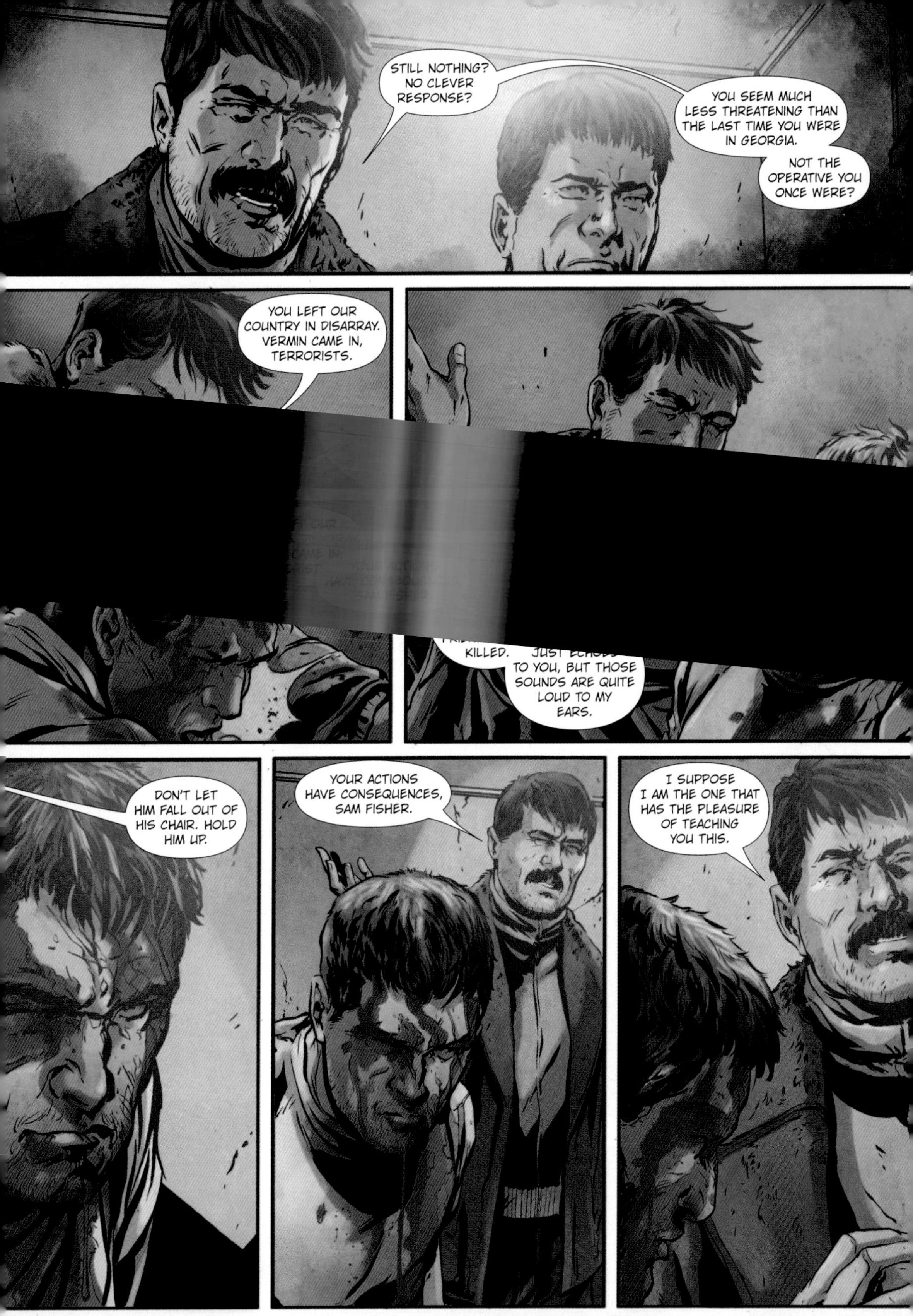
STILL NOTHING? NO CLEVER RESPONSE?
YOU SEEM MUCH LESS THREATENING THAN THE LAST TIME YOU WERE IN GEORGIA.
NOT THE OPERATIVE YOU ONCE WERE?
YOU LEFT OUR COUNTRY IN DISARRAY. VERMIN CAME IN, TERRORISTS.
KILLED.
TO YOU, BUT THOSE SOUNDS ARE QUITE LOUD TO MY EARS.
DON'T LET HIM FALL OUT OF HIS CHAIR. HOLD HIM UP.
YOUR ACTIONS HAVE CONSEQUENCES, SAM FISHER.
I SUPPOSE I AM THE ONE THAT HAS THE PLEASURE OF TEACHING YOU THIS.

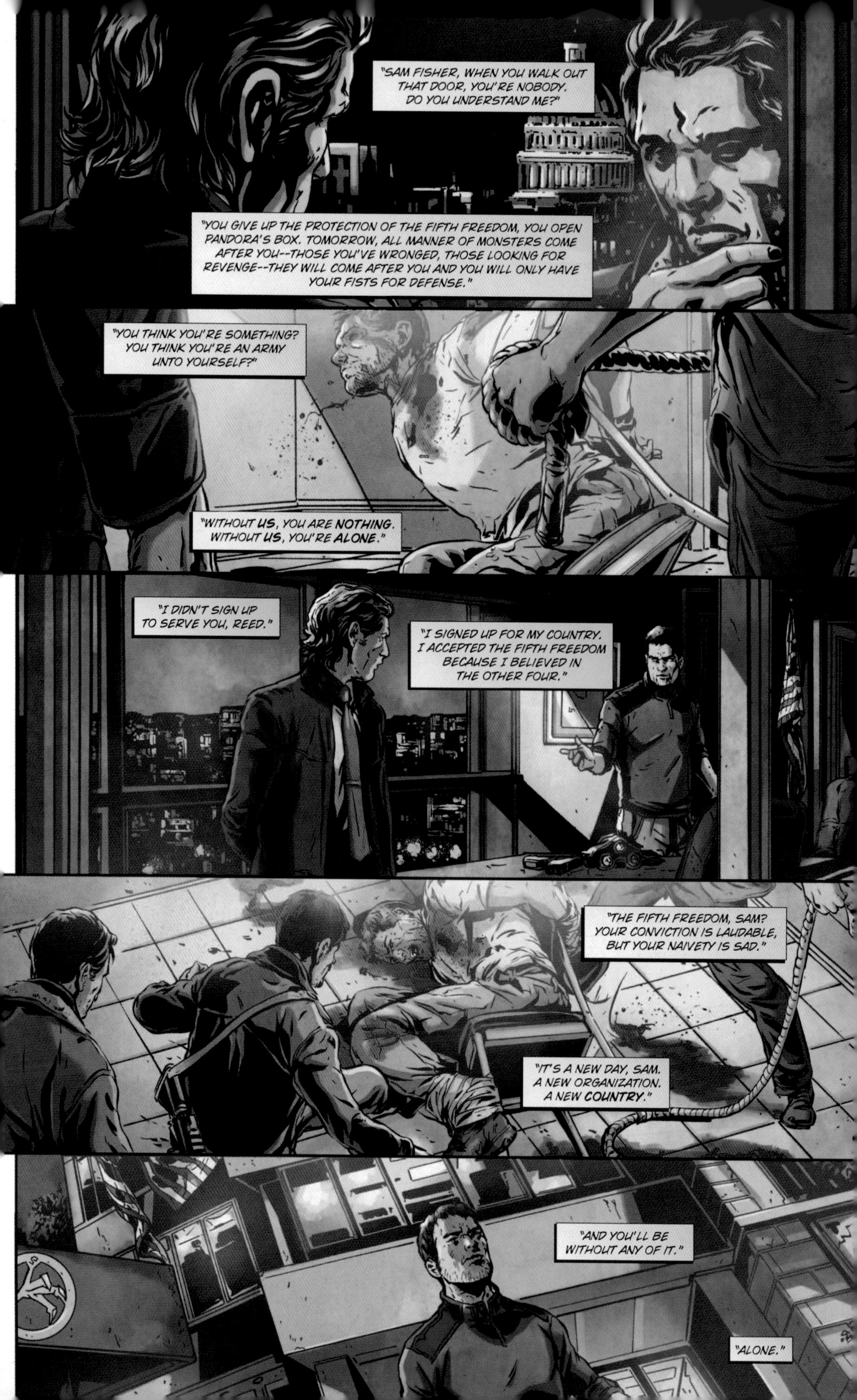
"SAM FISHER, WHEN YOU WALK OUT THAT DOOR, YOU'RE NOBODY. DO YOU UNDERSTAND ME?"
"YOU GIVE UP THE PROTECTION OF THE FIFTH FREEDOM, YOU OPEN PANDORA'S BOX. TOMORROW, ALL MANNER OF MONSTERS COME AFTER YOU--THOSE YOU'VE WRONGED, THOSE LOOKING FOR REVENGE--THEY WILL COME AFTER YOU AND YOU WILL ONLY HAVE YOUR FISTS FOR DEFENSE."
"YOU THINK YOU'RE SOMETHING? YOU THINK YOU'RE AN ARMY UNTO YOURSELF?"
"WITHOUT **US**, YOU ARE **NOTHING**. WITHOUT **US**, YOU'RE **ALONE**."
"I DIDN'T SIGN UP TO SERVE YOU, REED."
"I SIGNED UP FOR MY COUNTRY. I ACCEPTED THE FIFTH FREEDOM BECAUSE I BELIEVED IN THE OTHER FOUR."
"THE FIFTH FREEDOM, SAM? YOUR CONVICTION IS LAUDABLE, BUT YOUR NAIVETY IS SAD."
"IT'S A NEW DAY, SAM. A NEW ORGANIZATION. A NEW **COUNTRY**."
"AND YOU'LL BE WITHOUT ANY OF IT."
"ALONE."

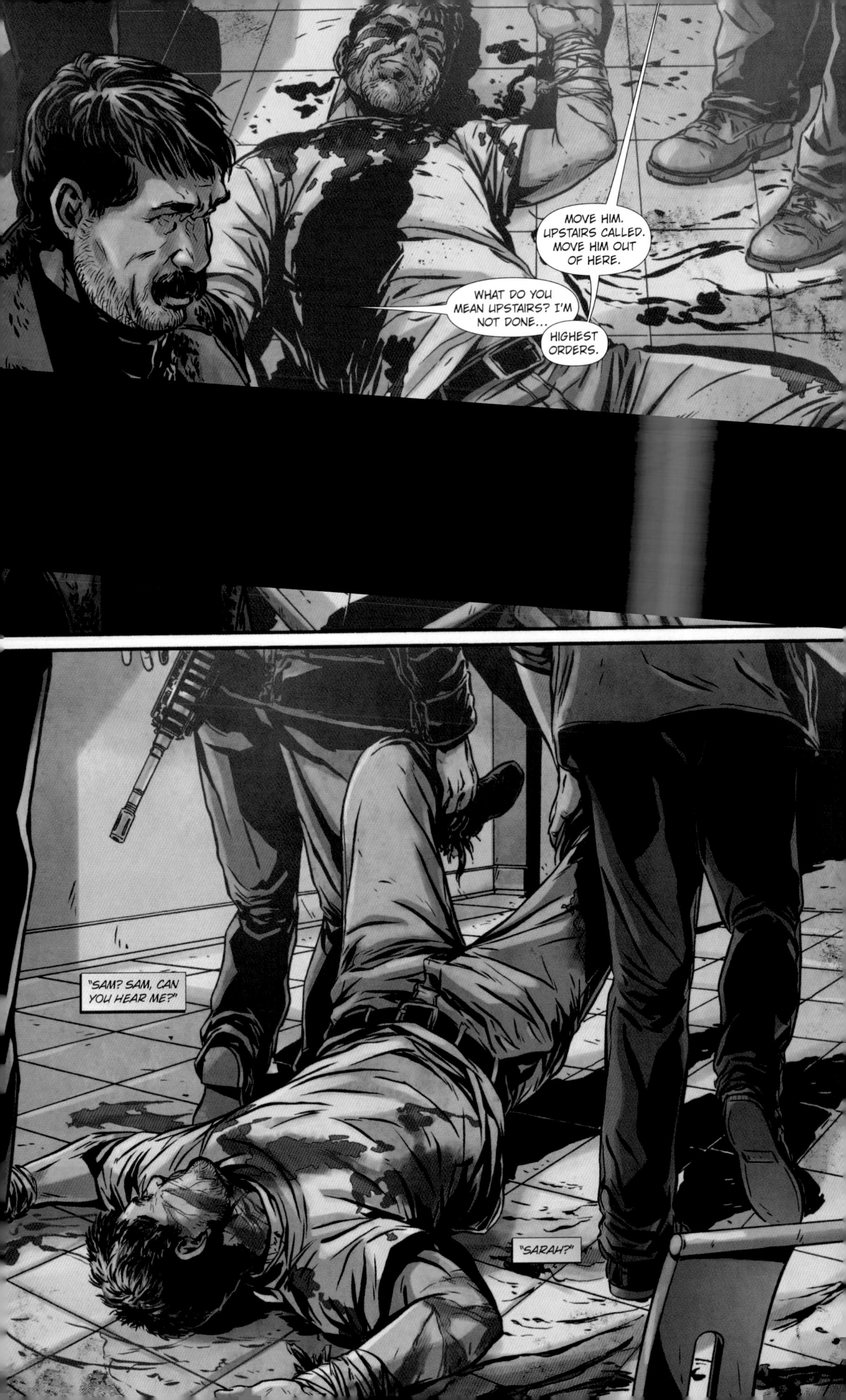
MOVE HIM. UPSTAIRS CALLED. MOVE HIM OUT OF HERE.
WHAT DO YOU MEAN UPSTAIRS? I'M NOT DONE…
HIGHEST ORDERS.
"SAM? SAM, CAN YOU HEAR ME?"
"SARAH?"

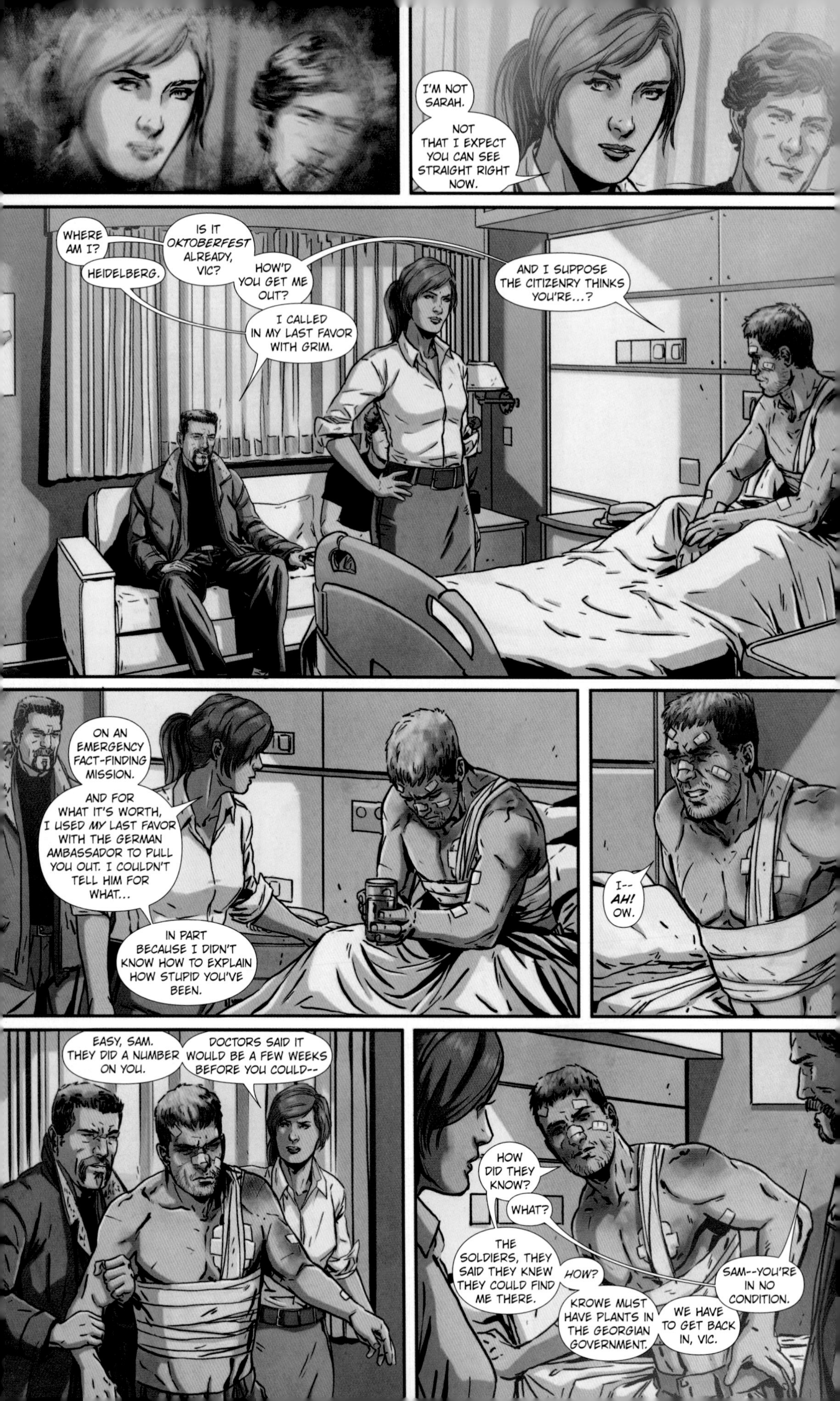

I'M NOT SARAH.
NOT THAT I EXPECT YOU CAN SEE STRAIGHT RIGHT NOW.
WHERE AM I?
HEIDELBERG.
IS IT *OKTOBERFEST* ALREADY, VIC?
HOW'D YOU GET ME OUT?
I CALLED IN MY LAST FAVOR WITH GRIM.
AND I SUPPOSE THE CITIZENRY THINKS YOU'RE...?
ON AN EMERGENCY FACT-FINDING MISSION.
AND FOR WHAT IT'S WORTH, I USED *MY* LAST FAVOR WITH THE GERMAN AMBASSADOR TO PULL YOU OUT. I COULDN'T TELL HIM FOR WHAT...
IN PART BECAUSE I DIDN'T KNOW HOW TO EXPLAIN HOW STUPID YOU'VE BEEN.
I-- **AH!** OW.
EASY, SAM. THEY DID A NUMBER ON YOU.
DOCTORS SAID IT WOULD BE A FEW WEEKS BEFORE YOU COULD--
HOW DID THEY KNOW?
WHAT?
THE SOLDIERS, THEY SAID THEY KNEW THEY COULD FIND ME THERE.
HOW?
KROWE MUST HAVE PLANTS IN THE GEORGIAN GOVERNMENT.
WE HAVE TO GET BACK IN, VIC.
SAM--YOU'RE IN NO CONDITION.

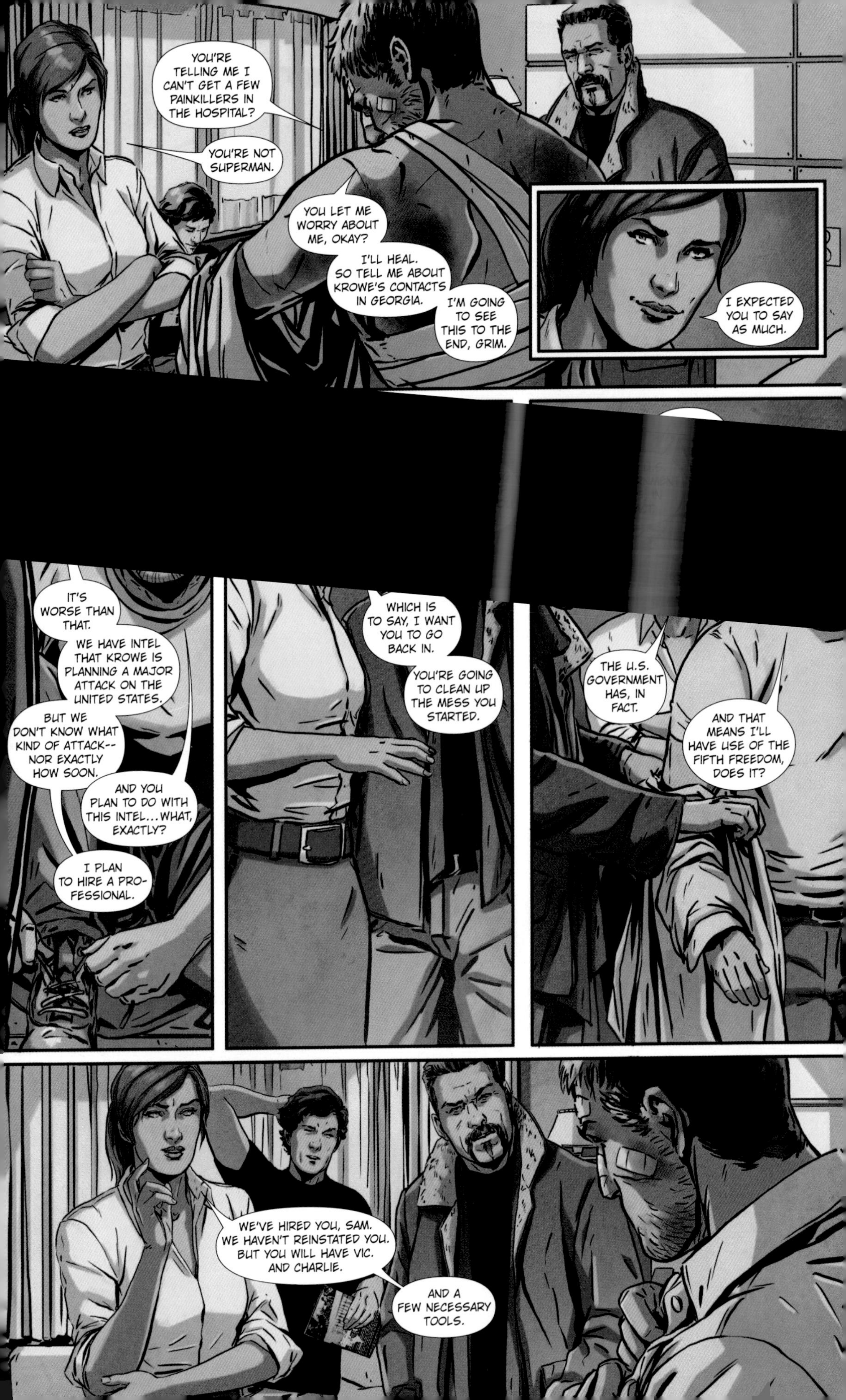
YOU'RE TELLING ME I CAN'T GET A FEW PAINKILLERS IN THE HOSPITAL?
YOU'RE NOT SUPERMAN.
YOU LET ME WORRY ABOUT ME, OKAY?
I'LL HEAL. SO TELL ME ABOUT KROWE'S CONTACTS IN GEORGIA.
I'M GOING TO SEE THIS TO THE END, GRIM.
I EXPECTED YOU TO SAY AS MUCH.
[redacted]
IT'S WORSE THAN THAT.
WE HAVE INTEL THAT KROWE IS PLANNING A MAJOR ATTACK ON THE UNITED STATES.
BUT WE DON'T KNOW WHAT KIND OF ATTACK-- NOR EXACTLY HOW SOON.
AND YOU PLAN TO DO WITH THIS INTEL...WHAT, EXACTLY?
I PLAN TO HIRE A PRO-FESSIONAL.
WHICH IS TO SAY, I WANT YOU TO GO BACK IN.
YOU'RE GOING TO CLEAN UP THE MESS YOU STARTED.
THE U.S. GOVERNMENT HAS, IN FACT.
AND THAT MEANS I'LL HAVE USE OF THE FIFTH FREEDOM, DOES IT?
WE'VE HIRED YOU, SAM. WE HAVEN'T REINSTATED YOU. BUT YOU WILL HAVE VIC. AND CHARLIE.
AND A FEW NECESSARY TOOLS.

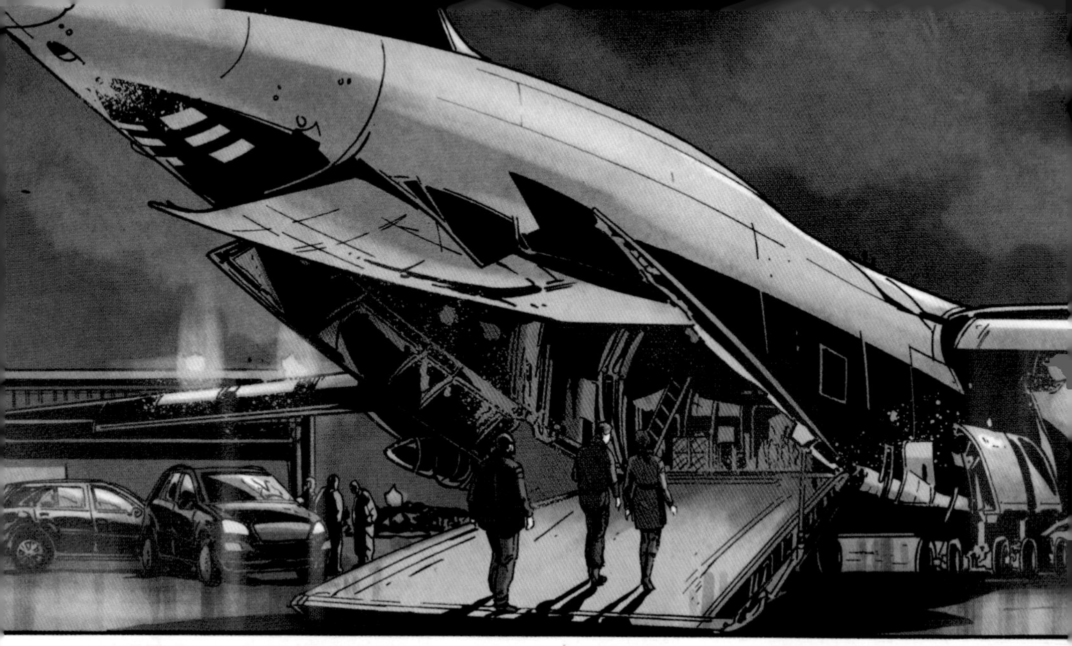

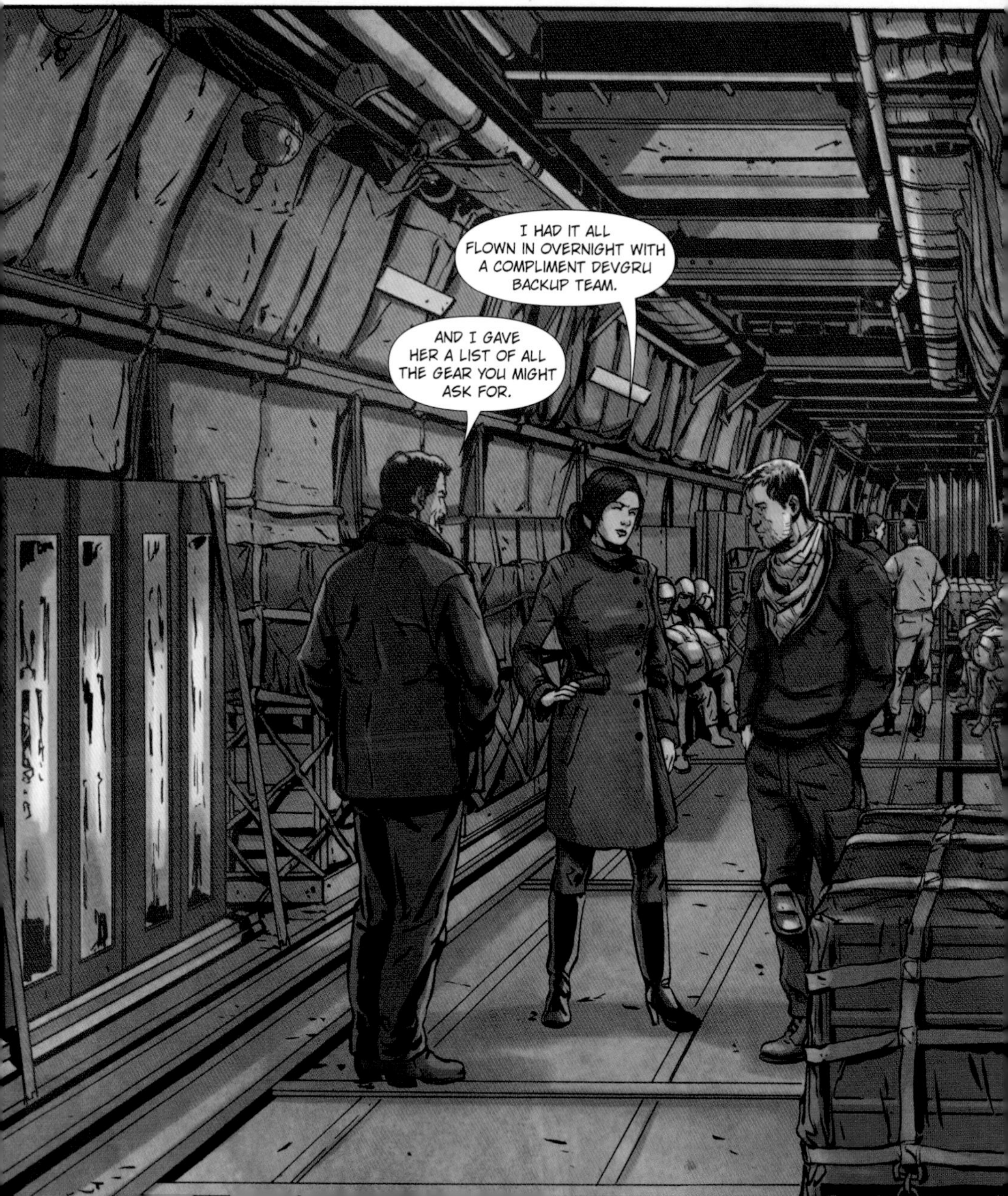
I HAD IT ALL FLOWN IN OVERNIGHT WITH A COMPLIMENT DEVGRU BACKUP TEAM.
AND I GAVE HER A LIST OF ALL THE GEAR YOU MIGHT ASK FOR.

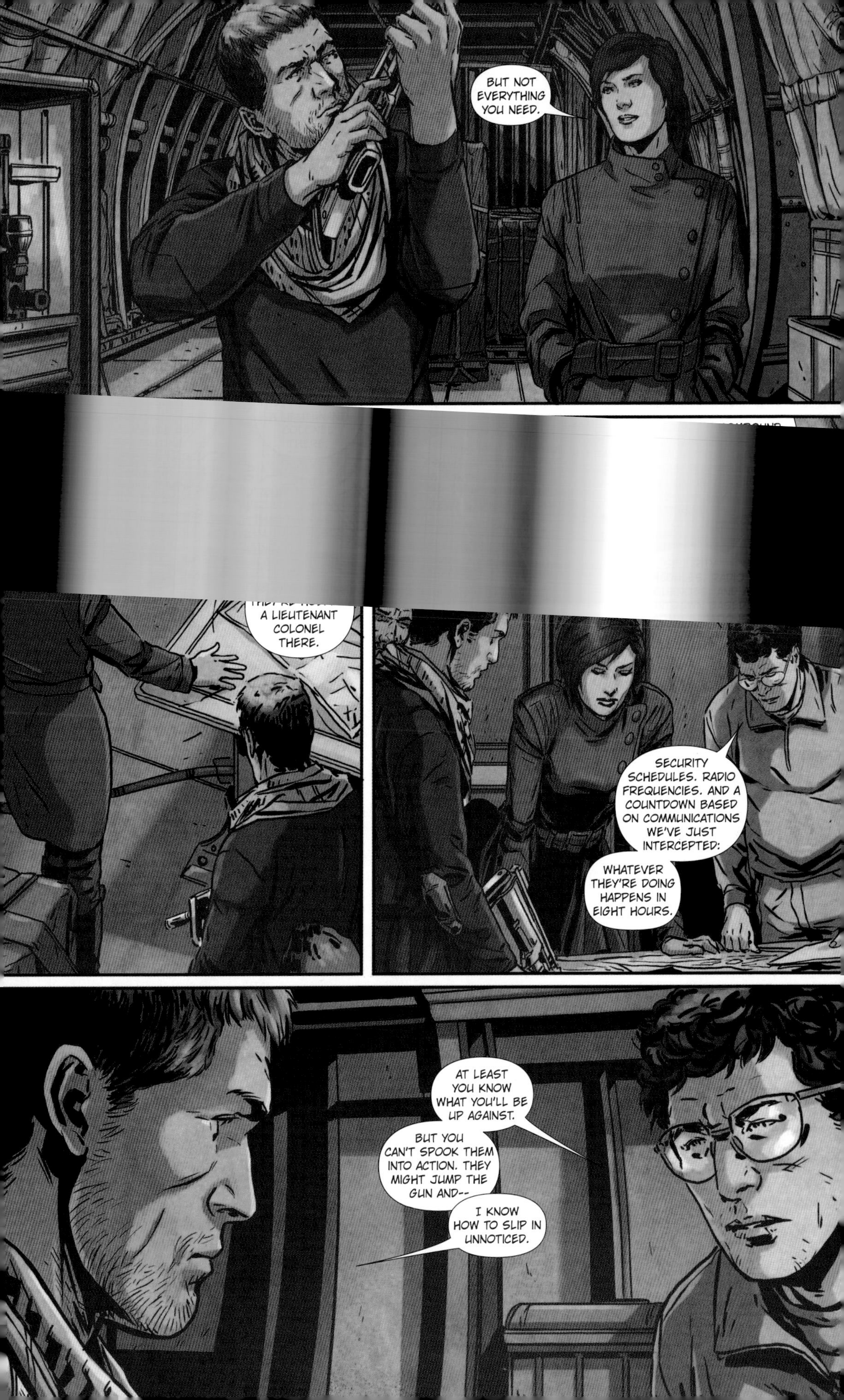
BUT NOT EVERYTHING YOU NEED.
A LIEUTENANT COLONEL THERE.
SECURITY SCHEDULES. RADIO FREQUENCIES. AND A COUNTDOWN BASED ON COMMUNICATIONS WE'VE JUST INTERCEPTED:
WHATEVER THEY'RE DOING HAPPENS IN EIGHT HOURS.
AT LEAST YOU KNOW WHAT YOU'LL BE UP AGAINST.
BUT YOU CAN'T SPOOK THEM INTO ACTION. THEY MIGHT JUMP THE GUN AND--
I KNOW HOW TO SLIP IN UNNOTICED.

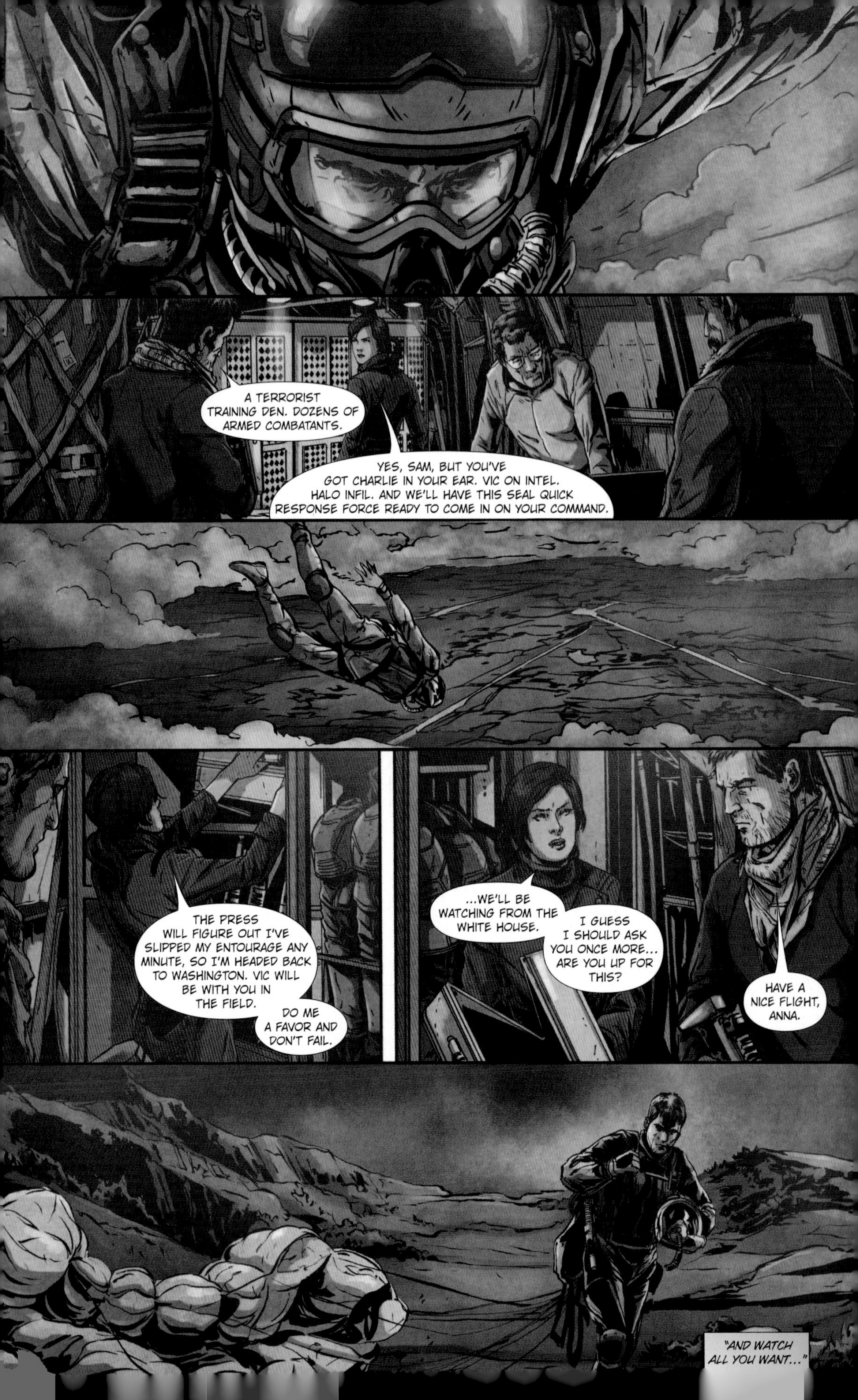
A TERRORIST TRAINING DEN. DOZENS OF ARMED COMBATANTS.
YES, SAM, BUT YOU'VE GOT CHARLIE IN YOUR EAR. VIC ON INTEL. HALO INFIL. AND WE'LL HAVE THIS SEAL QUICK RESPONSE FORCE READY TO COME IN ON YOUR COMMAND.
THE PRESS WILL FIGURE OUT I'VE SLIPPED MY ENTOURAGE ANY MINUTE, SO I'M HEADED BACK TO WASHINGTON. VIC WILL BE WITH YOU IN THE FIELD.
DO ME A FAVOR AND DON'T FAIL.
...WE'LL BE WATCHING FROM THE WHITE HOUSE.
I GUESS I SHOULD ASK YOU ONCE MORE... ARE YOU UP FOR THIS?
HAVE A NICE FLIGHT, ANNA.
"AND WATCH ALL YOU WANT..."

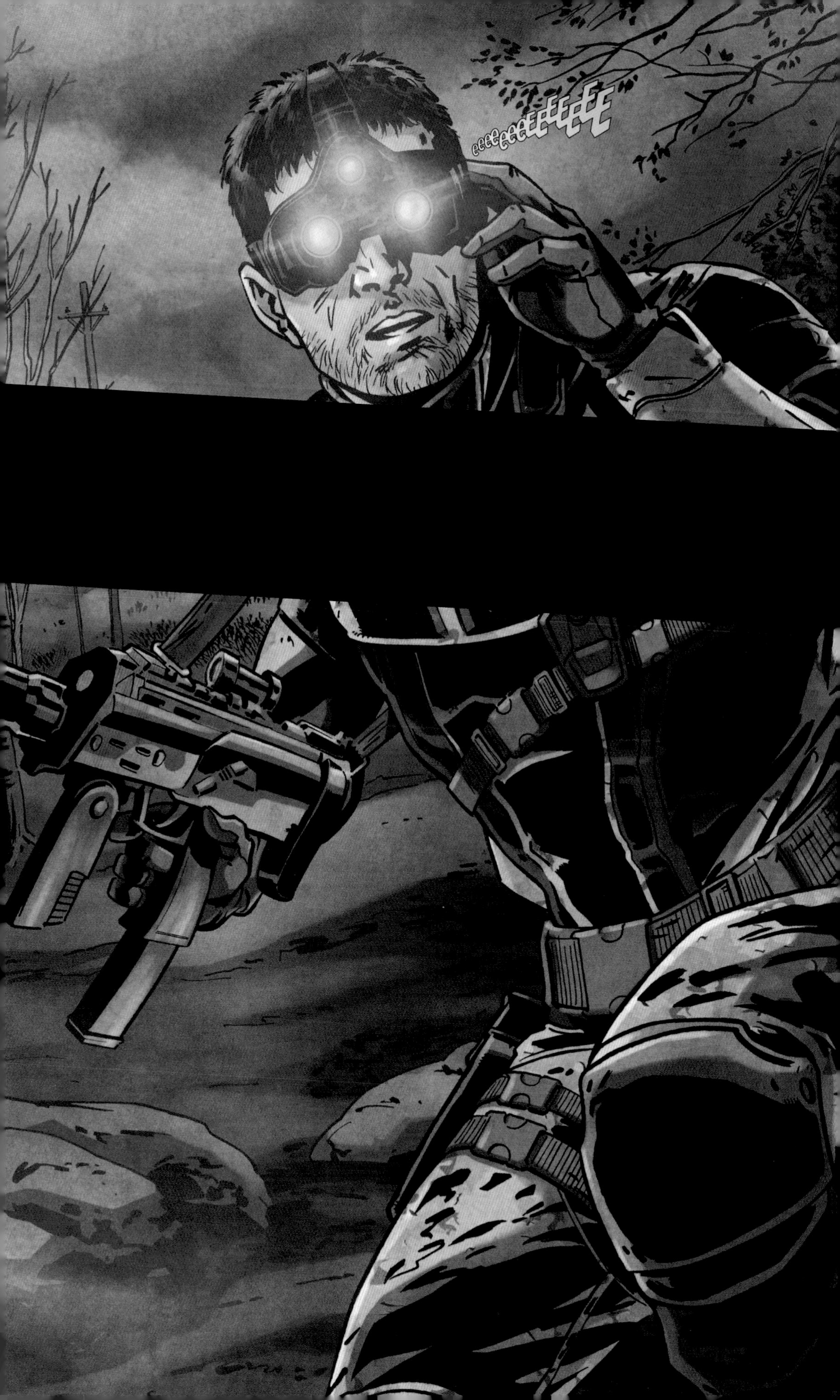
eeeeeeeEEEEEEE

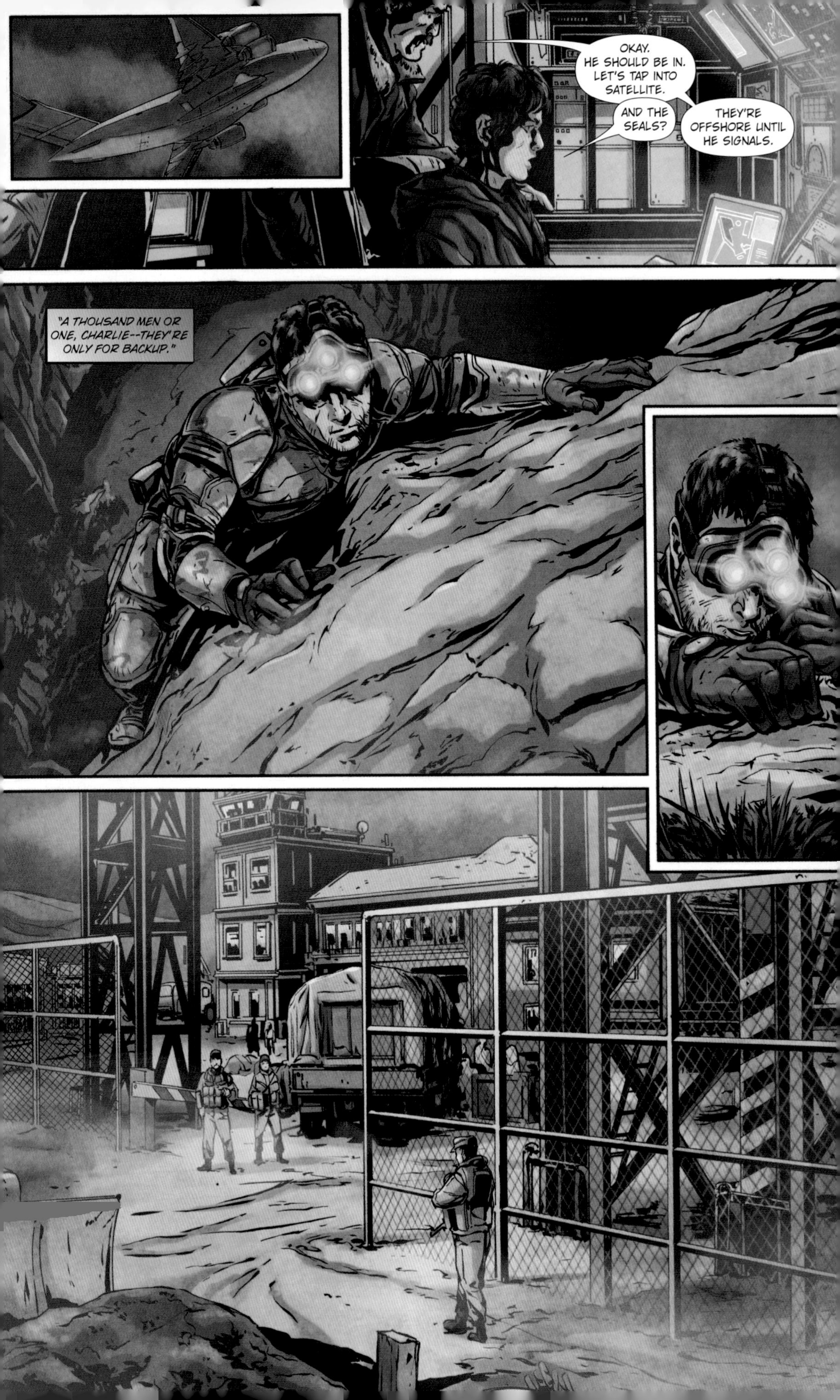
OKAY. HE SHOULD BE IN. LET'S TAP INTO SATELLITE.
AND THE SEALS?
THEY'RE OFFSHORE UNTIL HE SIGNALS.
"A THOUSAND MEN OR ONE, CHARLIE--THEY'RE ONLY FOR BACKUP."

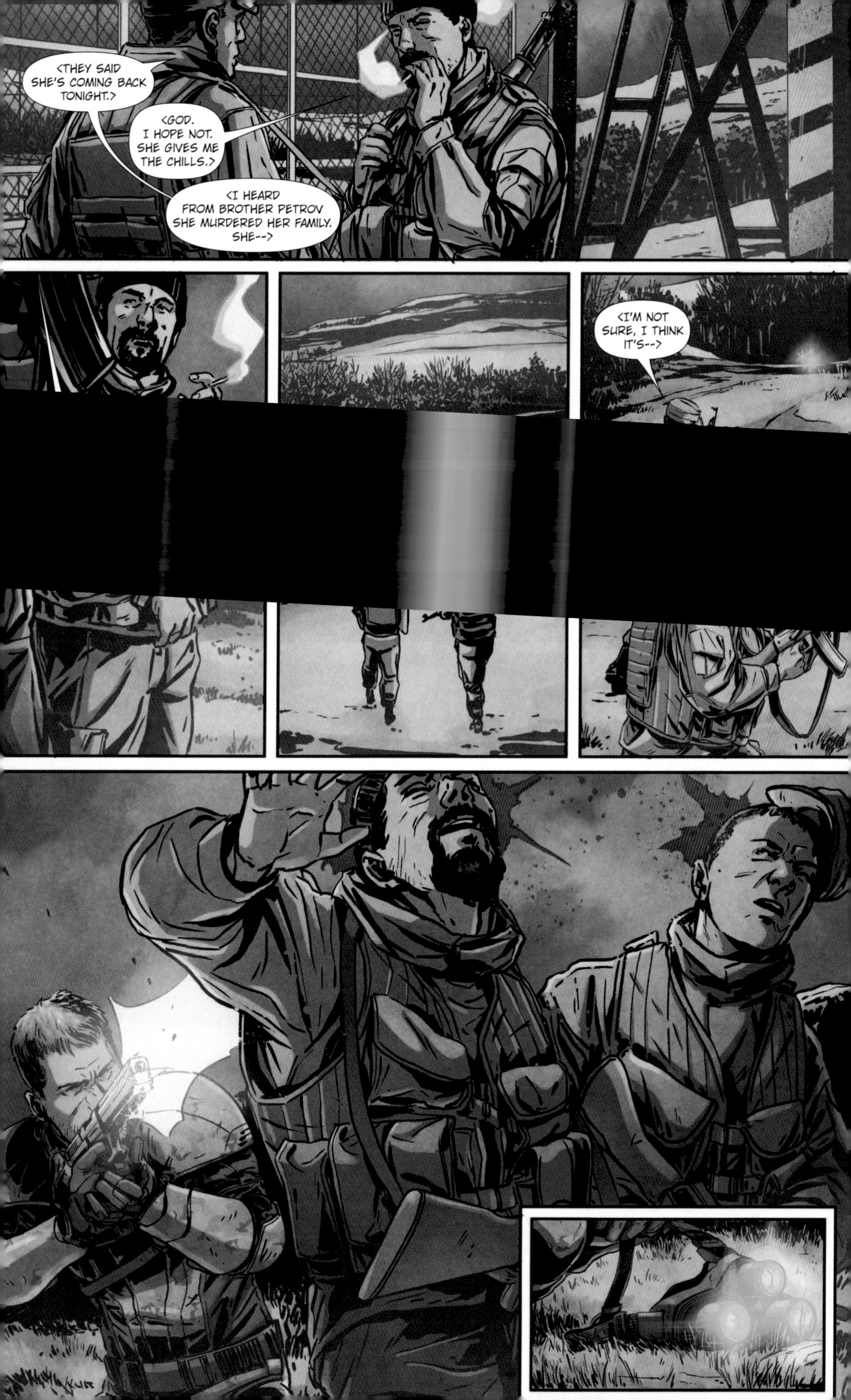
<THEY SAID SHE'S COMING BACK TONIGHT.>
<GOD. I HOPE NOT. SHE GIVES ME THE CHILLS.>
<I HEARD FROM BROTHER PETROV SHE MURDERED HER FAMILY. SHE-->
<I'M NOT SURE, I THINK IT'S-->

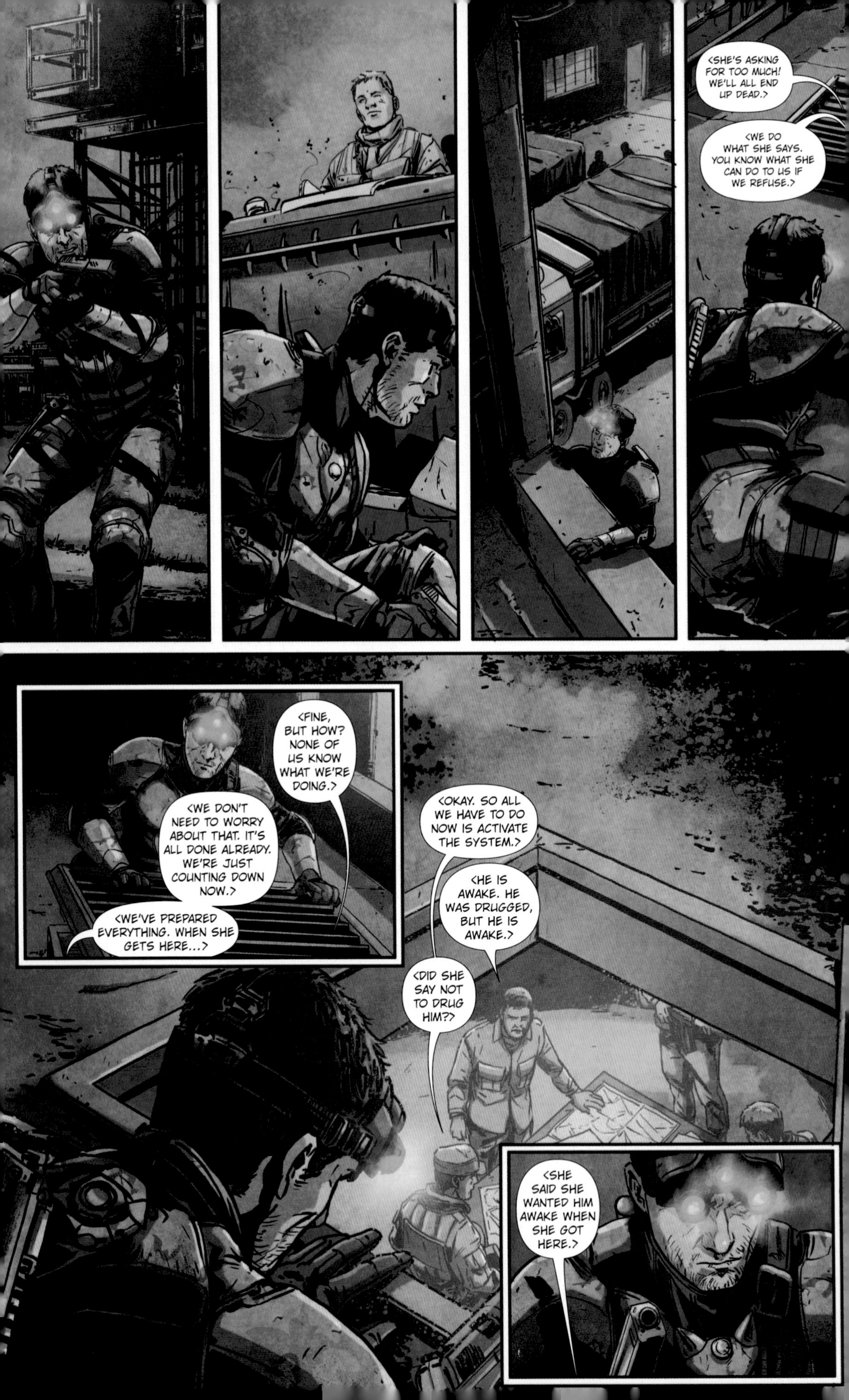

<SHE'S ASKING FOR TOO MUCH! WE'LL ALL END UP DEAD.>
<WE DO WHAT SHE SAYS. YOU KNOW WHAT SHE CAN DO TO US IF WE REFUSE.>
<FINE, BUT HOW? NONE OF US KNOW WHAT WE'RE DOING.>
<WE DON'T NEED TO WORRY ABOUT THAT. IT'S ALL DONE ALREADY. WE'RE JUST COUNTING DOWN NOW.>
<WE'VE PREPARED EVERYTHING. WHEN SHE GETS HERE...>
<OKAY. SO ALL WE HAVE TO DO NOW IS ACTIVATE THE SYSTEM.>
<HE IS AWAKE. HE WAS DRUGGED, BUT HE IS AWAKE.>
<DID SHE SAY NOT TO DRUG HIM?>
<SHE SAID SHE WANTED HIM AWAKE WHEN SHE GOT HERE.>

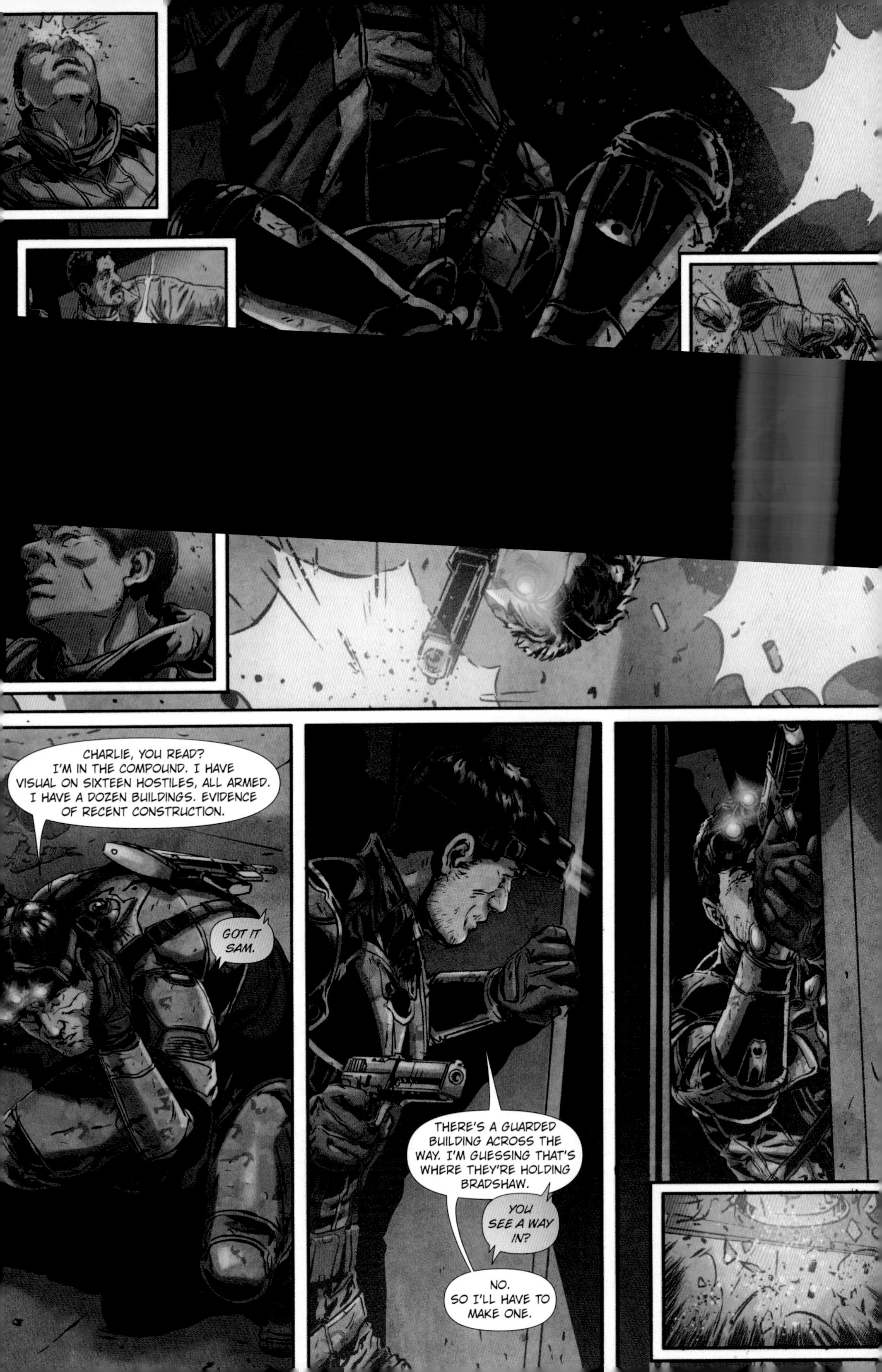
CHARLIE, YOU READ? I'M IN THE COMPOUND. I HAVE VISUAL ON SIXTEEN HOSTILES, ALL ARMED. I HAVE A DOZEN BUILDINGS. EVIDENCE OF RECENT CONSTRUCTION.
GOT IT SAM.
THERE'S A GUARDED BUILDING ACROSS THE WAY. I'M GUESSING THAT'S WHERE THEY'RE HOLDING BRADSHAW.
YOU SEE A WAY IN?
NO. SO I'LL HAVE TO MAKE ONE.

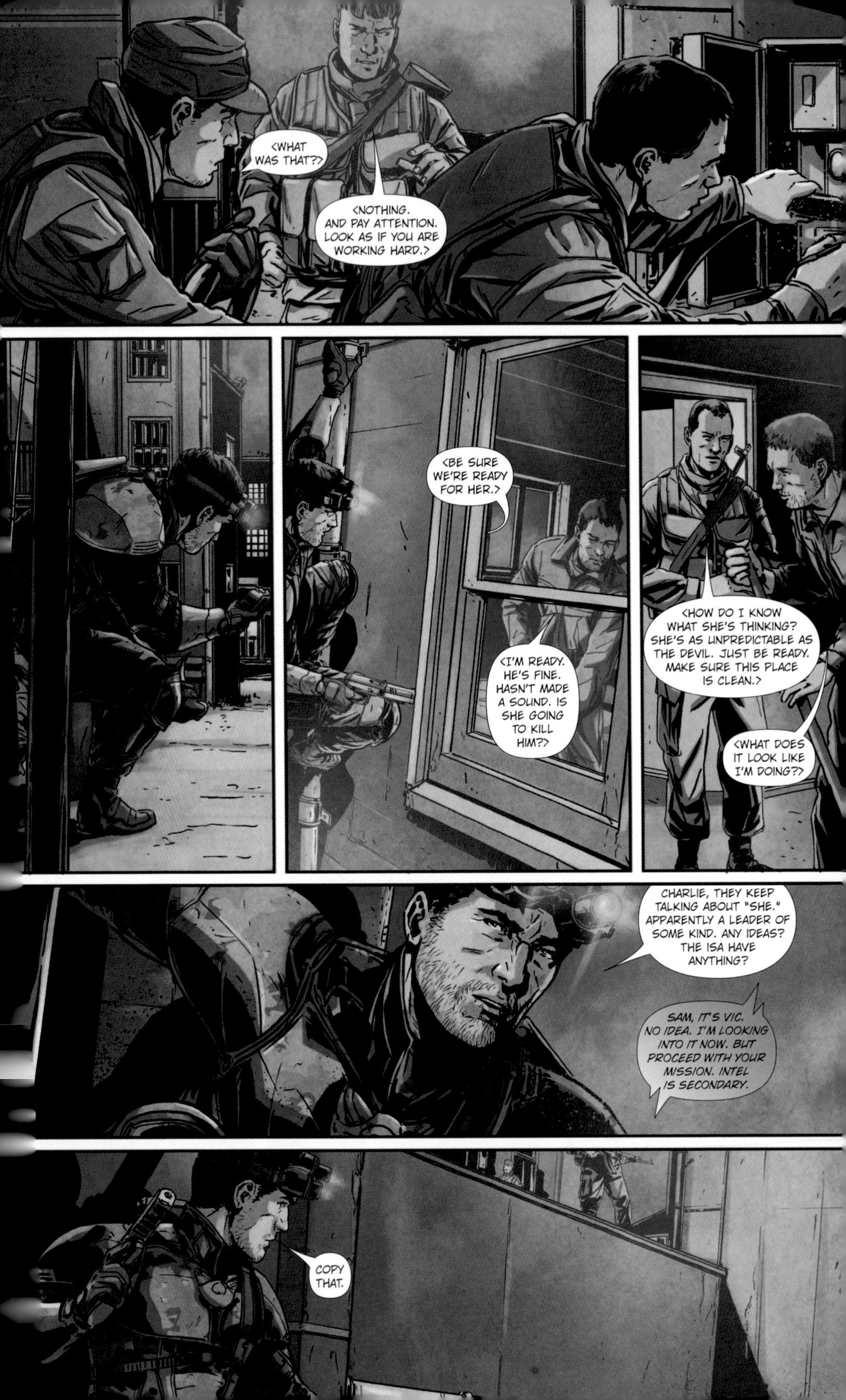
<WHAT WAS THAT?>
<NOTHING. AND PAY ATTENTION. LOOK AS IF YOU ARE WORKING HARD.>
<BE SURE WE'RE READY FOR HER.>
<I'M READY. HE'S FINE. HASN'T MADE A SOUND. IS SHE GOING TO KILL HIM?>
<HOW DO I KNOW WHAT SHE'S THINKING? SHE'S AS UNPREDICTABLE AS THE DEVIL. JUST BE READY. MAKE SURE THIS PLACE IS CLEAN.>
<WHAT DOES IT LOOK LIKE I'M DOING?>
CHARLIE, THEY KEEP TALKING ABOUT "SHE." APPARENTLY A LEADER OF SOME KIND. ANY IDEAS? THE ISA HAVE ANYTHING?
SAM, IT'S VIC. NO IDEA. I'M LOOKING INTO IT NOW. BUT PROCEED WITH YOUR MISSION. INTEL IS SECONDARY.
COPY THAT.

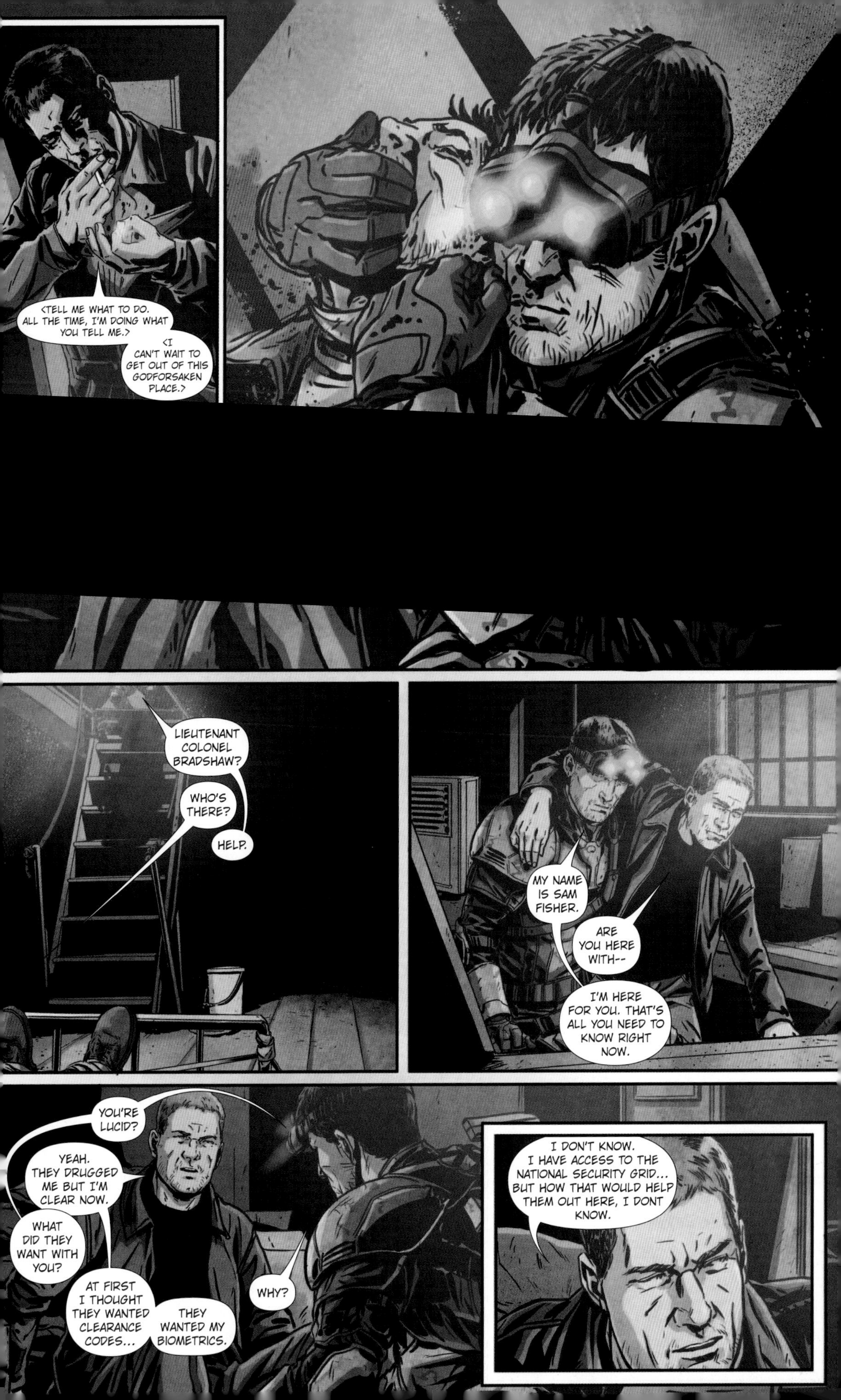
<TELL ME WHAT TO DO. ALL THE TIME, I'M DOING WHAT YOU TELL ME.>
<I CAN'T WAIT TO GET OUT OF THIS GODFORSAKEN PLACE.>
LIEUTENANT COLONEL BRADSHAW?
WHO'S THERE?
HELP.
MY NAME IS SAM FISHER.
ARE YOU HERE WITH--
I'M HERE FOR YOU. THAT'S ALL YOU NEED TO KNOW RIGHT NOW.
YOU'RE LUCID?
YEAH. THEY DRUGGED ME BUT I'M CLEAR NOW.
WHAT DID THEY WANT WITH YOU?
AT FIRST I THOUGHT THEY WANTED CLEARANCE CODES...
THEY WANTED MY BIOMETRICS.
WHY?
I DON'T KNOW. I HAVE ACCESS TO THE NATIONAL SECURITY GRID... BUT HOW THAT WOULD HELP THEM OUT HERE, I DONT KNOW.

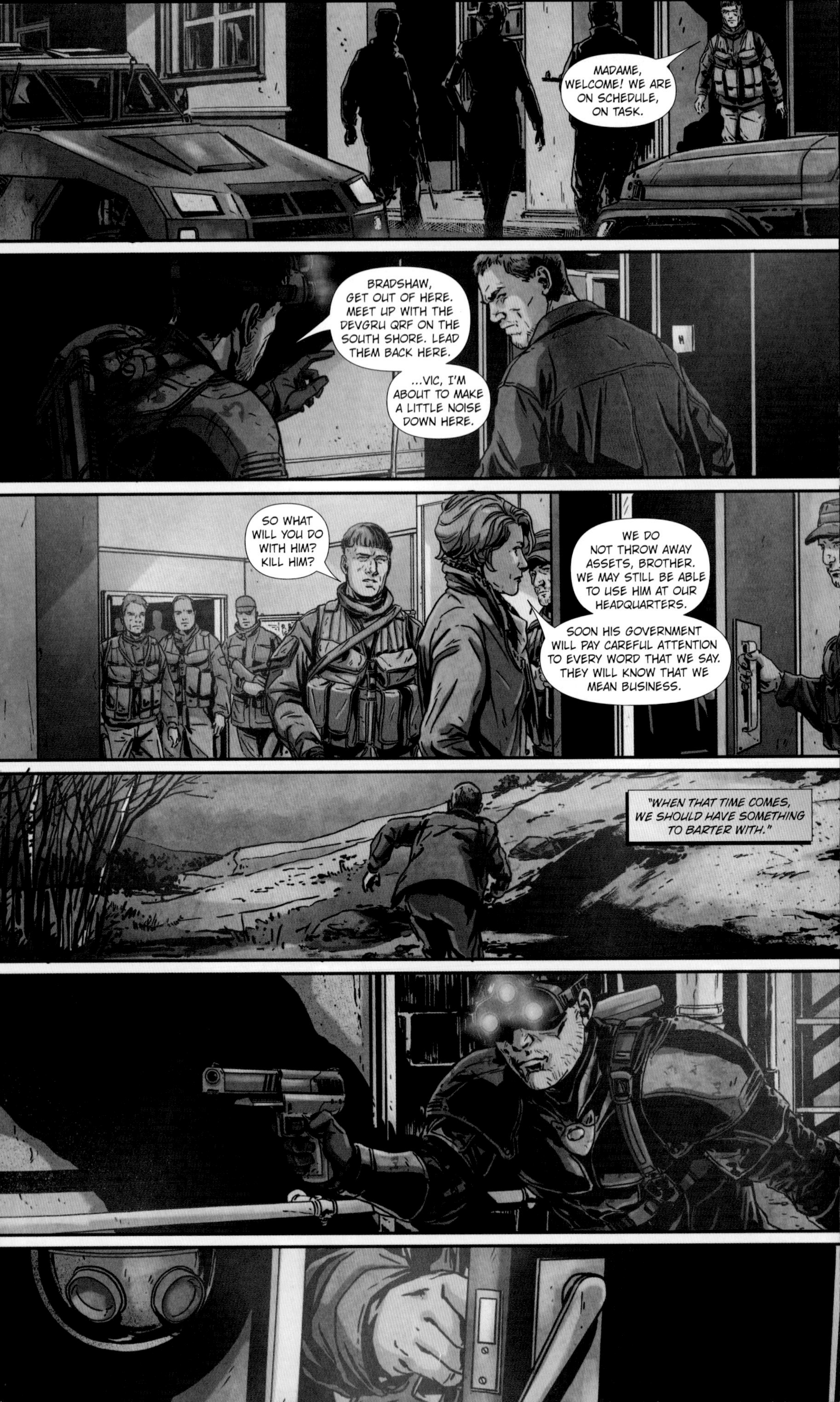
MADAME, WELCOME! WE ARE ON SCHEDULE, ON TASK.
BRADSHAW, GET OUT OF HERE. MEET UP WITH THE DEVGRU QRF ON THE SOUTH SHORE. LEAD THEM BACK HERE.
...VIC, I'M ABOUT TO MAKE A LITTLE NOISE DOWN HERE.
SO WHAT WILL YOU DO WITH HIM? KILL HIM?
WE DO NOT THROW AWAY ASSETS, BROTHER. WE MAY STILL BE ABLE TO USE HIM AT OUR HEADQUARTERS.
SOON HIS GOVERNMENT WILL PAY CAREFUL ATTENTION TO EVERY WORD THAT WE SAY. THEY WILL KNOW THAT WE MEAN BUSINESS.
"WHEN THAT TIME COMES, WE SHOULD HAVE SOMETHING TO BARTER WITH."

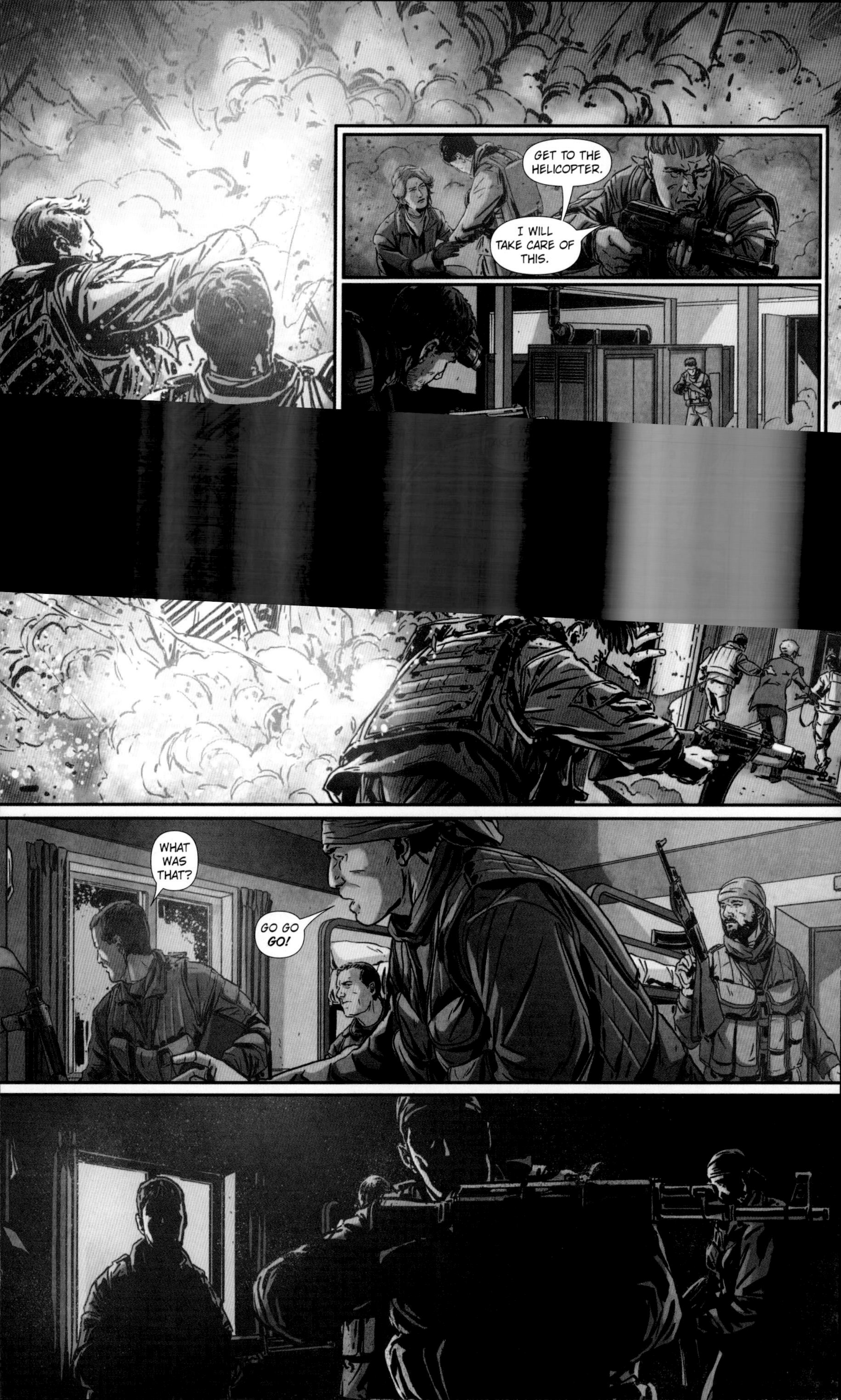
GET TO THE HELICOPTER.
I WILL TAKE CARE OF THIS.
WHAT WAS THAT?
GO GO GO!

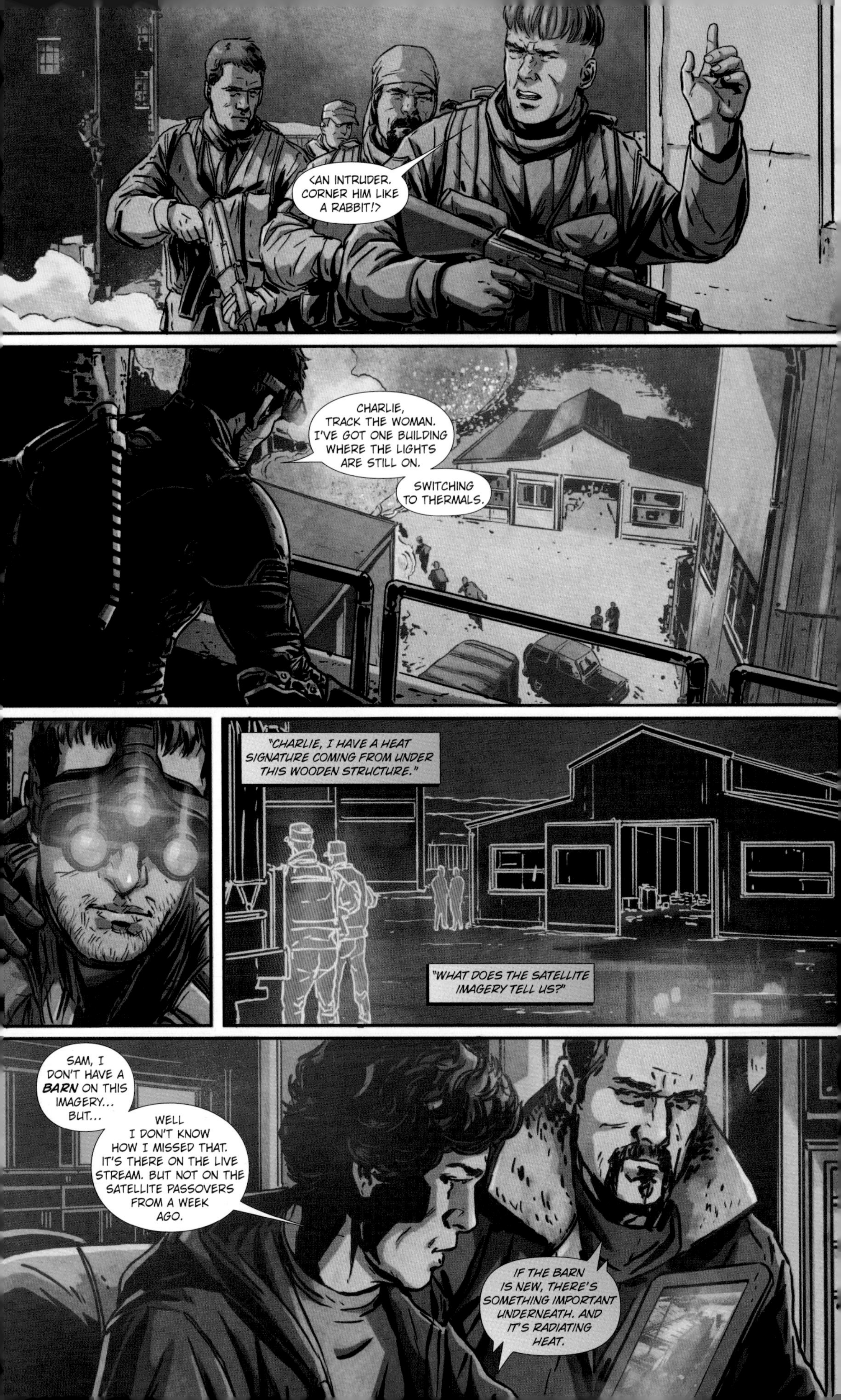
<AN INTRUDER. CORNER HIM LIKE A RABBIT!>
CHARLIE, TRACK THE WOMAN. I'VE GOT ONE BUILDING WHERE THE LIGHTS ARE STILL ON.
SWITCHING TO THERMALS.
"CHARLIE, I HAVE A HEAT SIGNATURE COMING FROM UNDER THIS WOODEN STRUCTURE."
"WHAT DOES THE SATELLITE IMAGERY TELL US?"
SAM, I DON'T HAVE A *BARN* ON THIS IMAGERY... BUT...
WELL I DON'T KNOW HOW I MISSED THAT. IT'S THERE ON THE LIVE STREAM. BUT NOT ON THE SATELLITE PASSOVERS FROM A WEEK AGO.
IF THE BARN IS NEW, THERE'S SOMETHING IMPORTANT UNDERNEATH. AND IT'S RADIATING HEAT.

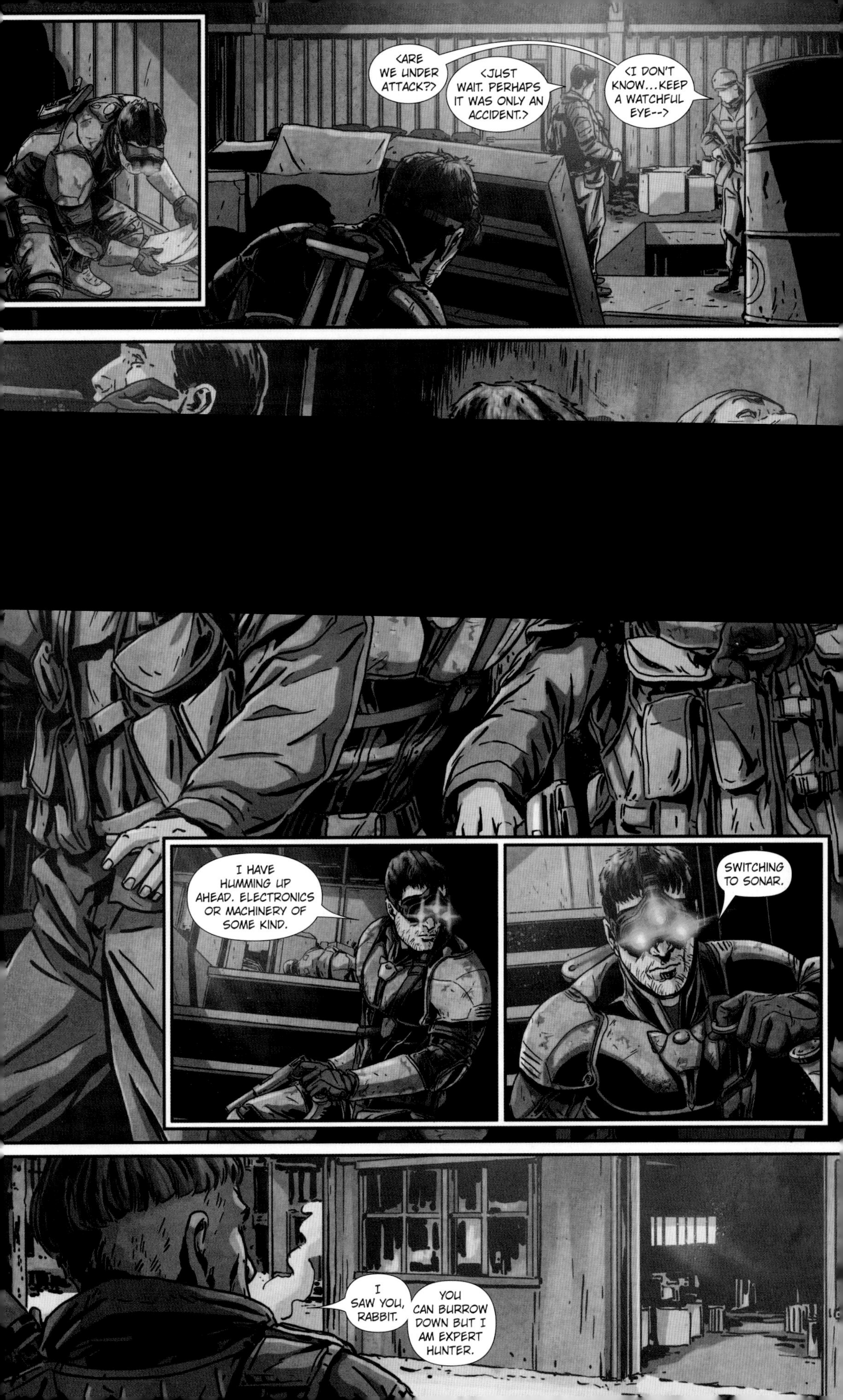

<ARE WE UNDER ATTACK?>
<JUST WAIT. PERHAPS IT WAS ONLY AN ACCIDENT.>
<I DON'T KNOW...KEEP A WATCHFUL EYE-->
[redacted]
I HAVE HUMMING UP AHEAD. ELECTRONICS OR MACHINERY OF SOME KIND.
SWITCHING TO SONAR.
I SAW YOU, RABBIT.
YOU CAN BURROW DOWN BUT I AM EXPERT HUNTER.

CHARLIE, I'VE GOT SOME SORT OF NETWORKING ROOM...

...COMPUTER STATIONS. MAJOR MACHINES. NOT SURE WHAT I'VE GOT HERE.

PLUG YOUR THUMB DRIVE IN. I'LL SEE WHAT WE'VE GOT.

OKAY.

OKAY. THEY'VE RECODED THEIR IP, THEY'RE REROUTING-- WOW, THROUGH ABOUT TWO DOZEN DIFFERENT REDIRECTS, AND--

WE'RE NOT ALL VIDEO GAME PLAYING, COMPUTER HACKING NERDS, CHARLIE.

WHAT I MEAN IS, THEY'RE MAKING IT LOOK LIKE THIS STATION IS...IN THE UNITED STATES. LIKE IT'S PART OF OUR DEFENSE NETWORK.

THAT'S LIKE REALLY HAR TO DO.

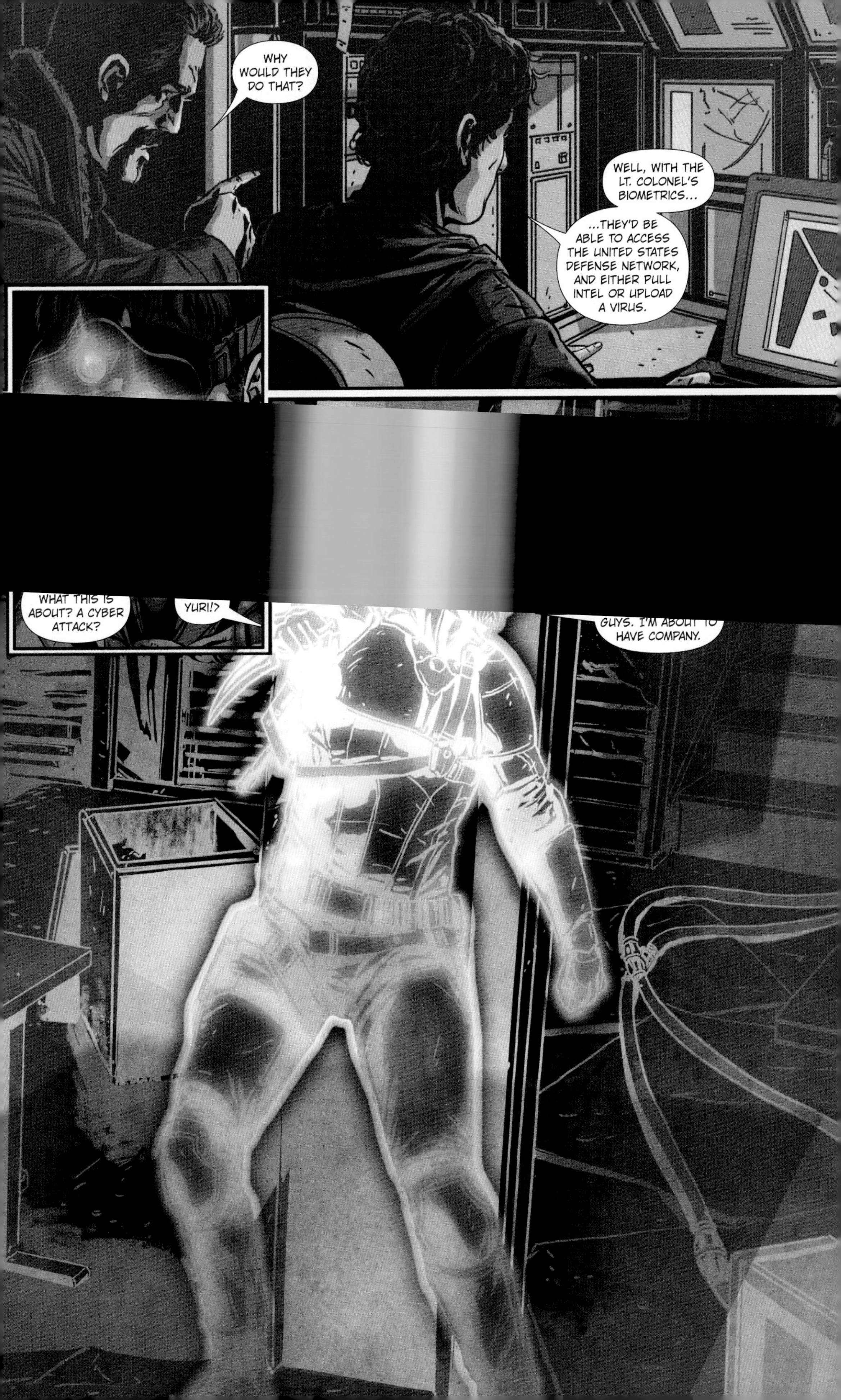
WHY WOULD THEY DO THAT?
WELL, WITH THE LT. COLONEL'S BIOMETRICS...
...THEY'D BE ABLE TO ACCESS THE UNITED STATES DEFENSE NETWORK, AND EITHER PULL INTEL OR UPLOAD A VIRUS.
[redacted]
WHAT THIS IS ABOUT? A CYBER ATTACK?
YURI!?
GUYS. I'M ABOUT TO HAVE COMPANY.

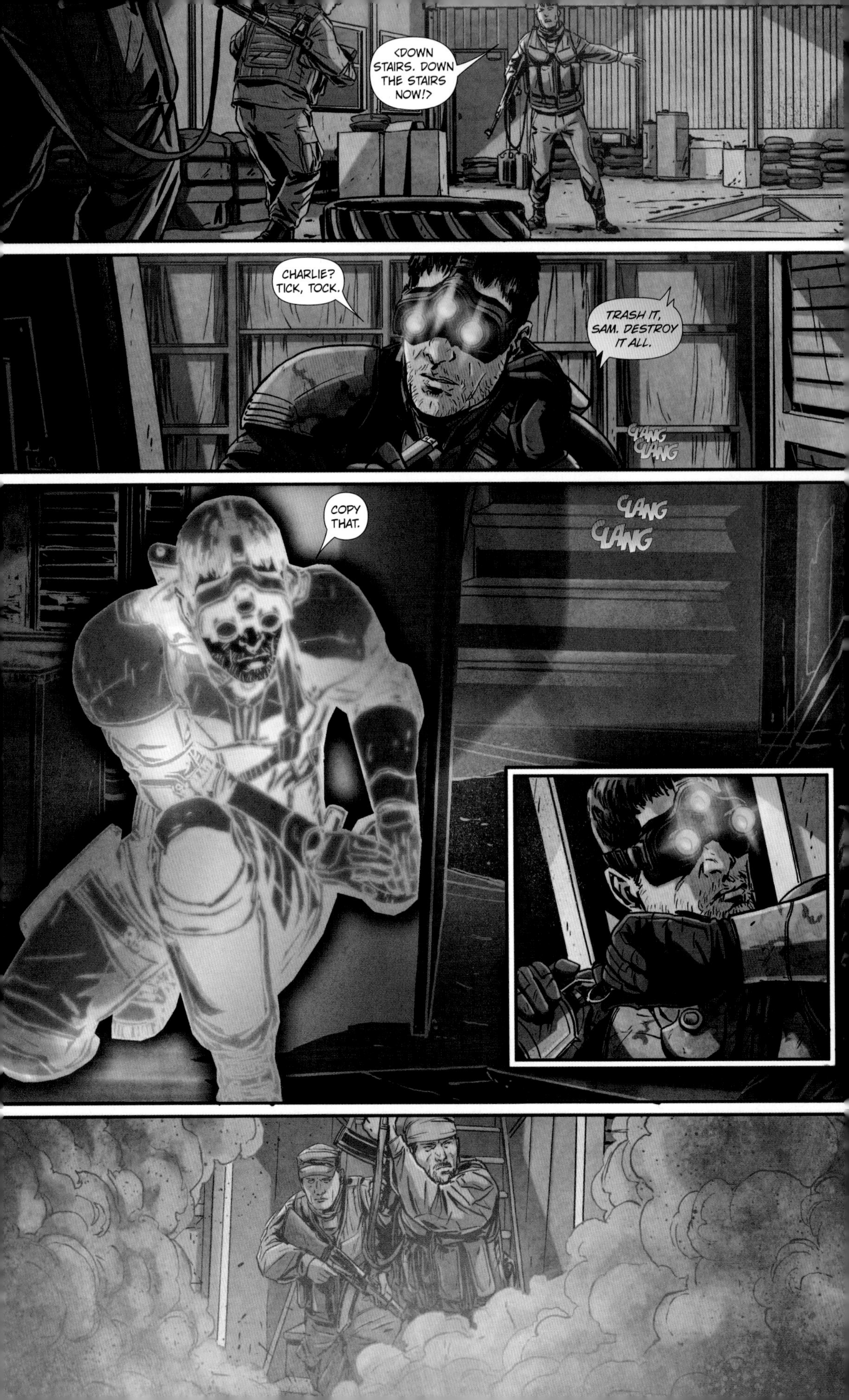

<DOWN STAIRS. DOWN THE STAIRS NOW!>
CHARLIE? TICK, TOCK.
TRASH IT, SAM. DESTROY IT ALL.
CLANG CLANG
COPY THAT.
CLANG CLANG

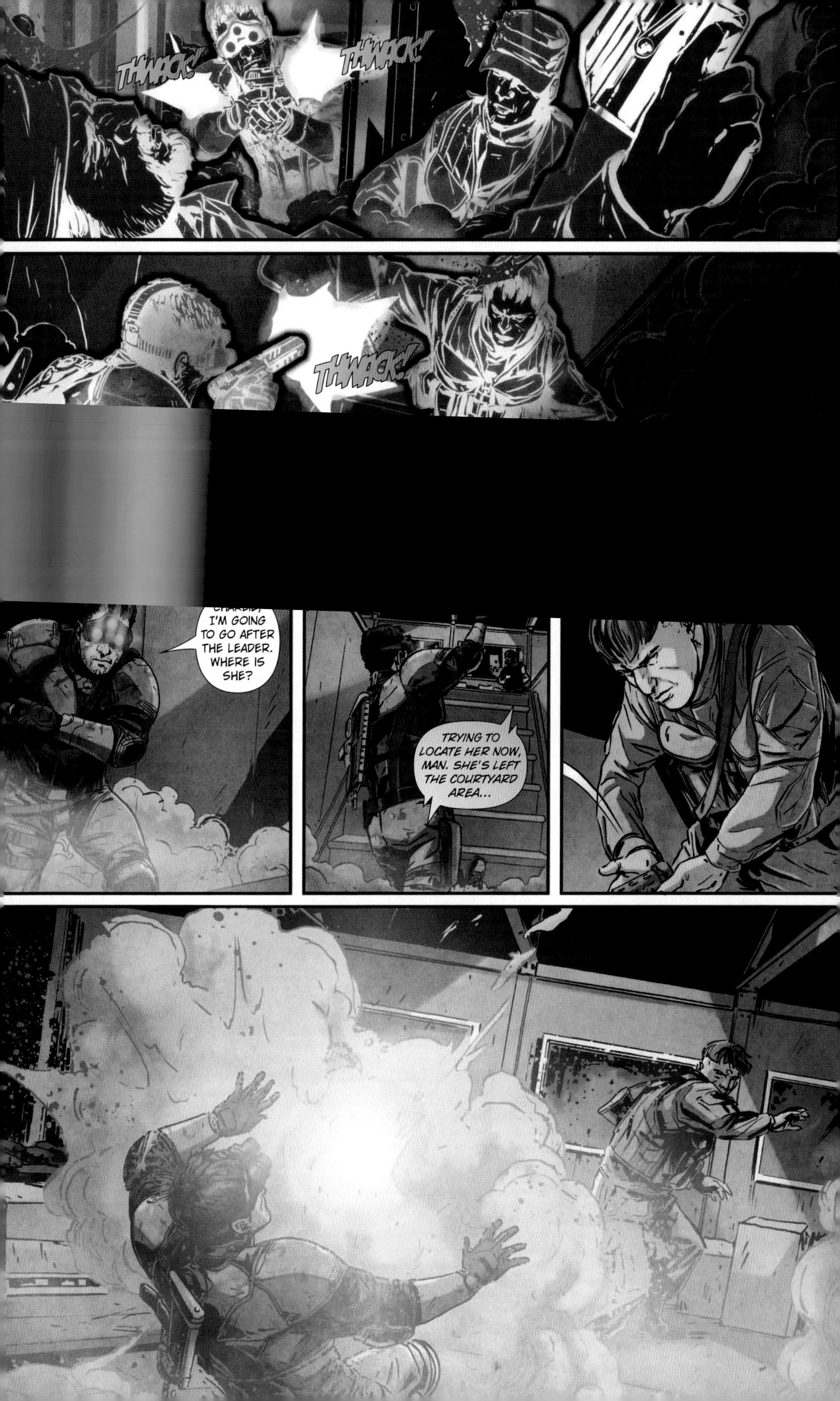
THWACK!
THWACK!
THWACK!
[redacted]
I'M GOING TO GO AFTER THE LEADER. WHERE IS SHE?
TRYING TO LOCATE HER NOW, MAN. SHE'S LEFT THE COURTYARD AREA...

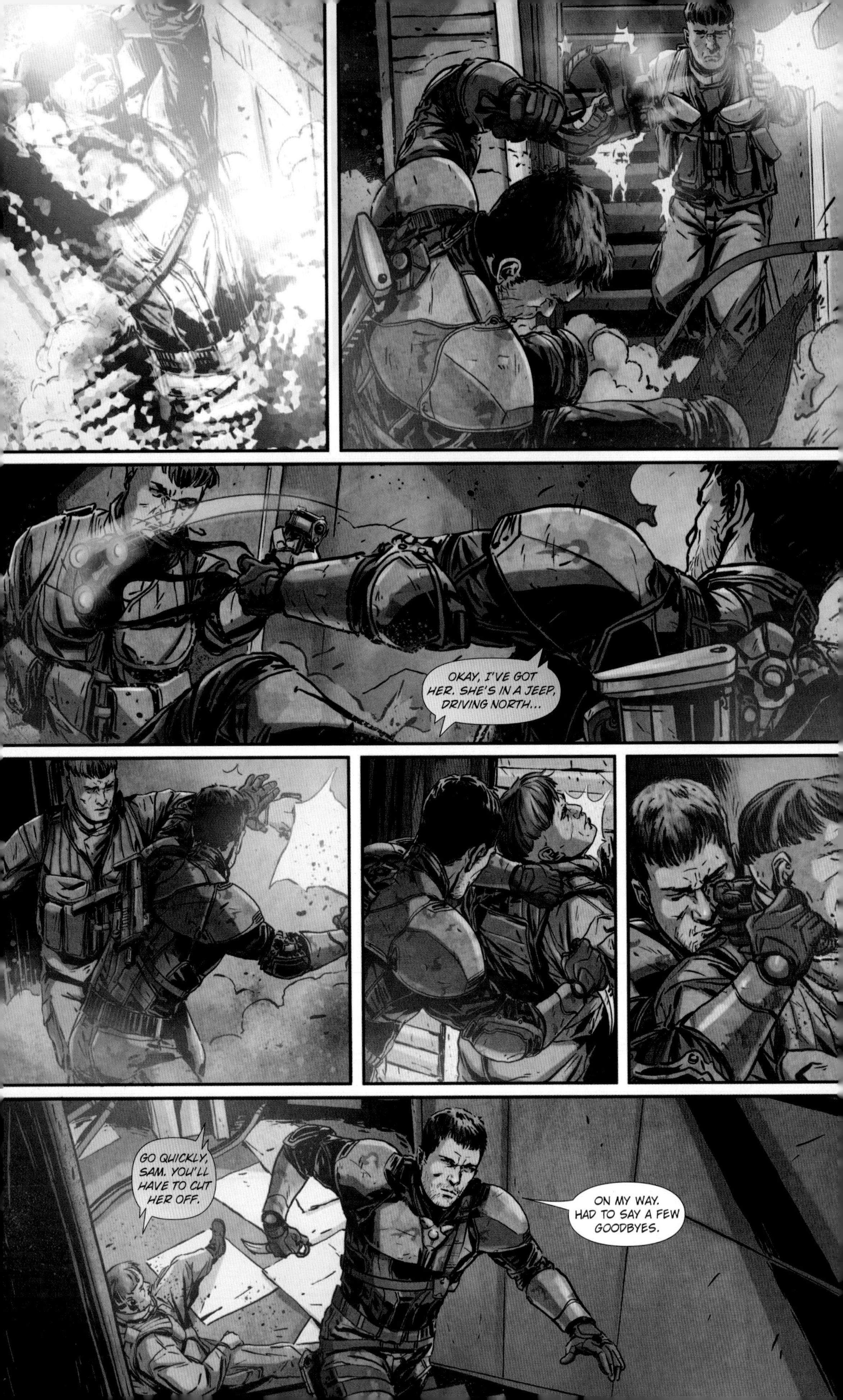
OKAY, I'VE GOT HER. SHE'S IN A JEEP, DRIVING NORTH...
GO QUICKLY, SAM. YOU'LL HAVE TO CUT HER OFF.
ON MY WAY. HAD TO SAY A FEW GOODBYES.

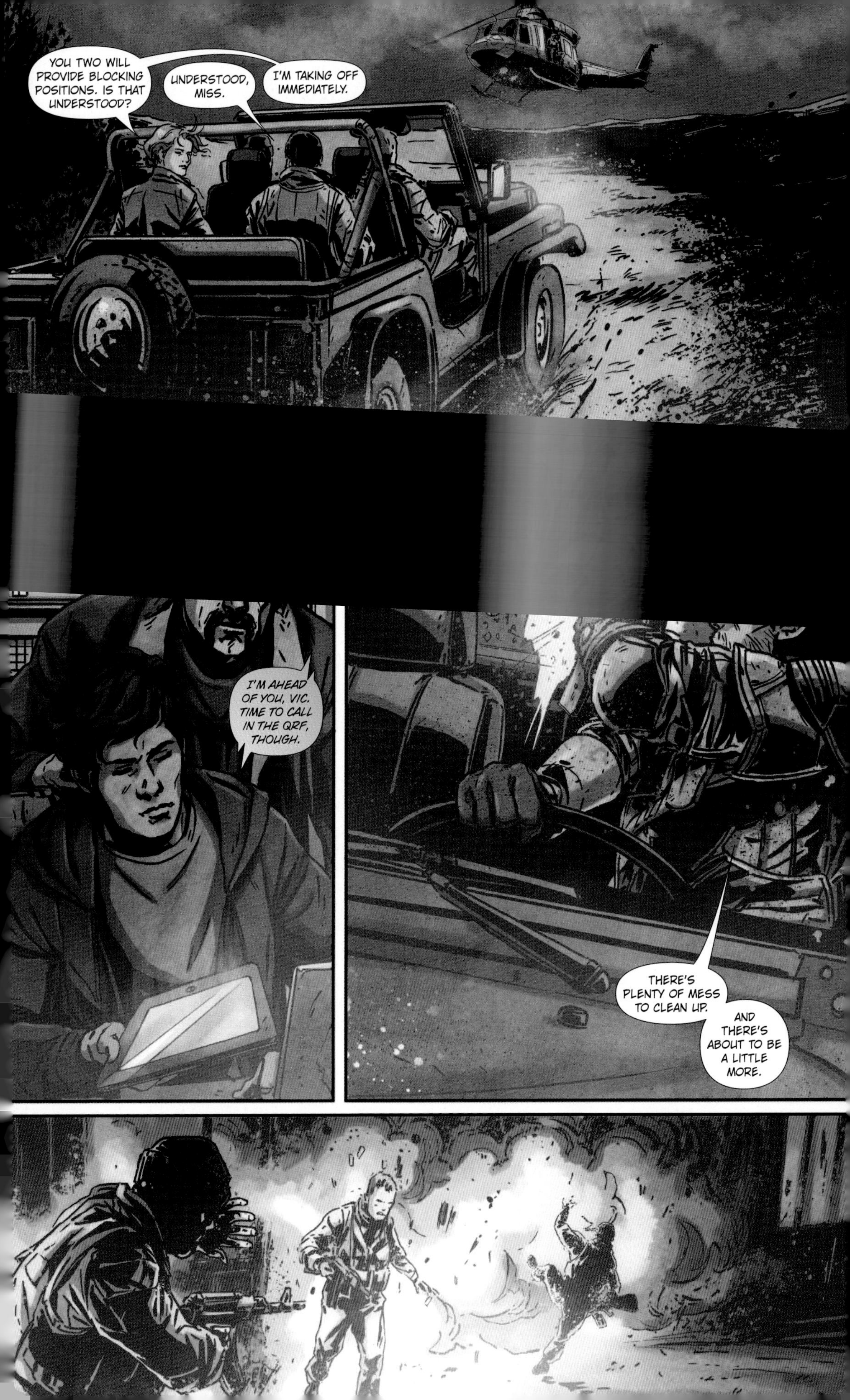
YOU TWO WILL PROVIDE BLOCKING POSITIONS. IS THAT UNDERSTOOD?
UNDERSTOOD, MISS.
I'M TAKING OFF IMMEDIATELY.
I'M AHEAD OF YOU, VIC. TIME TO CALL IN THE QRF, THOUGH.
THERE'S PLENTY OF MESS TO CLEAN UP.
AND THERE'S ABOUT TO BE A LITTLE MORE.

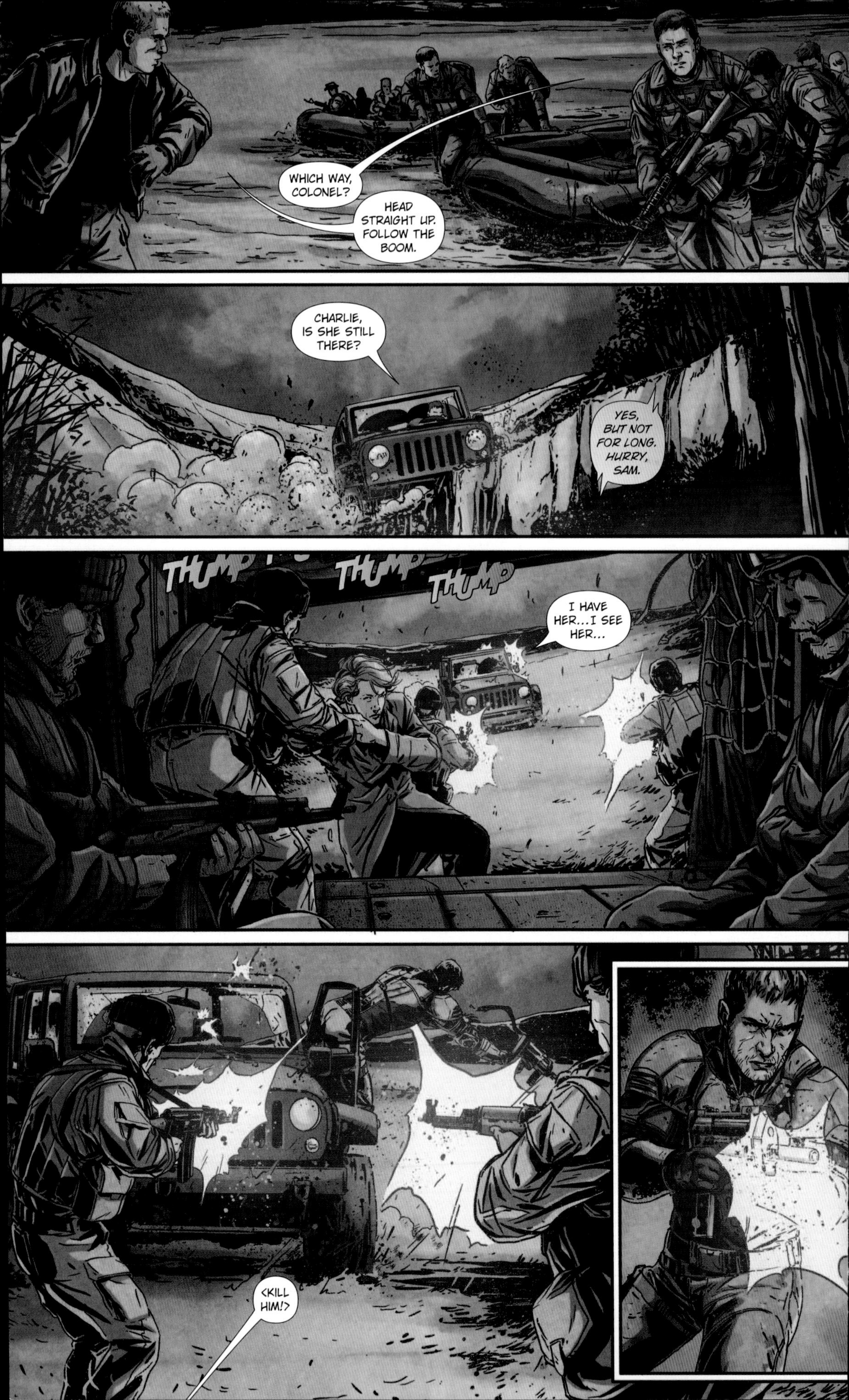
WHICH WAY, COLONEL?
HEAD STRAIGHT UP. FOLLOW THE BOOM.
CHARLIE, IS SHE STILL THERE?
YES, BUT NOT FOR LONG. HURRY, SAM.
THUMP
THUMP
THUMP
I HAVE HER...I SEE HER...
<KILL HIM!>

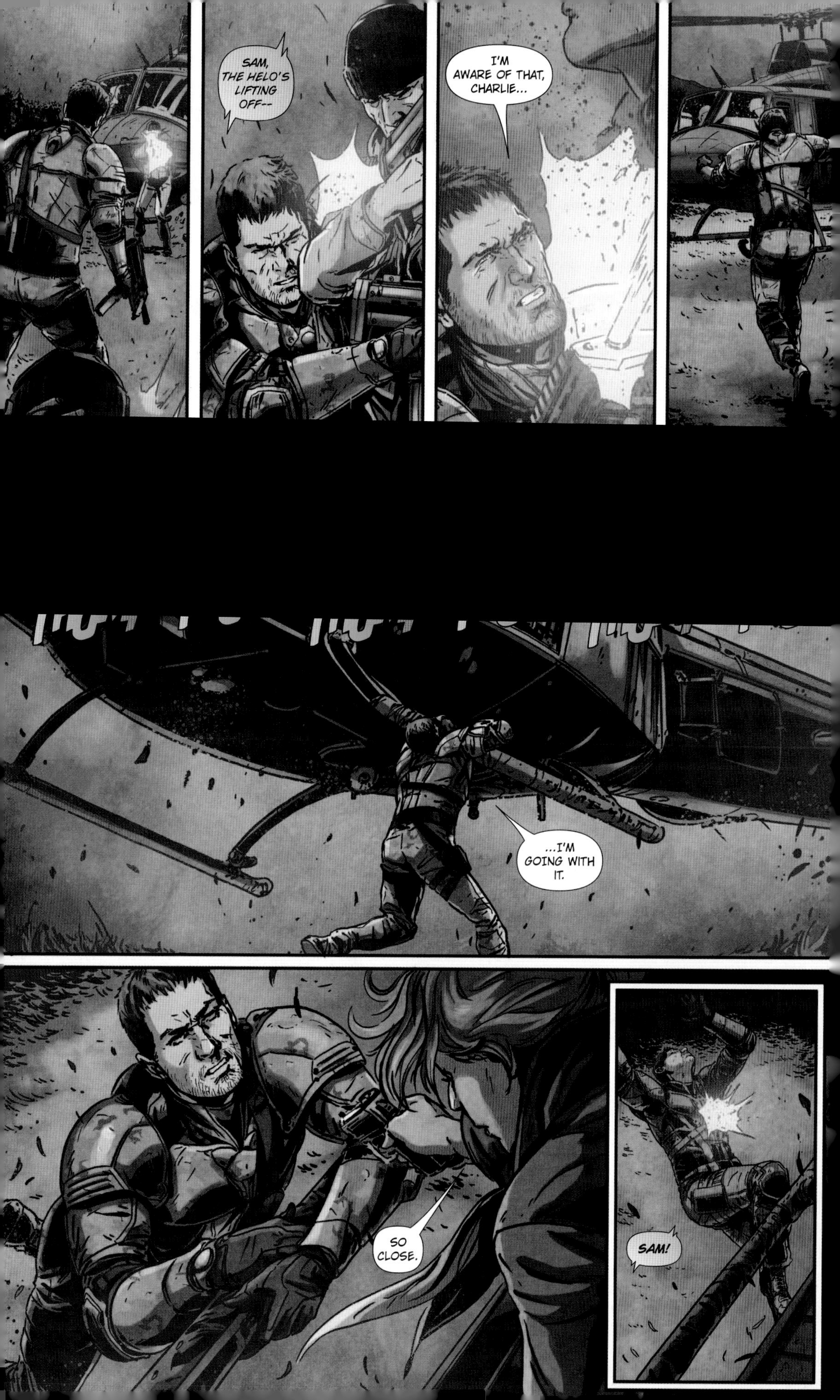
SAM, THE HELO'S LIFTING OFF--
I'M AWARE OF THAT, CHARLIE...
[redacted]
...I'M GOING WITH IT.
SO CLOSE.
SAM!

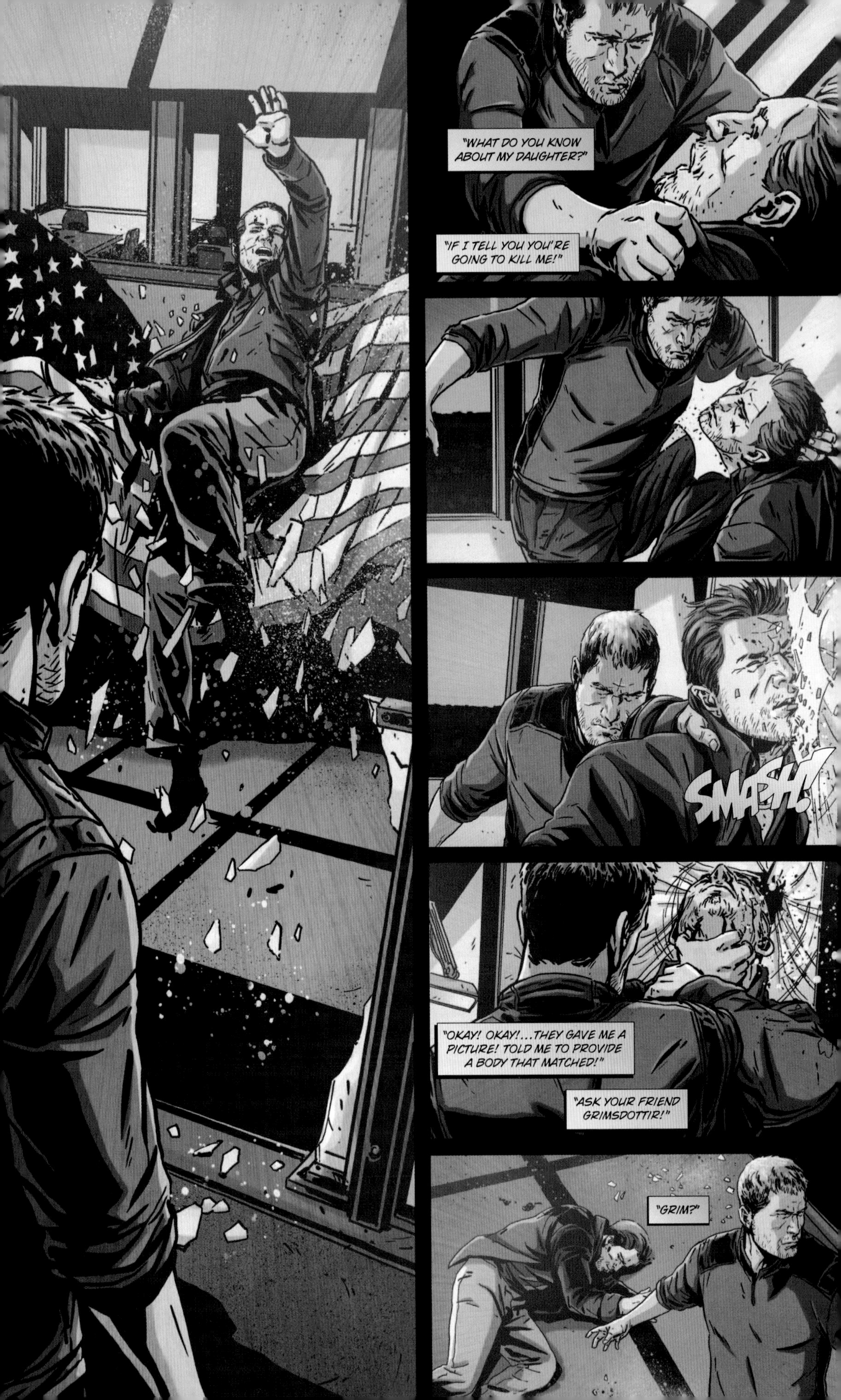
"WHAT DO YOU KNOW ABOUT MY DAUGHTER?"
"IF I TELL YOU YOU'RE GOING TO KILL ME!"
SMASH!
"OKAY! OKAY!...THEY GAVE ME A PICTURE! TOLD ME TO PROVIDE A BODY THAT MATCHED!"
"ASK YOUR FRIEND GRIMSDOTTIR!"
"GRIM?"

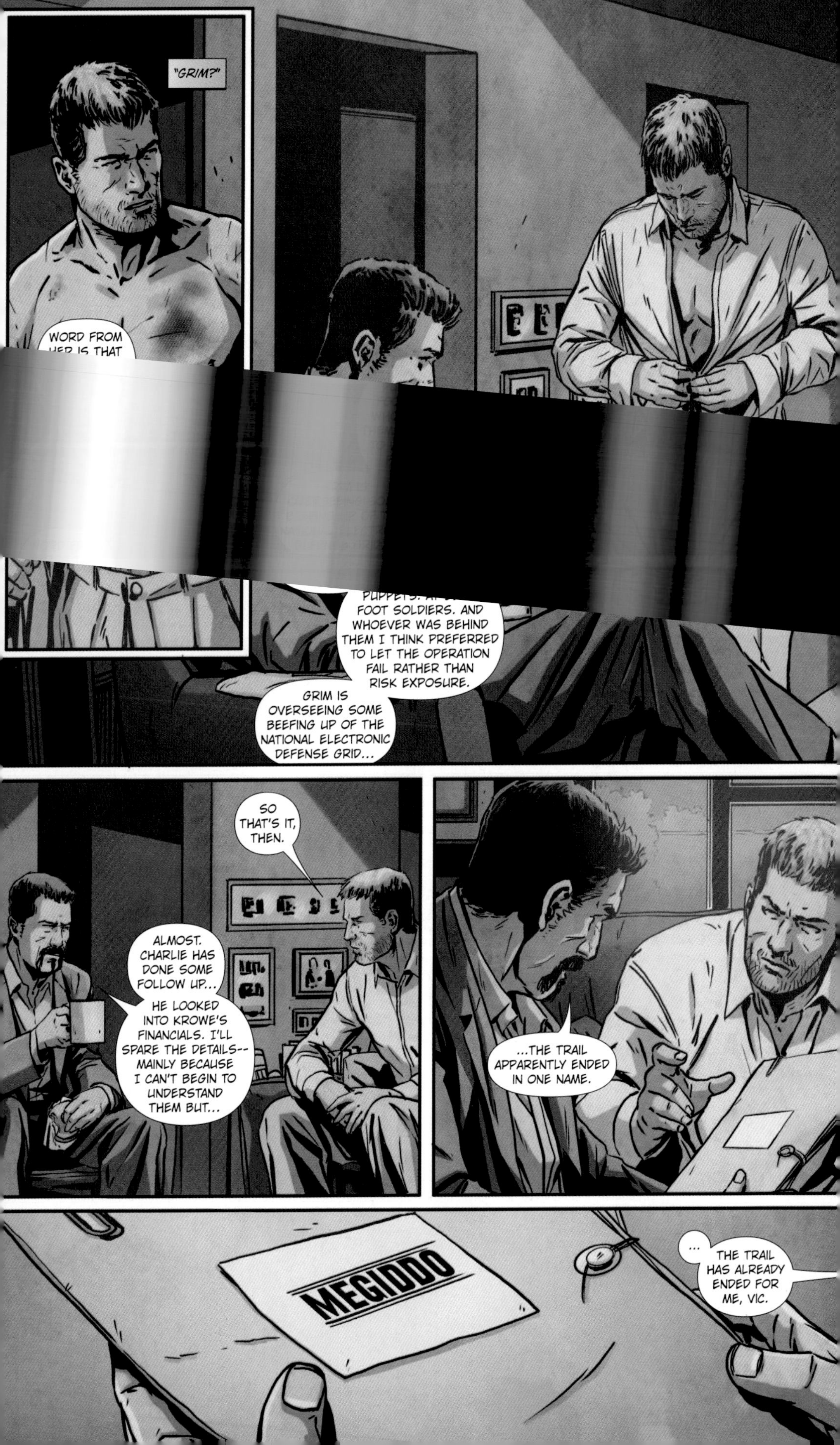
"GRIM?"
WORD FROM
FOOT SOLDIERS. AND WHOEVER WAS BEHIND THEM I THINK PREFERRED TO LET THE OPERATION FAIL RATHER THAN RISK EXPOSURE.
GRIM IS OVERSEEING SOME BEEFING UP OF THE NATIONAL ELECTRONIC DEFENSE GRID...
SO THAT'S IT, THEN.
ALMOST. CHARLIE HAS DONE SOME FOLLOW UP...
HE LOOKED INTO KROWE'S FINANCIALS. I'LL SPARE THE DETAILS-- MAINLY BECAUSE I CAN'T BEGIN TO UNDERSTAND THEM BUT...
...THE TRAIL APPARENTLY ENDED IN ONE NAME.
MEGIDDO
... THE TRAIL HAS ALREADY ENDED FOR ME, VIC.

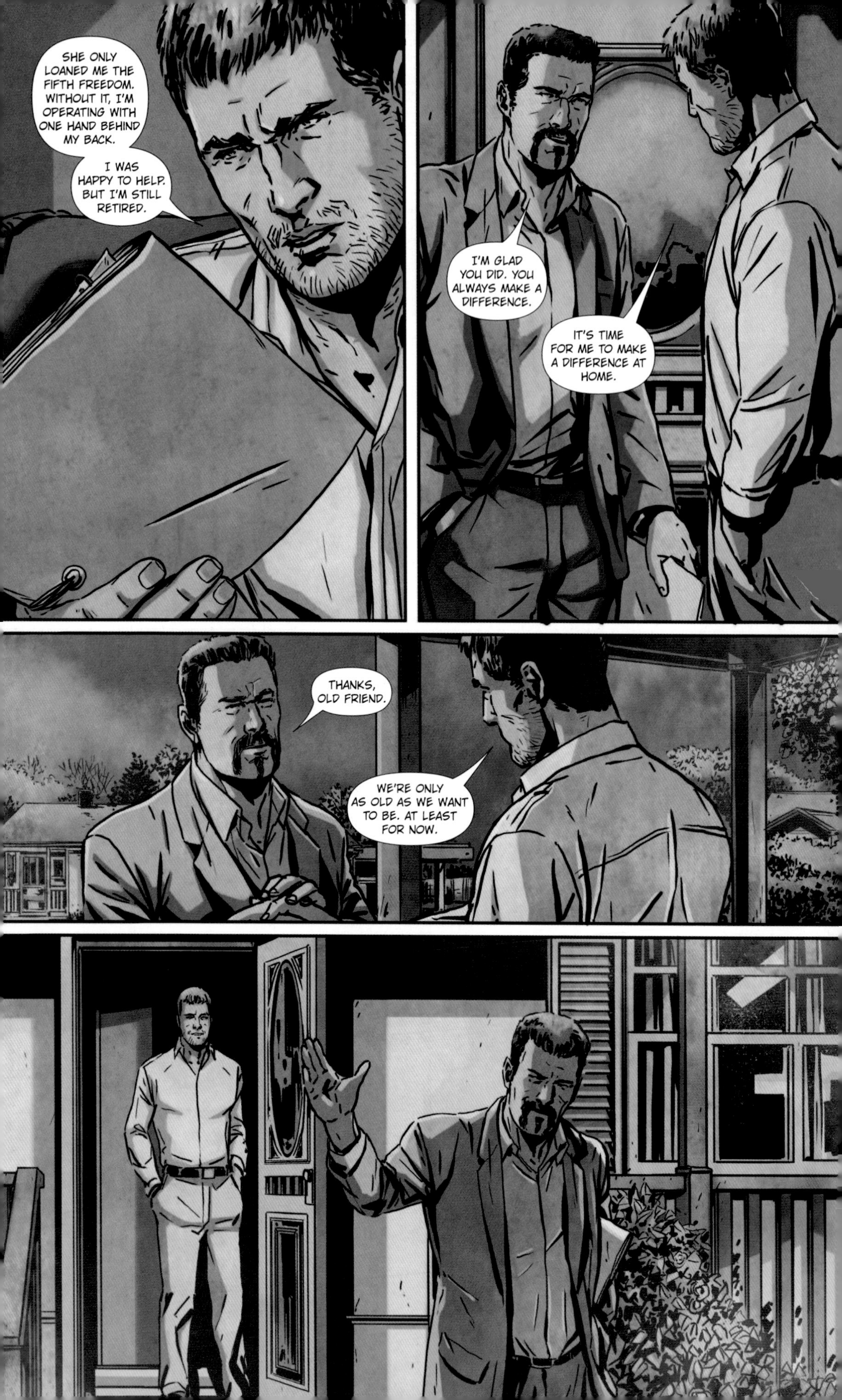
SHE ONLY LOANED ME THE FIFTH FREEDOM. WITHOUT IT, I'M OPERATING WITH ONE HAND BEHIND MY BACK.
I WAS HAPPY TO HELP. BUT I'M STILL RETIRED.
I'M GLAD YOU DID. YOU ALWAYS MAKE A DIFFERENCE.
IT'S TIME FOR ME TO MAKE A DIFFERENCE AT HOME.
THANKS, OLD FRIEND.
WE'RE ONLY AS OLD AS WE WANT TO BE. AT LEAST FOR NOW.

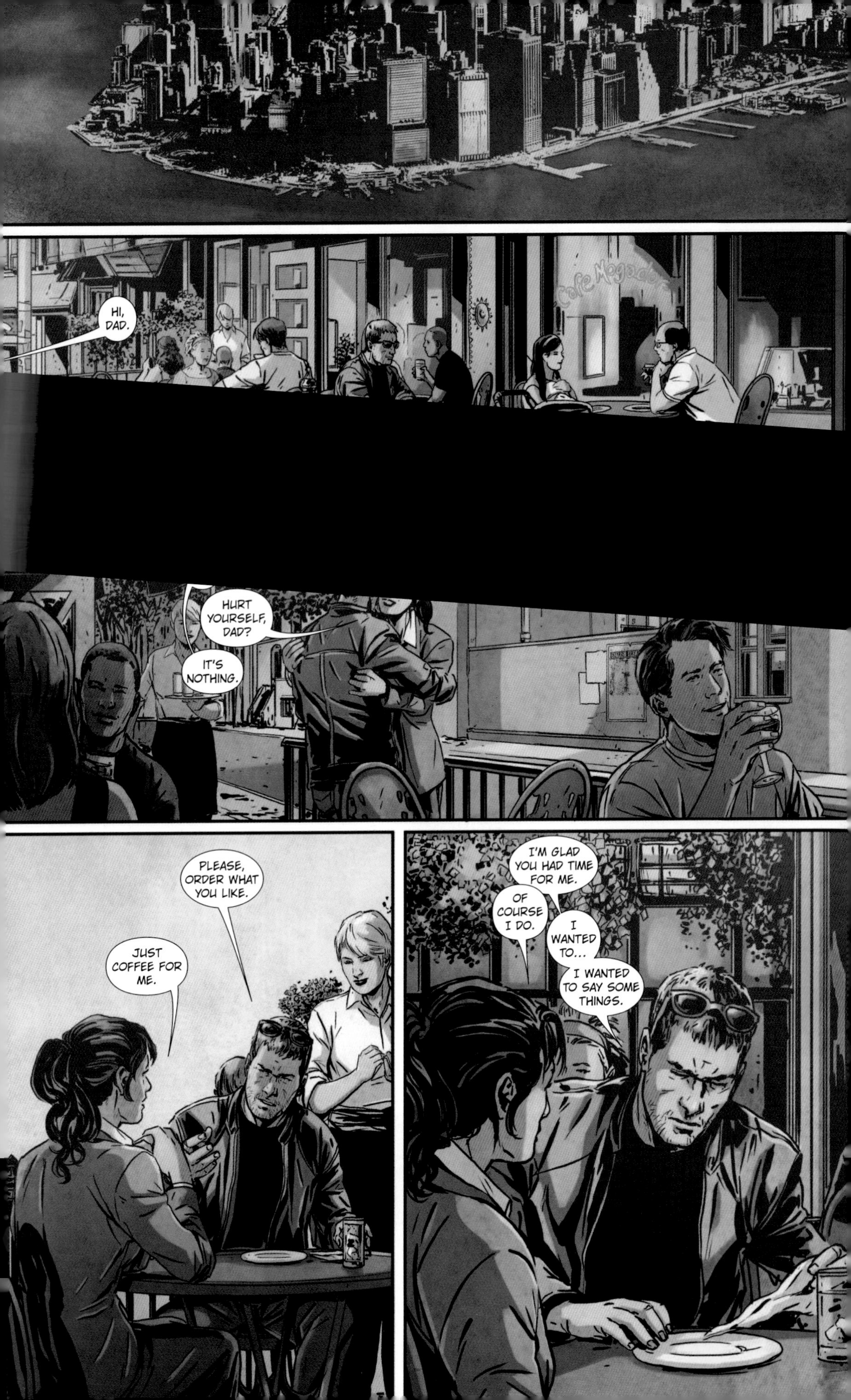
HI, DAD.
[redacted]
HURT YOURSELF, DAD?
IT'S NOTHING.
PLEASE, ORDER WHAT YOU LIKE.
JUST COFFEE FOR ME.
I'M GLAD YOU HAD TIME FOR ME.
OF COURSE I DO.
I WANTED TO...
I WANTED TO SAY SOME THINGS.

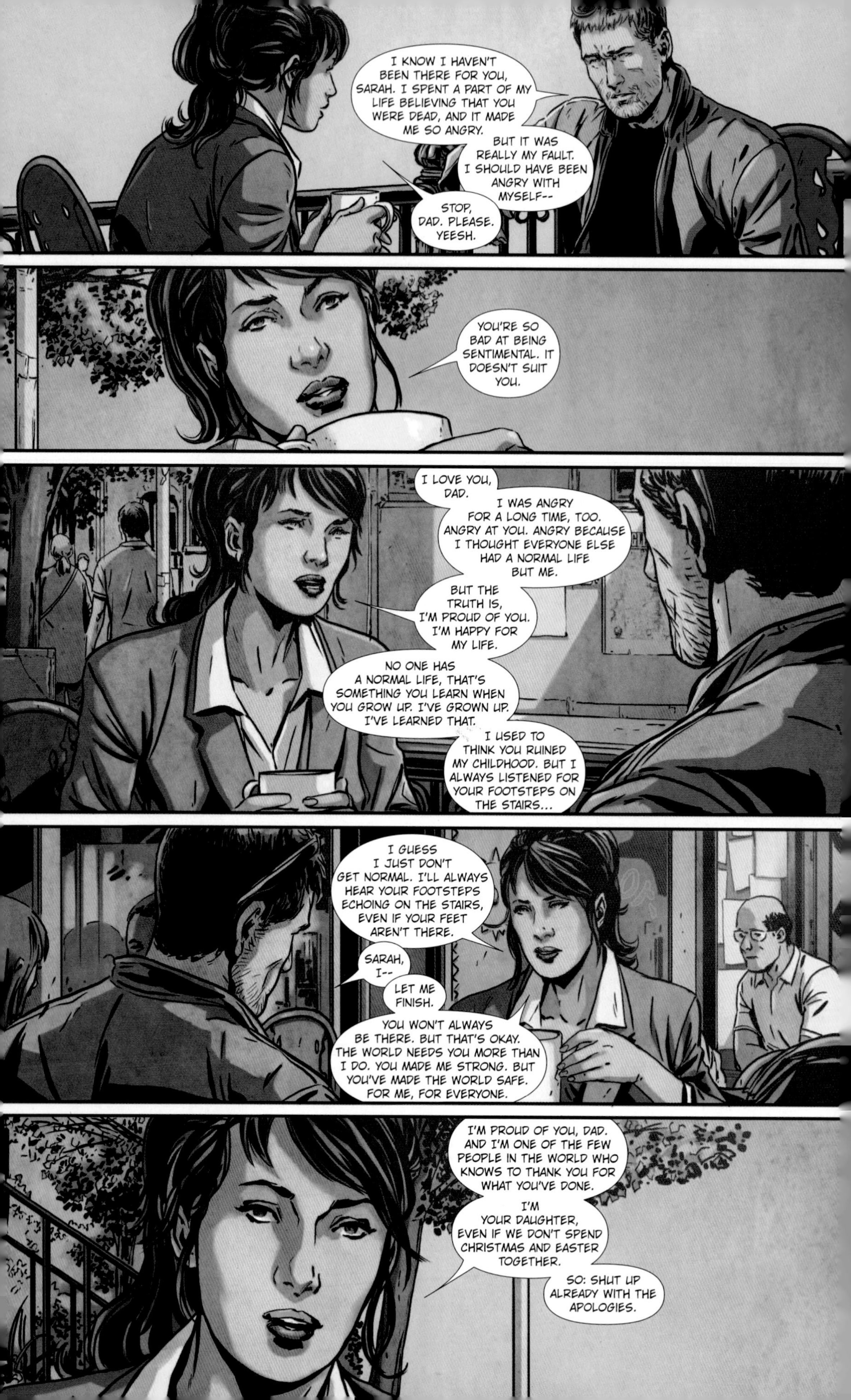
I KNOW I HAVEN'T BEEN THERE FOR YOU, SARAH. I SPENT A PART OF MY LIFE BELIEVING THAT YOU WERE DEAD, AND IT MADE ME SO ANGRY.
BUT IT WAS REALLY MY FAULT. I SHOULD HAVE BEEN ANGRY WITH MYSELF--
STOP, DAD. PLEASE. YEESH.
YOU'RE SO BAD AT BEING SENTIMENTAL. IT DOESN'T SUIT YOU.
I LOVE YOU, DAD.
I WAS ANGRY FOR A LONG TIME, TOO. ANGRY AT YOU. ANGRY BECAUSE I THOUGHT EVERYONE ELSE HAD A NORMAL LIFE BUT ME.
BUT THE TRUTH IS, I'M PROUD OF YOU. I'M HAPPY FOR MY LIFE.
NO ONE HAS A NORMAL LIFE, THAT'S SOMETHING YOU LEARN WHEN YOU GROW UP. I'VE GROWN UP. I'VE LEARNED THAT.
I USED TO THINK YOU RUINED MY CHILDHOOD. BUT I ALWAYS LISTENED FOR YOUR FOOTSTEPS ON THE STAIRS...
I GUESS I JUST DON'T GET NORMAL. I'LL ALWAYS HEAR YOUR FOOTSTEPS ECHOING ON THE STAIRS, EVEN IF YOUR FEET AREN'T THERE.
SARAH, I--
LET ME FINISH.
YOU WON'T ALWAYS BE THERE. BUT THAT'S OKAY. THE WORLD NEEDS YOU MORE THAN I DO. YOU MADE ME STRONG. BUT YOU'VE MADE THE WORLD SAFE. FOR ME, FOR EVERYONE.
I'M PROUD OF YOU, DAD. AND I'M ONE OF THE FEW PEOPLE IN THE WORLD WHO KNOWS TO THANK YOU FOR WHAT YOU'VE DONE.
I'M YOUR DAUGHTER, EVEN IF WE DON'T SPEND CHRISTMAS AND EASTER TOGETHER.
SO: SHUT UP ALREADY WITH THE APOLOGIES.

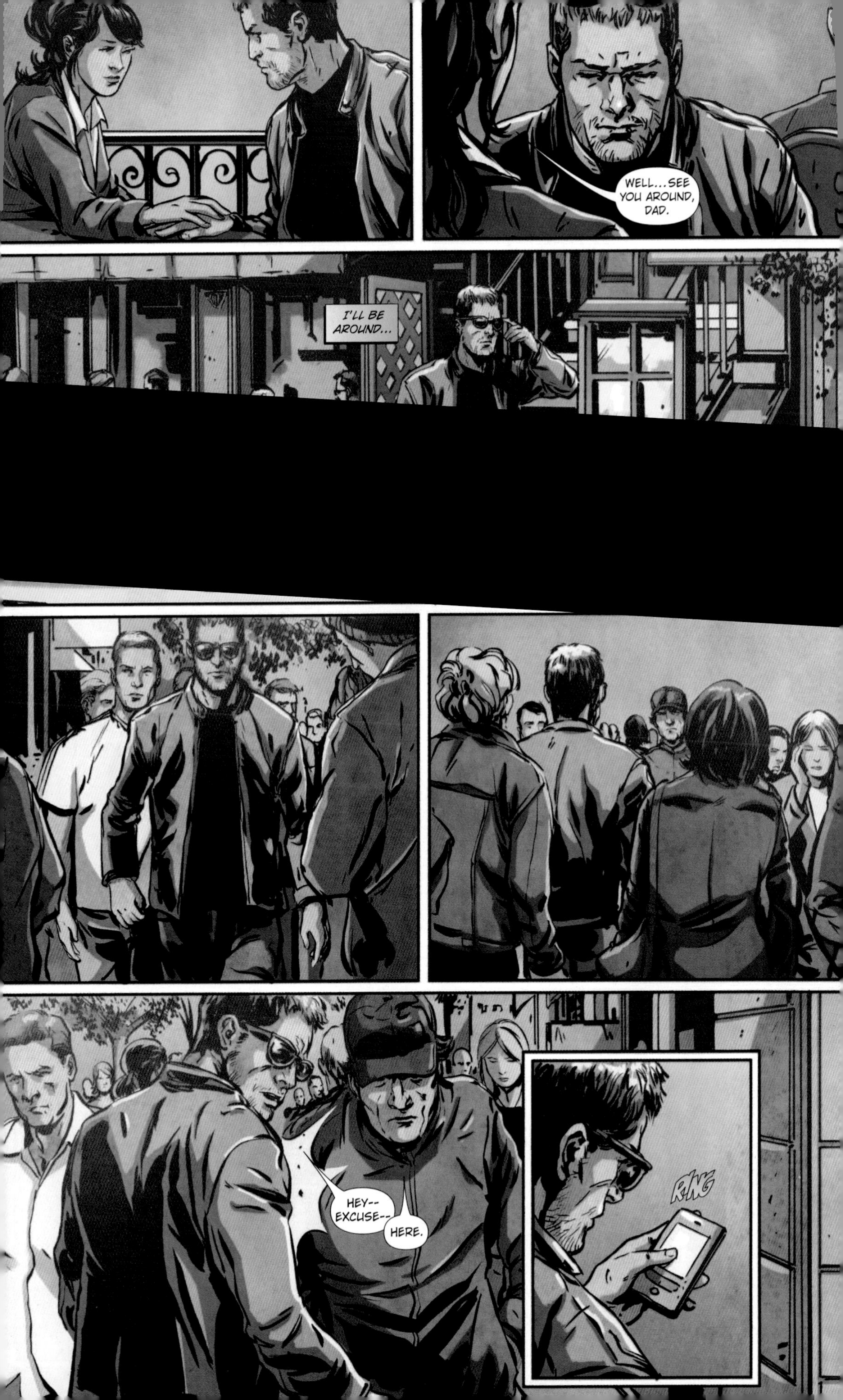
WELL...SEE YOU AROUND, DAD.
I'LL BE AROUND...
HEY-- EXCUSE--
HERE.
RING

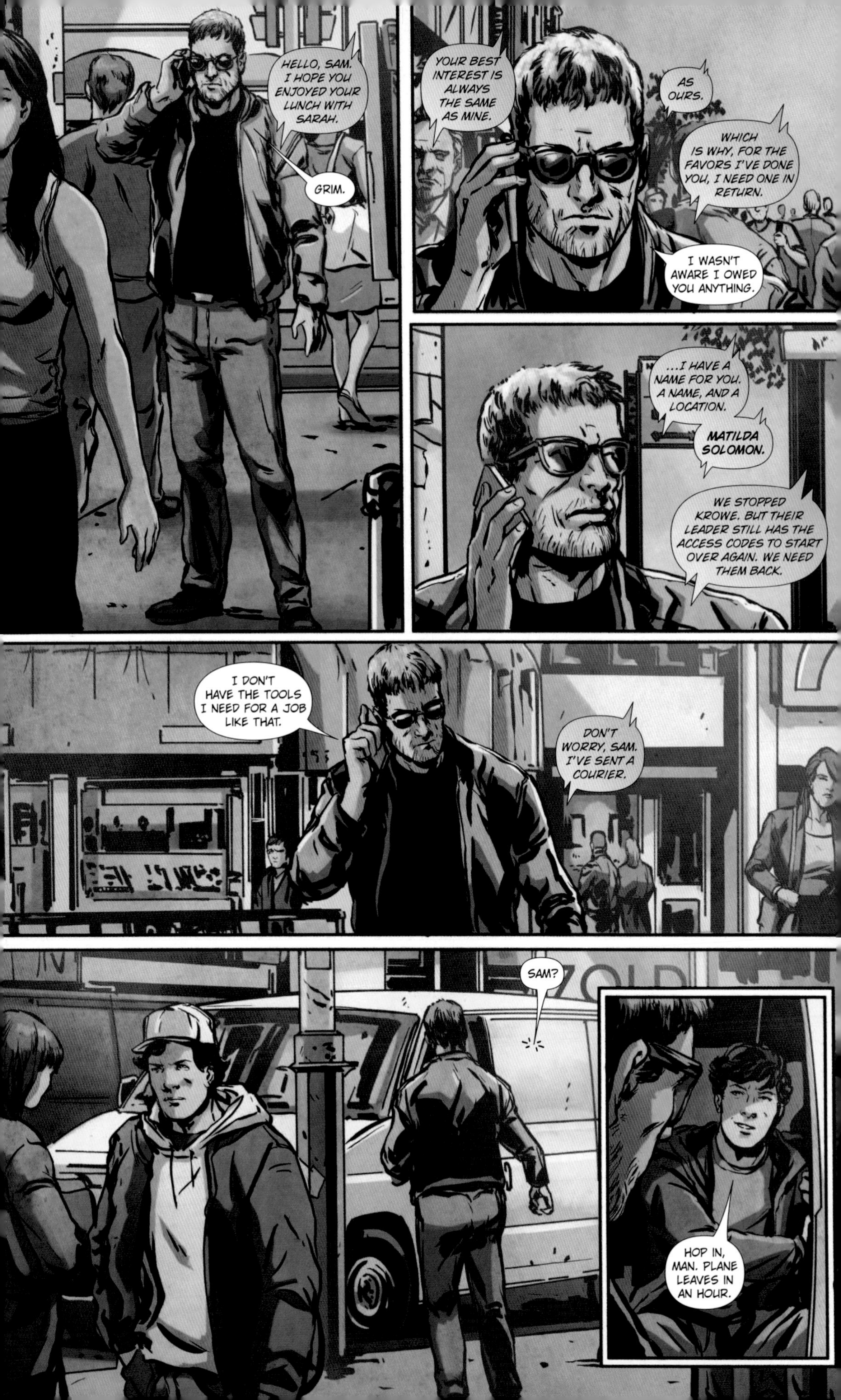
HELLO, SAM. I HOPE YOU ENJOYED YOUR LUNCH WITH SARAH.
GRIM.
YOUR BEST INTEREST IS ALWAYS THE SAME AS MINE.
AS OURS.
WHICH IS WHY, FOR THE FAVORS I'VE DONE YOU, I NEED ONE IN RETURN.
I WASN'T AWARE I OWED YOU ANYTHING.
...I HAVE A NAME FOR YOU. A NAME, AND A LOCATION.
MATILDA SOLOMON.
WE STOPPED KROWE. BUT THEIR LEADER STILL HAS THE ACCESS CODES TO START OVER AGAIN. WE NEED THEM BACK.
I DON'T HAVE THE TOOLS I NEED FOR A JOB LIKE THAT.
DON'T WORRY, SAM. I'VE SENT A COURIER.
SAM?
HOP IN, MAN. PLANE LEAVES IN AN HOUR.

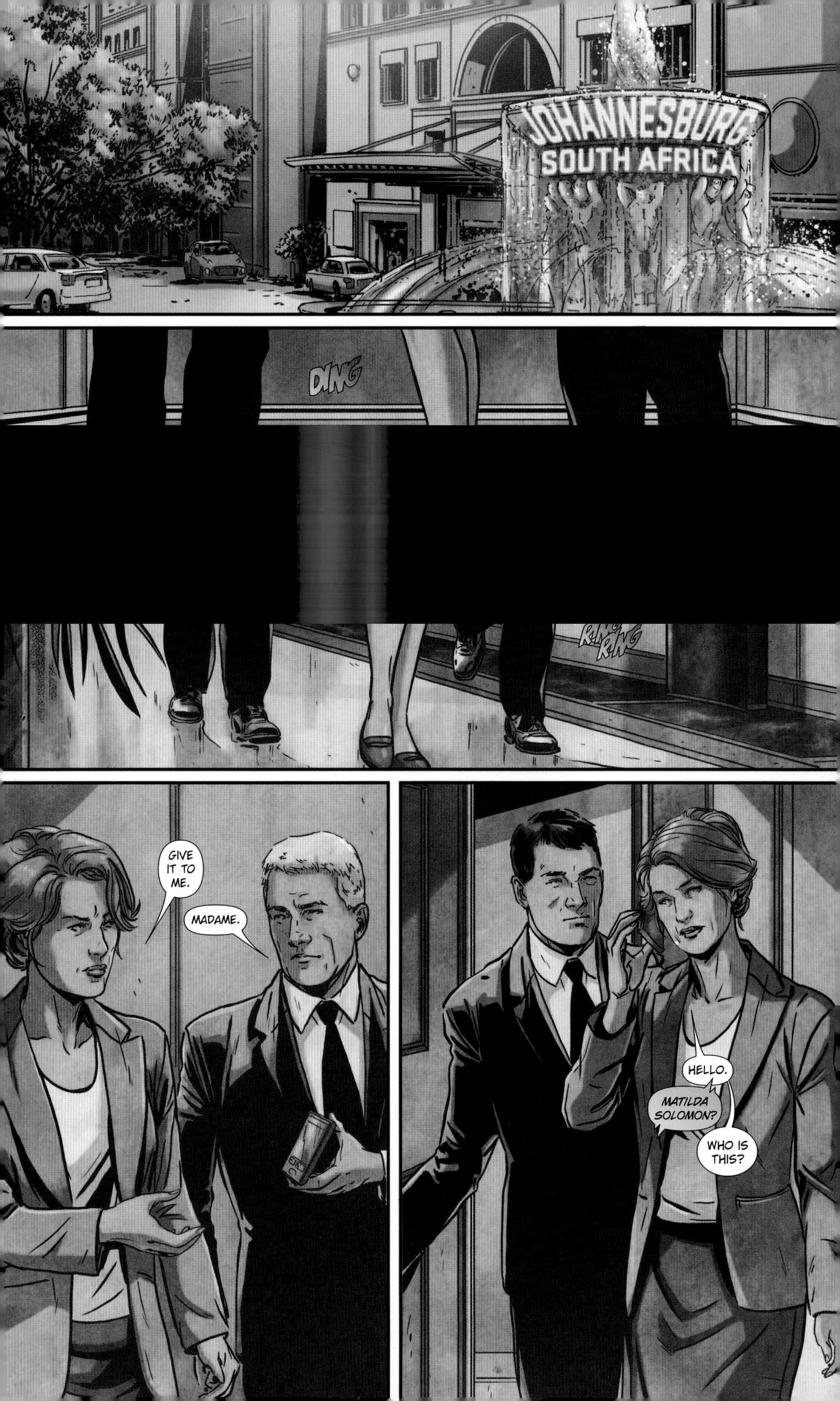
JOHANNESBURG
SOUTH AFRICA
DING
RING RING
GIVE IT TO ME.
MADAME.
HELLO.
MATILDA SOLOMON?
WHO IS THIS?

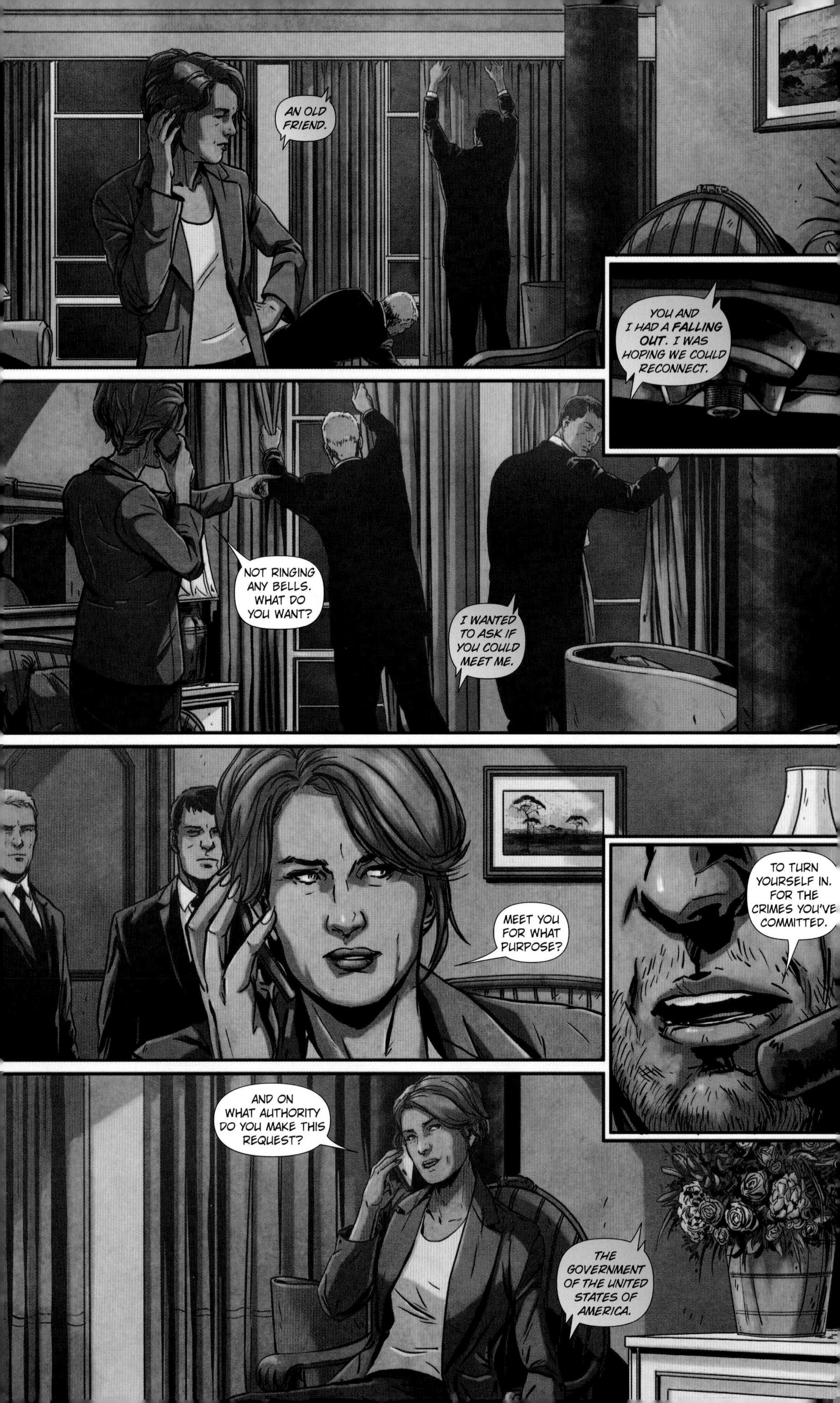
AN OLD FRIEND.
YOU AND I HAD A **FALLING OUT**. I WAS HOPING WE COULD RECONNECT.
NOT RINGING ANY BELLS. WHAT DO YOU WANT?
I WANTED TO ASK IF YOU COULD MEET ME.
MEET YOU FOR WHAT PURPOSE?
TO TURN YOURSELF IN. FOR THE CRIMES YOU'VE COMMITTED.
AND ON WHAT AUTHORITY DO YOU MAKE THIS REQUEST?
THE GOVERNMENT OF THE UNITED STATES OF AMERICA.

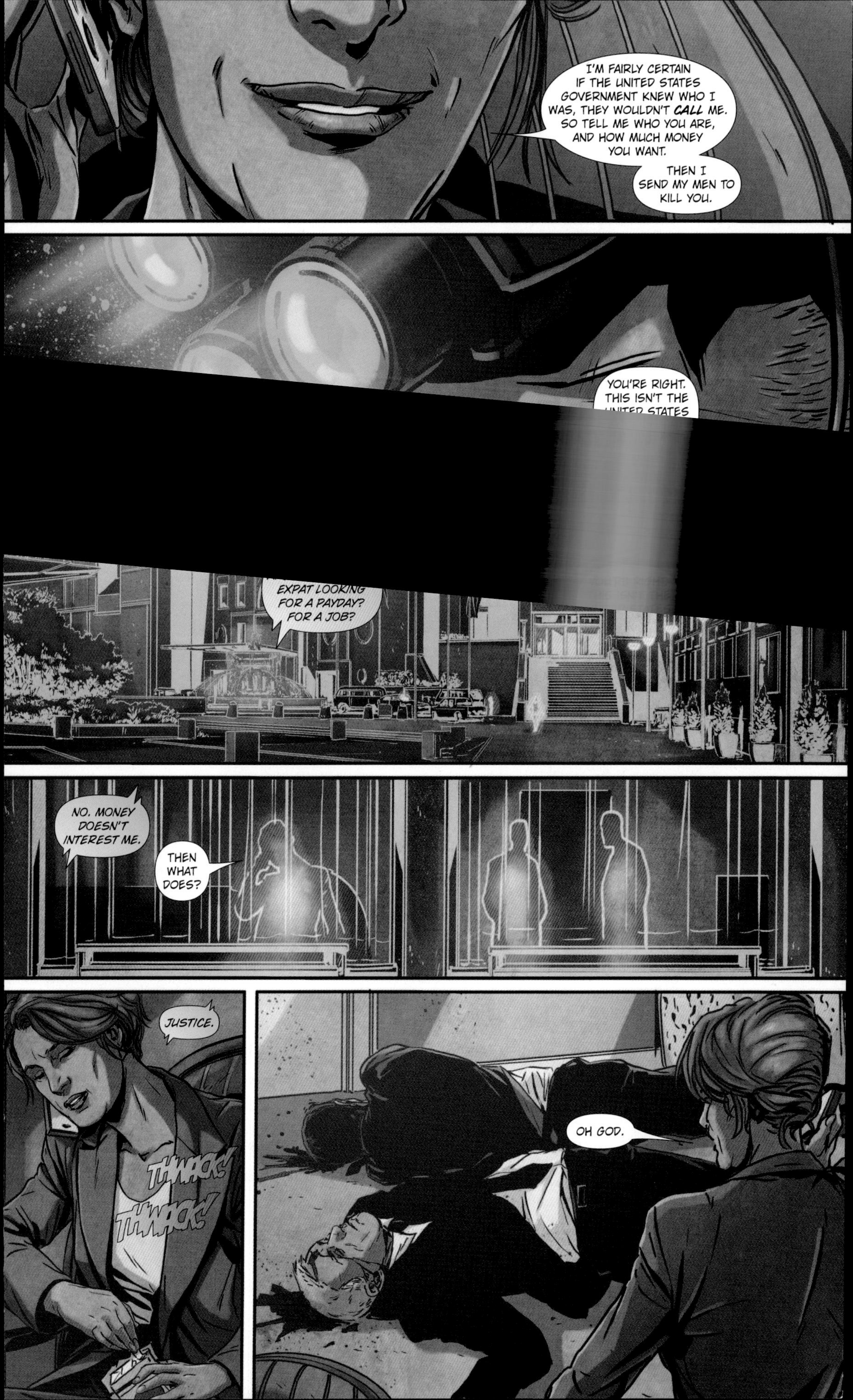
I'M FAIRLY CERTAIN IF THE UNITED STATES GOVERNMENT KNEW WHO I WAS, THEY WOULDN'T **CALL** ME. SO TELL ME WHO YOU ARE, AND HOW MUCH MONEY YOU WANT.
THEN I SEND MY MEN TO KILL YOU.
YOU'RE RIGHT. THIS ISN'T THE [redacted]
EXPAT LOOKING FOR A PAYDAY? FOR A JOB?
NO. MONEY DOESN'T INTEREST ME.
THEN WHAT DOES?
JUSTICE.
THWACK!
THWACK!
OH GOD.

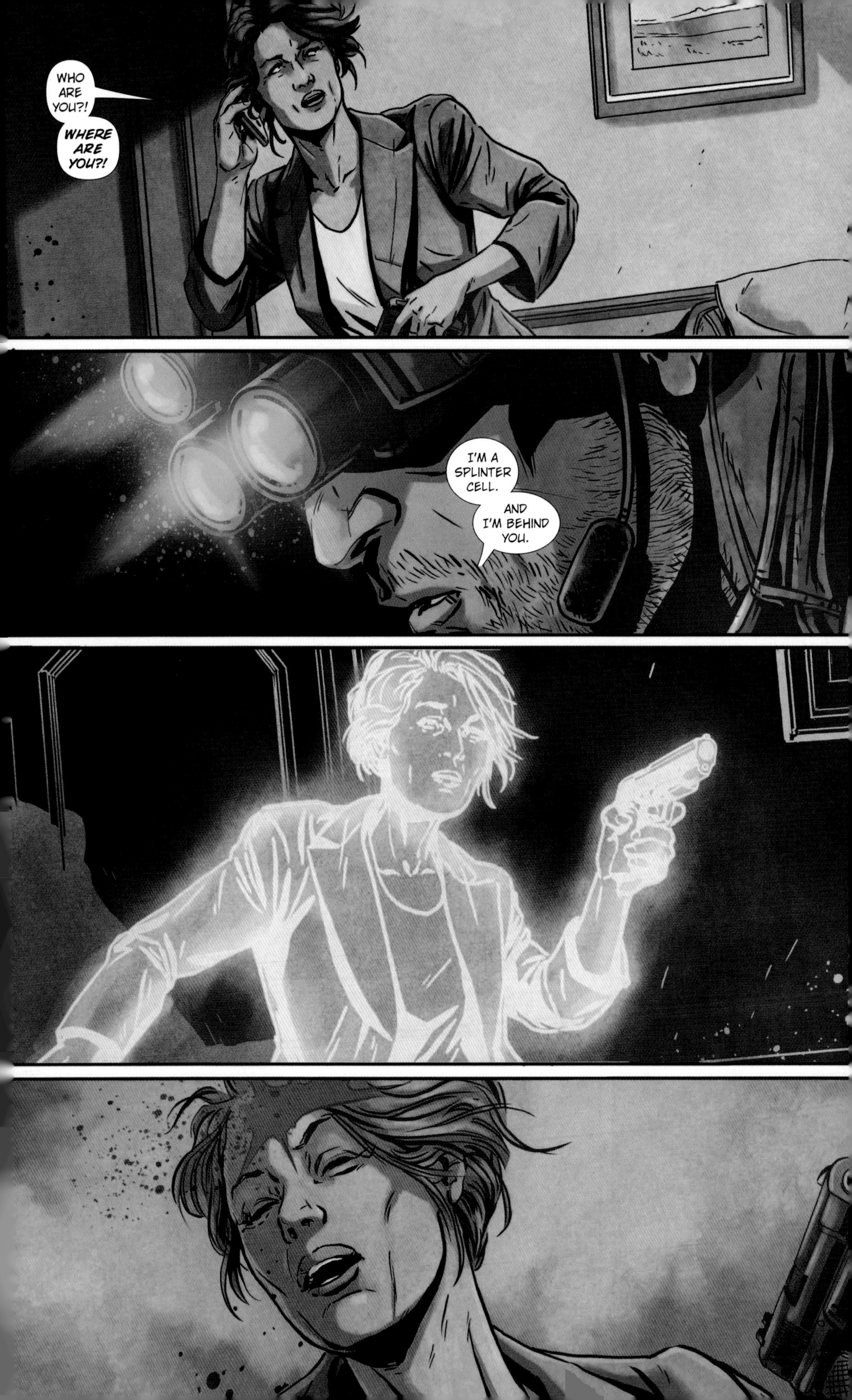

WHO ARE YOU?!
WHERE ARE YOU?!
I'M A SPLINTER CELL.
AND I'M BEHIND YOU.

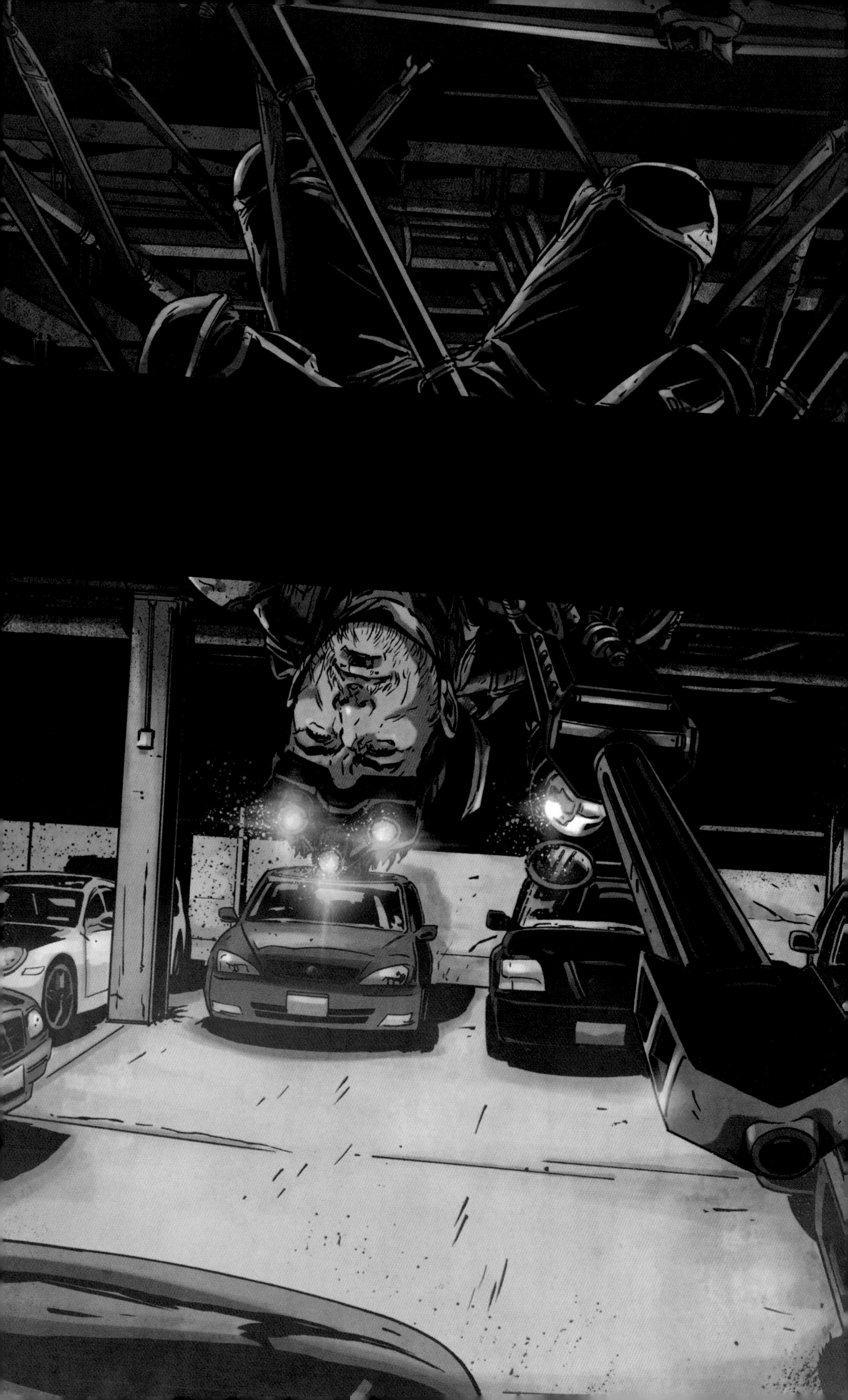

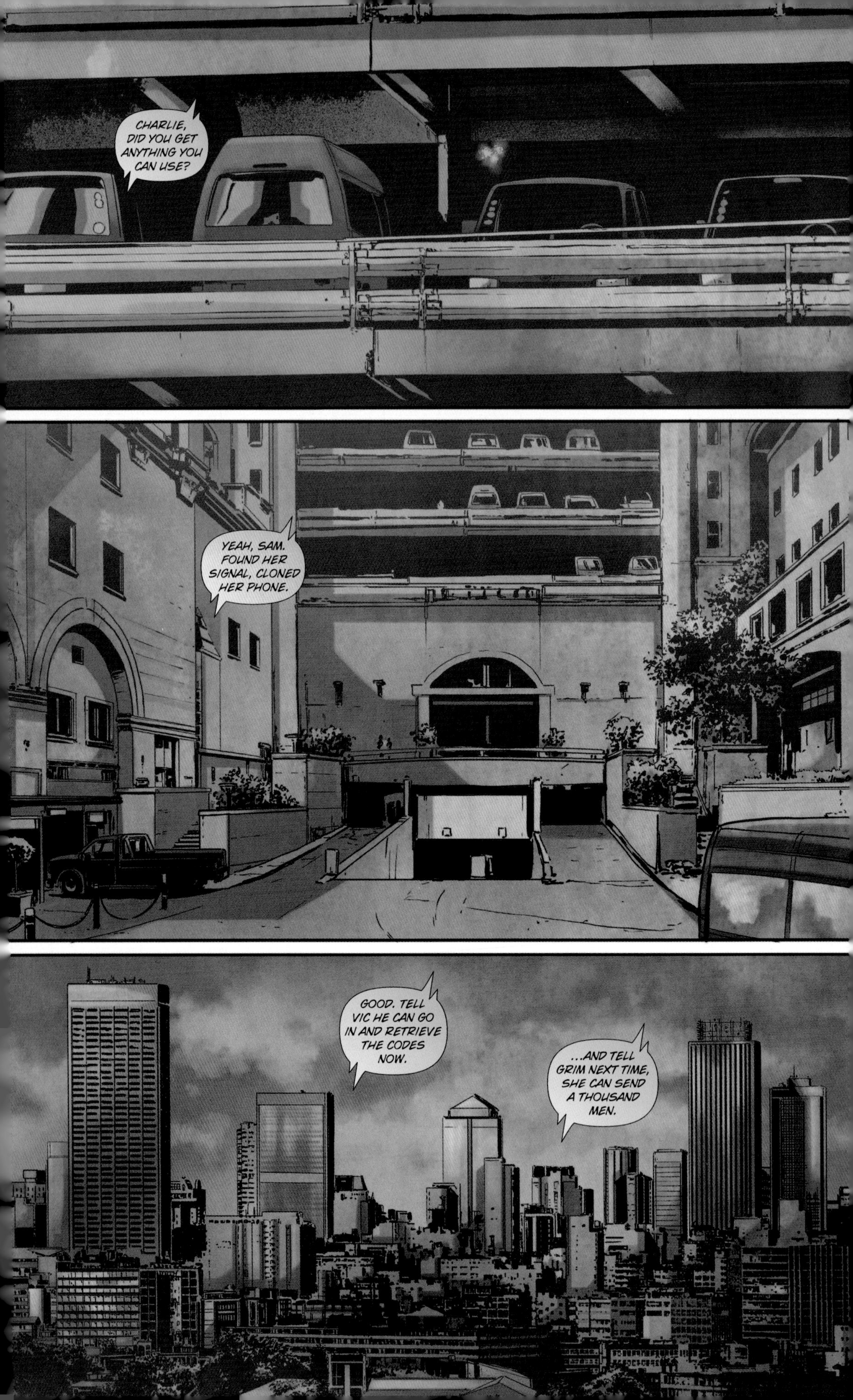
CHARLIE, DID YOU GET ANYTHING YOU CAN USE?
YEAH, SAM. FOUND HER SIGNAL, CLONED HER PHONE.
GOOD. TELL VIC HE CAN GO IN AND RETRIEVE THE CODES NOW.
...AND TELL GRIM NEXT TIME, SHE CAN SEND A THOUSAND MEN.

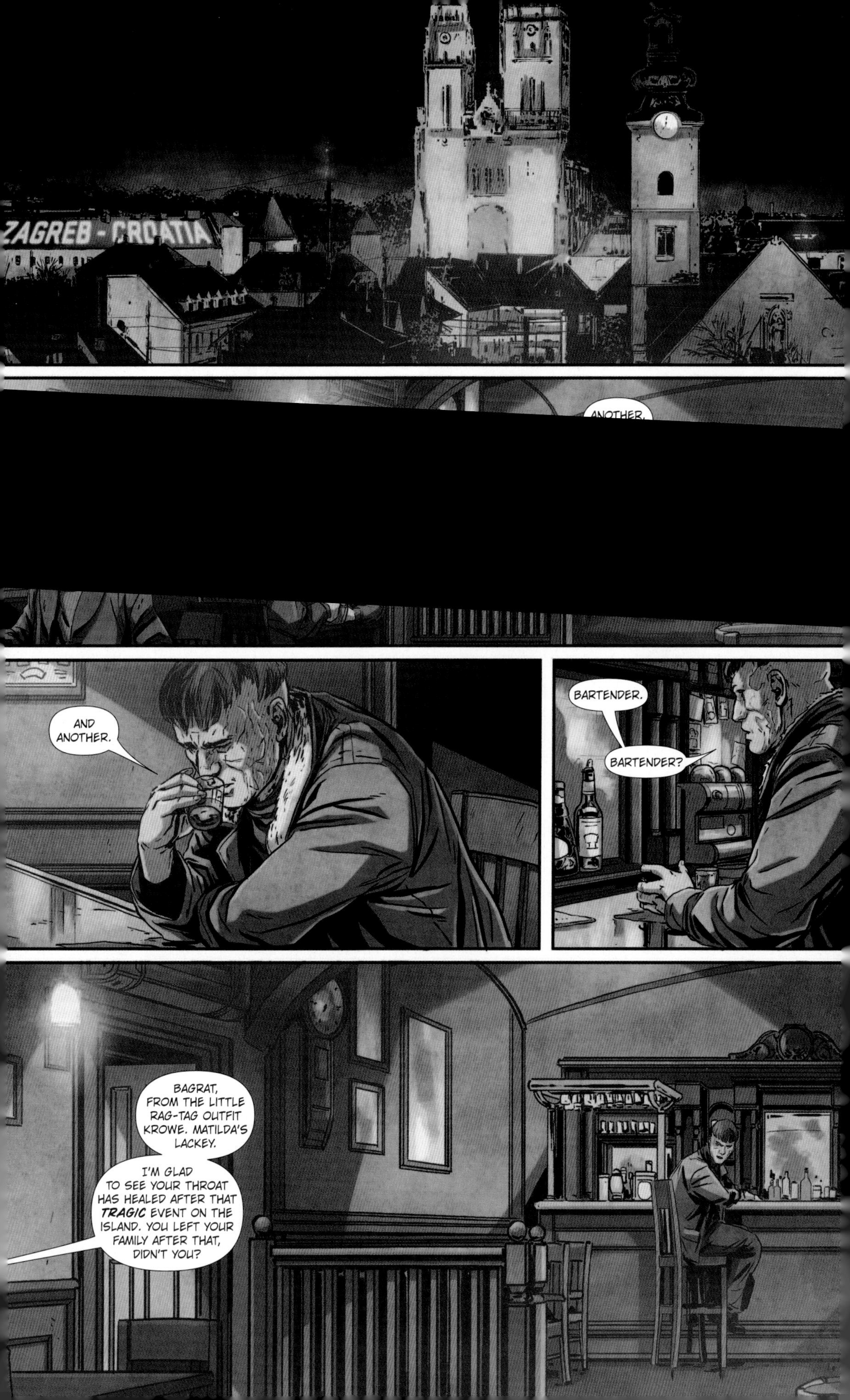
ZAGREB - CROATIA
[redacted]
AND ANOTHER.
BARTENDER.
BARTENDER?
BAGRAT, FROM THE LITTLE RAG-TAG OUTFIT KROWE. MATILDA'S LACKEY.
I'M GLAD TO SEE YOUR THROAT HAS HEALED AFTER THAT *TRAGIC* EVENT ON THE ISLAND. YOU LEFT YOUR FAMILY AFTER THAT, DIDN'T YOU?

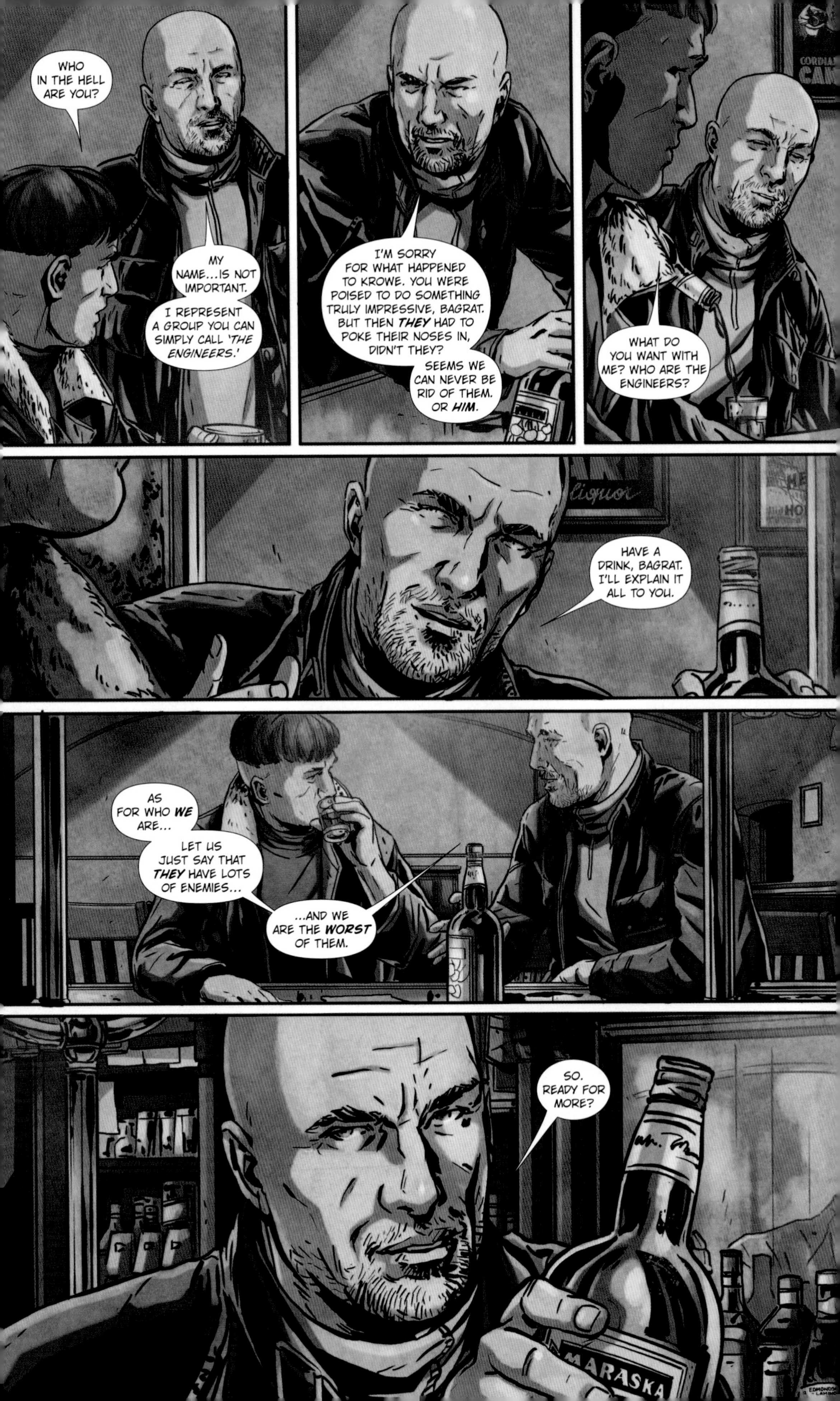
WHO IN THE HELL ARE YOU?
MY NAME...IS NOT IMPORTANT.
I REPRESENT A GROUP YOU CAN SIMPLY CALL 'THE ENGINEERS.'
I'M SORRY FOR WHAT HAPPENED TO KROWE. YOU WERE POISED TO DO SOMETHING TRULY IMPRESSIVE, BAGRAT. BUT THEN THEY HAD TO POKE THEIR NOSES IN, DIDN'T THEY?
SEEMS WE CAN NEVER BE RID OF THEM. OR HIM.
WHAT DO YOU WANT WITH ME? WHO ARE THE ENGINEERS?
HAVE A DRINK, BAGRAT. I'LL EXPLAIN IT ALL TO YOU.
AS FOR WHO WE ARE...
LET US JUST SAY THAT THEY HAVE LOTS OF ENEMIES...
...AND WE ARE THE WORST OF THEM.
SO. READY FOR MORE?
MARASKA

IN THE SHADOW OF SPLINTER CELL ∴ ECHOES

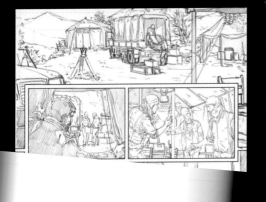

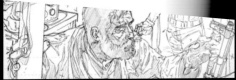

Test page pencils by Marc Laming

«When we presented Marc with an art test it was never about his ability to make Sam look good in a comic page, this we had no doubt. It was really about our vision for the storytelling and how our intentions could translate onto the page.

«So for Echoes we were searching for a turn of the head, that curl of the lip, that sullen look over heavy eyes that spells doom for the bad guys.

These are the elusive qualities that make a quality comic book artist a great storyteller.

A quick glance at the test page and it's clear that Marc has mastered it.»

Scott Lee
Splinter Cell Blacklist art director

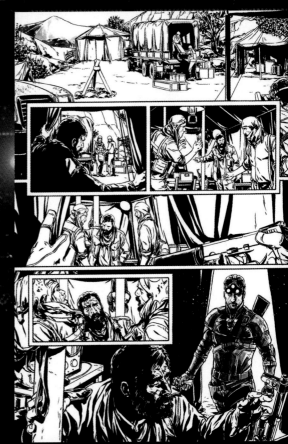

Test page inks by Marc Laming

IN THE SHADOW OF SPLINTER CELL ∴ ECHOES

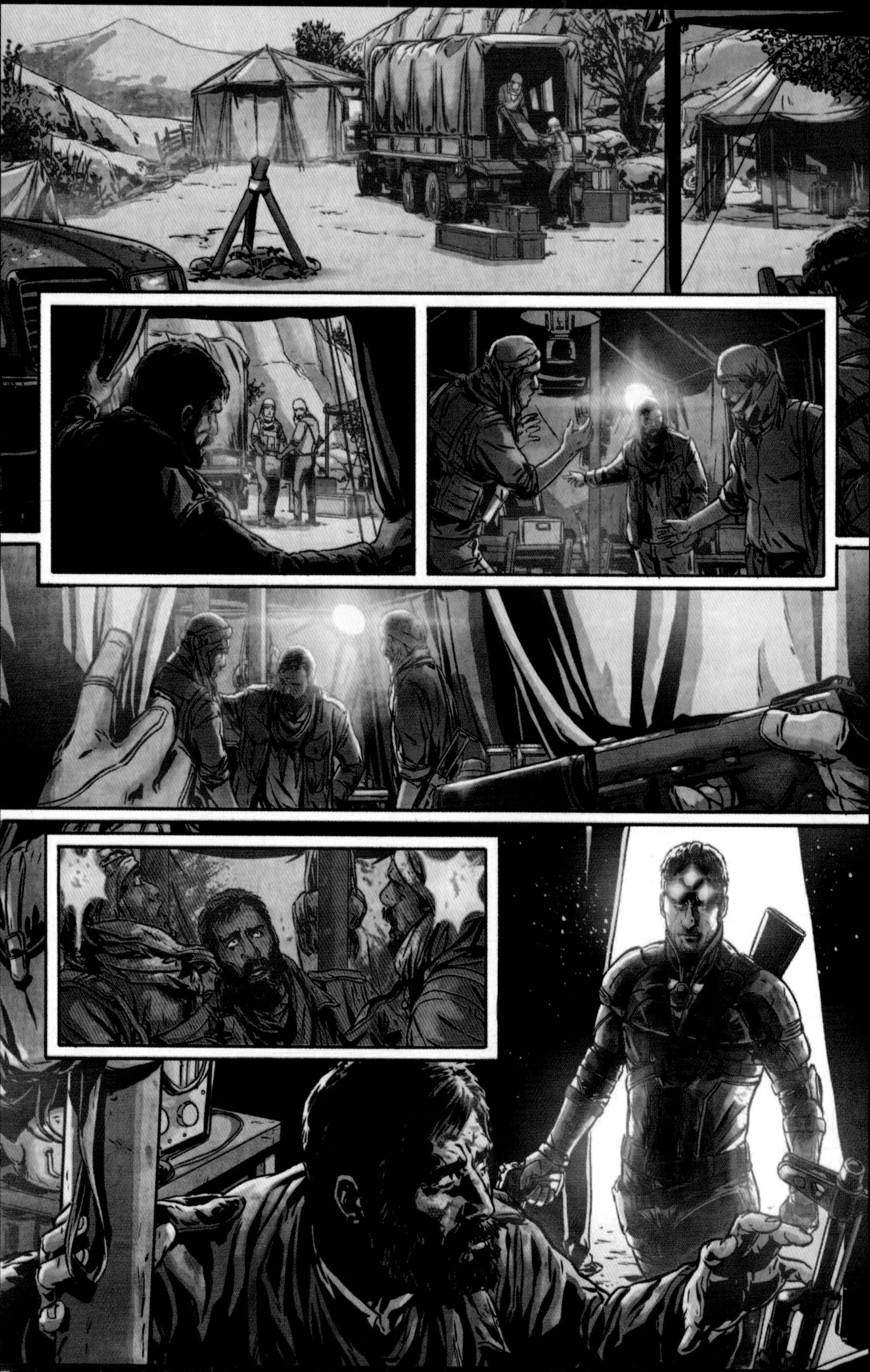

Test page colours by Ian Herring

TOM CLANCY'S®

SPLINTER CELL®

ECHOES

A SPECIAL INTERVIEW WITH WRITER NATHAN EDMONDSON

- Nathan, you are critically acclaimed as a writer, but are you a gamer as well? Were you familiar with the Tom Clancy *Splinter Cell* video game franchise [illegible]

[illegible]

The book does fall within the continuity of game [illegible] stands on its own as an espionage and combat thriller, accessible to anyone.

- For the uninitiated – and the franchise has sold more than 27 million copies worldwide since its introduction in 2002, so I do not know who those uninitiated would be – tell us about Sam Fisher.

Sam Fisher is a Splinter Cell — a counter-terrorism cover operative who engages alone using high-tech skills and subterfuge with a small support staff.

- This seems to be a rather personal story for your protagonist Fisher. Tell us a little bit about what he has gone through and will be going through in this limited series.

When the story opens, Sam has stepped out of the field and is trying to recover some of his life at home. It isn't long before he learns that his real home is out in the world, fighting terrorists.

- What is KROWE and what are they up to? (*No spoilers!*)

KROWE is a kind of terrorist group upstart that gets the chance to play in the big leagues.

- What (besides playing the games, lol) type of research did you do for *Echoes*? Did you work with central Clancy writer Richard Dansky at all?

We did work with Dansky, who is really the master of Sam's voice and that universe. We worked closely with Scott Lee, Patrick Redding and

others over at Ubisoft as well. Most other research was rather specific, but we kept in close consult with Ubisoft the whole way through.

‣ Will we get the espionage feel of *Black Widow* or *Punisher* in these pages? And conversely, should we look for Sam Fisher-like maneuvers in your Marvel spy books?

ECHOES is a unique book with its own tone, pace and voice. I wouldn't look to closely at my other titles for similarities — not intentional ones, anyone. The stories are about the characters and Sam is such a unique character, with his own past and universe and mythology that he carries onto the page.

‣ All tolled, what has been the biggest challenge in bringing a video game world into a comic book? Was there any works you looked to for inspiration?

The biggest challenge was finding Sam's voice. So many people have heard it — literally — in their heads and it was vital to translate that correctly in the comic in a way that didn't contradict the gaming experience but also spoke clearly to new readers.

‣ How was it like working with Marc Laming? Did he interpret your script in the manner you expected?

Marc is a fantastic illustrator and once we got our stride, he did his thing. He continued to collaborate with Ubisoft along the way to keep the story and game visuals consistent but he was in his zone and he did his thing.

‣ Marc was so good at establishing just the right atmosphere for *Exile on the Planet of the Apes* and in *Kings Watch*. Do you feel he succeeded for *Echoes*?

Absolutely, the look and feel of the book are perfect, and Ian Herring's colors of course added to that.

‣ If memory serves, you once worked in Washington D.C. before returning to Georgia. That time in our nation's capital explain why you are so good at spy/espionage sagas? (*laughs*)

I did, and most of my work was international. My time in that tenure certainly adds something to how I approach these kinds of stories.

‣ Nathan, tell us how you entered the comic book industry.

With Christian Ward and Olympus via Image Comics!

‣ As a writer, how does it feel to have one of your properties – the five-issue Image limited series *Who is Jake Ellis?* – be optioned for a film? And with David Yates attached to direct!

And Seth Lochhead writing! And Peter Chernin producing! An starring—

wait, I'm getting ahead of myself here. We're thrilled about what Ford Gilmore and David Yates and everyone have put together for us. With Jake Ellis — and a couple of other projects in film and TV — it's a true honor and thrill.

♣ Will you be doing any writing/consulting for the film? At what stage is the picture now?

I can't talk too much about all that, but I can say I'm pretty heavily involved in some film work now on different levels.

♣ You were on board with DC's New 52 relaunch, but it never seemed *Grifter* got off the ground concept-wise. You departed after eight issues. Can you discuss the problems there?

I try not to think about things like that, to be honest. You put together a book with an illustrator and it's all joy after the delivery. I try to be a better writer with each work and learn from each illustrator. And I've worked — and I'm working — with some very talented illustrators.

♣ Compare *Ellis'* Jon Moore and *Echoes'* Sam Fisher.

I think they're radically different. Jon Moore is a young analyst skating by in the espionage world with the aid of Jake Ellis, whereas Sam is a veteran bad ass who is best when he's on his own.

♣ What is it about stories like *Splinter Cell: Echoes* that excites you as a writer?

I feel with stories like this that I'm taking a pry bar to the world and looking at some of the dirty, lethal mechanics that make it turn. It's a thrill to see the shadows of covert warfare come alive around whatever character I can let loose into one of those worlds.

♣ So, do your tastes in other media (novels, films) tilt toward the noir?

Not especially, no.

♣ What is new on the horizon for Nathan Edmondson?

Stay tuned and I'm sure you'll see some announcements on twitter!

♣

TOM CLANCY'S
SPLINTER CELL
ECHOES
A SPECIAL INTERVIEW WITH ARTIST
MARC LAMING
INTERVIEW BY BYRON BREWER

❖ I first became aware of your art, Marc, around 2001 when you were penciling the great DC/Vertigo experiment by Howard Chaykin and David Tischman, *American Century.* The story of Harry Block/Kraft kind of had that espionage feel. Any comparisons of that work with Tom Clancy's *Splinter Cell: Echoes*?

The only comparisons I can draw are that both books are very grounded in their respective periods and therefore they required a great deal of research and reference to ensure that they feel 'real' enough to the reader. After working on SC:E I'm sure I'll be on serval government's watch lists just from my googling search requests. ;)

❖ Why are these noir tales of personal risk and shadow governments stories at which you excel? Is it your favorite fictional genre?

I really don't know and I guess that's really for others to answer but I guess that because I have quite an old fashioned comic strip like style that editors see my work suiting noir/action adventures stories most. I do enjoy drawing stories that contain quiet character moments and I've always liked the challenge of making 'talking head' pages interesting for the reader. And who doesn't like a troubled/flawed lead character?

I read all genres of fiction and I'm a veracious reader. The books I've most in enjoyed recently are Carlos Ruiz Zafon's 'Cemetery Of Lost Books' series and there's a huge slice of noir in those suppose.

❖ Did you study the *Splinter Cell* games in putting the character studies for *Echoes* together, or are the images we will be seeing in this four-issue limited series mostly Laming imagination?

My brief from Ubisoft was to bring the look & feel of Blacklist to SC:E so I immersed myself in the artwork and animatics that they sent me until I came up with what you see the book. Nathan & I were also guests at Ubisoft's Toronto studio for a few days so we got to see the game being developed and that fully allowed us to see how they were imagining Sam Fisher's world in Blacklist.

❖ Are there any characters in the limited series you wholly designed yourself? Not just tweaked, but virtually created?

There are a few, mostly the Krowe agents but Nathan & I were very aware of wanting to give Splinter Cell fans loads of Easter eggs to enjoy so must are tweaks from Sam's previous game adventures.

  ❖ Are you a gamer? If so, have you played *Blacklist, Chaos Theory* or any of the franchise?

Unfortunately drawing comic books doesn't allow much time for gaming these days although I did play 'Conviction' before we began the project to familarise myself with Sam's fighting style and stealth tactics.

  ❖ How similar will gamers familiar with the Tom Clancy *Splinter Cell* games find the art's "feel" in the books from Dynamite/Ubisoft?

·· ⸱ ⸱ ⸱ᵢₜₕ all the research and the conscious effort we made as
ₐₙd fₐₙ'ₛ ₒf

World. The art could not be less similar, yet beth the book. How do you develop that talent?

I think both of those series look like my work as a whole but I think I approached the atmosphere's of the books differently. POTA I saw as an intense WWII movie as directed by Corina Bechko & Gabriel Hardman and Jeff Parker's Kings Watch was a big splashy summer blockbuster so that lent itself to a more open illustration style.

  ❖ What is the greatest challenge in translating a video game into the comic book?

From my point of view it was staying 'on model' throughout the book.

  ❖ Was Sam Fisher your favorite character in *Echoes*?

Sam was fun to draw especially when in his ops suits but my favourite character to draw in the book was actually Sam's friend Victor Coste – he had a great mustache going on.

  ❖ What do you enjoy rendering most in such a book as this, one that has both high over-the-top action but also extremely character-suffering personal moments?

I enjoy both! Action scenes get you to stretch one set of muscles and the character stuff another and Nathan gave me plenty of both to draw in SC:E.

  ❖ Is Nathan Edmondson a hard writer with whom to work? How did you guys gel as a team on this limited series?

Nathan & I had already worked on an issue of his Image book 'The Activity' and we had worked together really well so we had a solid working relationship already before SC:E. We were also able to discuss the project face to face when Ubisoft had us visit them.

❖ Along the way, Marc, did you happen to work any with artists from the games, like Clancy art director Scott Lee?

I worked quite closely with Scott at the beginning of the project when we were still nailing down the mood and the look and feel of the artwork and he was extremely supportive and helpful during that process. Also, Scott tells the best stories...

❖ After this experience, do you think you would be interested in trying a stint as a game artist?

I can see the attraction of the games development world but I think I like the challenge of the storytelling in comics to much to dive in to being a games artist.

❖ To your understanding, the main difference between being a comic book artist vs. a game artist is ...?

The average pay scale hahahaha. ;)

❖ Tell me the story of how you became an artist? What comic book artists did you admire/emulate as a youth?

I've always read and always drawn since I could hold a crayon and I almost can't remember a time when comics weren't in my life. My Dad would often buy comics for me on his way home from work -UK weekly comics like with great titles like Victor, Shiver & Shake, Valiant, Buster & TV Countdown and the British Marvel reprints like Mighty World of Marvel & Spider-Man Weekly. My love of comics continued to grow and like I was with book I read everything regardless of genre. At the age of 10 we were asked to write a piece for school about 'what we wanted to be when we grew up' and my answer was 'an artist or inker for Marvel Comics' and I don't think my mind ever changed from that point on.

I went on to study illustration & graphic design at a college that didn't consider comics a career so I spent three years not thinking about comics and doing as much drawing & painting as I could. But comics never really went away and thanks to being able to put comics by the likes of Bill Sienkiewicz and Dave McKean under my tutors noses they let me do a comics based project for my final show. Pretty soon after I graduated I got my first work in comics on the strength of that project working on the Revolver anthology Romance Special. I was totally out of my depth and really needed to go away and learn how to do comics properly! I worked as a graphic designer for a few years which taught me loads about design and page layout but it wasn't comics and it wasn't long before I was putting a portfolio of samples together and self pub-lishing comics. That lead to meeting Andy Lanning at a UK convention who was, and still is, very encouraging about my work and he introduced me to Shelly Bond which lead eventually to me working for DC.

I've always been a fan of the artists like Al Williamson, Howard Chaykin, Alex Toth, Gil Kane, Jack Kirby, Jeff Jones, Charles Schultz, Giles, Barry Windsor-Smith, Frank Belamy, Frank Hampson, Milton Caniff, Dave Sim, Frank Robbins – the list could go on and on and they have all been an influence in one way or another

> ♣ If you could work on one existing comic book, what would it be and what about that character(s) attracts you?

I've been so lucky in the last few years and had a chance to work on characters that I've always been a big fan of. I'm currently getting to draw Captain America in the Invaders which is dream come true but I'd love to draw Solomon Kane, Conan or Shang Chi.

> ♣ What did you think of *Echoes'* big-bads, KROWE?

They were a lot of fun to draw and just the sort of very real nasties that Nathan is so good at writing.

> ♣ Who would be your dream writer with whom to work (aside from Nathan Edmondson, of course, lol)?

I've been blessed with the people I've had the great fortune to work with – Howard Chaykin, Bill Willingham, Garbiel & Corinna, Nathan, Jeff Parker, Gary Phillips, Nate Cosby, James Robinson, Rachel Deering – all such good writers so I've been spoilt already.

> ♣ Marc, any projects present or future you'd like to discuss?

I could tell you, but in Sam Fisher fashion, if I did I'd have to kill you. ;)

♣

TOM CLANCY'S
SPLINTER CELL
ECHOES
A SPECIAL INTERVIEW WITH
SCOTT LEE
INTERVIEW BY BYRON BREWER

❖ So, Scott, how does a guy with a degree in fine arts from the University of British Columbia wind up a Tom Clancy video game franchise art director and one of the creative minds behind *Splinter Cell: Echoes*?

I've been fortunate as an artist to have had such a long career with opportunities to work on exciting high profile projects across the entertainment spectrum. My experience as a comic book artist has helped me immensely in my role as an Art Director so I guess helping to create a comic book from a video game was a natural progression.

❖ Tell us a little about the process of designing/creating a video game. How is it, say, different from working/creating at DC Comics?

At the core, the creative process of creating games and comic books is very similar, however creating video games expands on the process exponentially. In comic books, storytelling is the focus. This is a very important part of video game development as well. When creating video games at Ubisoft, we start with the gameplay innovation, making sure that the game is fun for the player, and then we expand on it with the story. Above all, the biggest difference is the fact that a comic team consists of the artist and writer making decisions on the fly and with games there are a few...hundred more people involved.

❖ Did you design or were you a part of a team that designed Sam Fisher?

The opportunity to put your own spin on an iconic character is every artist's dream. For me, as a fan of the Splinter Cell series, I really wanted to bring the iconic silhouette of his original OPsuit back. I infused the old comic character tradition of giving airtight reason and function for everything on the character and recreated Sam's operations suit with this in mind – every piece of armour, every sensor, every gadget has a function and reason for being there. For his physical characteristics we really wanted to honor the previous iterations of Sam, all the while making him much more expressive than he had ever been before.

❖ What are the mechanics in visually translating a video game into a comic book? Did you work with *Echoes* artist Marc Laming?

Splinter Cell is a franchise that strives for absolute realism both in look and emotional tone, so translating that into a comic book we relied heavily on the aesthetic of the artist. We chose Mark because his art is subtle, subdued, and mature. So aside from the tenet of visual cues from the Splinter Cell universe, we made certain Mark's style stayed true and uncompromised. I really think comics lose their soul when art or writing styles are shoe horned to fit other mediums – I feel it's why adapted comics are often so poorly done.

❖ Tell about your involvement in the creation of *Echoes*.

From the moment I started at Ubisoft Toronto, Jade Raymond our Managing Director expressed her desire to deepen the Splinter Cell Franchise through other mediums including comic books. Creative ~~~ Poland. Game Director Pat Redding, and I set out with a ~~~~~~ suited to comic books. Most ~~~~~ful, enrich

❖ Rumor has it that things ~~~. Comic Con?

Actually, I began working as a comic book artist after attending my first ever San Diego Comicon in the 90s.

❖ How competitive was that, all out there by your lonesome?

I sort of went in oblivious and over-confident; until the first portfolio review line that is. After waiting in lineups the entire first day and getting a range of reviews from "it's not bad" to "you're not good enough to get published", I decided to just enjoy the Con and see the floor rather than wait in lines the entire weekend.

❖ How did you go to work with DC? Talk about some of your first assignments and experiences there. Most memorable to me as a reader is your tenure on *Teen Titans* with the great Marv Wolfman.

On the 2nd day of that Con, I happened to walk past the big DC booth and saw someone just sitting behind a table. I asked if he could have a look at my portfolio – as fate would have it, Neal Pozner, the late great DC Editor, flipped through my pages and offered me an issue of DC Showcase right on the spot. I was a huge Perez/Wolfman Titans fan so eventually getting to work with Marv was a huge honor.

❖ Tell us about those magic days of working with Joe Quesada, now Chief Creative Officer at Marvel Comics. How did that come about and was Joe Q.'s art something that influenced you as an artist?

Joe had just created Event Comics doing the incredible series Ash. He happened to get a hold of my portfolio at another San Diego Comicon and wanted to meet me. My portfolio had some fill in pages from X-Force among other things with an unusual Disney-esque alpine village in the double page splash. I was worried because I didn't have a whole lot of that 90s gritted teeth muscle-bound goodness but he actually loved the audaciousness of doing something so different. He took a chance and gave me the Ash spinoff series 22 Brides with Fabian Nicieza writing and Jimmy Palmiotti inking my pencils. Honestly Joe's love for originality and different styles really transformed the scape of the comic industry and made it what it is today. Joe was the most patient and sharing teacher a young artist could ever hope for and though I never emulated his art style he certainly was the biggest influence on my career in every other way.

❧ Speaking of influences, what other artists in any field influence your work today? Did you have a specific mentor?

Today I'm inspired constantly by great books, comics, movies, and games. The sophistication seen in today's comic book film adaptations is also evident in the latest video games. The audience now demands meaningful stories, limit pushing visual fidelity, and a rich experience in general. We are competing with all sorts of entertainment and I draw my inspirations from the same.

❧ Is it true that after graduation from the University of British Columbia, your second career choice was as a Wall Street broker? Usually creativity and mathematics do not mix! (laughs)

I was a huge fan of Oliver Stone's Wall Street. Suffice it to say that this career path lasted until I dropped out of 1st year Calculus.

❧ Scott, how did you come to enter the video game field? I heard something about … a dinner party?

Interestingly enough, I met my good friend Marc Baril, a video game music director and composer at a dinner. We had a chat about his work at Radical and he suggested I try my hand at concept art for one of the games he was working on. I loved games but I never gave any thought to working in it – Once I did, the medium just felt right and for an artist, getting your work seen by ever bigger audiences is really the ultimate goal.

❧ You worked on *Prototype* for Radical Entertainment?

I was brought on to Prototype in the final year of development to help ship the game. Radical was an internal Activision studio by then and all other projects were cancelled except for Prototype. Needless to say a lot weighed on this title. Ultimately I'm very proud of how it turned out – I think the innovation and fun factor was really underrated.

❧ As an artist, a creator, what are the differences between working in the video game industry from the comics industry? Which did you enjoy the most?

I think the biggest difference is scope. Both the scope of the work and the work process itself. Creating comics is by and large a solitary pursuit but the personal rewards and sense of achievement is immediate. Video games on the other hand are truly team efforts and enjoyed by a huge audience. I do miss the creative purity of comics but I'm in games for the long haul and enjoying it immensely.

❖ So how did you wind up at Ubisoft Toronto?

I was working on Max Payne 3 and the opportunity to come to Ubisoft Toronto came up. Having the chance to be part of the core team at a brand new studio is rare enough, but to do it with a company like Ubisoft was really something that comes once in a lifetime. The core crew here was a who's who of top flight action game veterans and that really sealed it for me.

designed the comic to be accessible to fans of the
universe. We knew instinctively that a four issue comic book run would be the perfect medium for us to tell that story.

❖ What do you think of Marc Laming's interpretations of the *Splinter Cell* universe?

Marc and Nathan Edmondson absolutely nailed our universe. Their interpretation really echoed the emotional tone we worked hard to establish in Blacklist. The sophistication I spoke of earlier, the maturity, and not giving into the temptation of over-the-top theatrics. Splinter Cell is about stealth, observation, and slowly building the tension to unbearable crescendos. I feel Echoes does the same and beautifully so.

❖ *Blacklist* and its launch are very important to Ubisoft Toronto, correct?

Splinter Cell Blacklist was definitely a studio builder. Being a new studio we absolutely needed to establish an incredibly high level of quality while reinvigorating the franchise at the same time. I'm very proud of the team and the project and the superlatives we received from fans and reviewers.

❖ What is your favorite part of *Splinter Cell: Echoes*?

It was seeing Sam Fisher at home, hanging out with his daughter Sarah, and having a cold one on his front porch. I can't tell you how much depth that adds to his character. In games we can rarely afford the opportunity to flesh out the lives of characters but comics can. It is the perfect medium to tell a side of his story that really couldn't be told in any other way.

⁂ So what is down the road for artist Scott Lee?

Bigger and better games of course and always following the pursuit of tearing apart boundaries when it comes to video game graphics and look. Doing one of the covers for Splinter Cell Echoes woke the old penciller in me. I'm actually itching to get back into creating comics! I'm hoping people may get to see some of my work.

⁂

TOM CLANCY'S
SPLINTER CELL
ECHOES

A SPECIAL INTERVIEW WITH
RICHARD DANSKY
INTERVIEW BY BYRON BREWER

❖ So, Richard, did the fact that you were a game master for *Villains and Vigilantes* back at Wesleyan University lead you into a life of writing video

games were the ...
chance to try my hand at them at Red Storm.

❖ Tell us how you came from White Wolf and developing *Wraith: The Oblivion* to chief Clancy writer for Ubisoft.

A friend of mine named David Weinstein, who was a networking engineer at Red Storm at the time, liked my work in tabletop and got on me to apply. I was starting to look around for new challenges at that point, and video games seemed like the logical way to go. I'd had a couple of near misses with other video game companies before that, but it was an amazing surprise to actually get the offer from RSE. That was back in 1999, or, to put it another way, so long ago that people in the game industry (myself included) had unironic mullets. But regardless, I was very lucky to find myself at a place where I could learn and transition from tabletop to video game design and writing, and where I got the chance to work on some remarkable games.

❖ How important is the *Splinter Cell: Blacklist* game to Ubisoft? Can you tell us how the idea for a bridging comic book like *Splinter Cell: Echoes* came about?

We'd actually done a small teaser comic before Conviction that showed Sam doing some of the legwork that ultimately led him to hunting down Andriy Kobin, and I was always kind of hoping we would expand on that. Even though we didn't, that sort of cleared the ground, as it were, on the idea of showing some of Sam's adventures between games.

Comics seemed like a great way to do this. One is that every medium has stories that it tells better than any other medium, and there were certain stories about Sam - the ones set in those gaps between games - that just worked perfectly as comics. Honestly, I think the story in Echoes works far better as a comic than it would as gameplay - the structure's perfectly in tune with what comics does so well.

❖ You had a lot to do with the creation of *Echoes*. Have you had any meetings with limited series writer Nathan Edmondson?

I had the pleasure of meeting Nathan in Toronto, and corresponding with him online. He's an incredible talent who flat-out knows his stuff. Seeing that kind of respect for getting the material right - both the tradecraft and the Splinter Cell-specific material - is just a great feeling. You know the stuff you've worked on is in good hands.

❖ I know you have published media tie-in novels before, like *Clan Novel Lasombra* and the *Trilogy of the Second Age*. Have you ever had a desire to perhaps script a comic book?

Funny you should say that, he said as he hastily closed the script he was working on. I've always been a big comics reader, to the point where I'm pretty sure I'm the only working game writer out there with a complete set of the Dennys O'Neal run on The Question, so writing comics has always been a wistful dream of mine. There's a couple of personal projects I'm working on now - not that I wouldn't drop them in a heart-beat to write The Mad Adventures of Andriy Kobin - that hopefully will see the light of day someday. I've gotten a lot of great encouragement from friends who work in comics, so with luck, one of these days I'll do them proud.

❖ How were you affected, as a game developer and personally, by the death of Tom Clancy? Did that change in any way the manner in which you see your role as Clancy head writer?

Honestly, it was more as a reader and a fan that it impacted me. One of the nice things about working on the Tom Clancy's games is that the hallmarks of what makes a Clancy game are so very clear that they make fantastic guidelines. It's easy to tell if what you're doing fits in his paradigm or not. Mr. Clancy hadn't been directly involved in the games for quite some time when he passed away, but his influence was always present and clear.

I will say, incidentally, that one of the unexpected benefits of the role has been getting to know Mr Clancy's son, Thom, who's a game dev himself and a great guy. I'm looking forward to seeing what he does in our medium.

❖ You have said in the past that your parents were both voracious readers and that you were encouraged to read at an early age. Is that where the desire to tell your own stories developed?

Very much so. The first fiction I read as fiction was *The Chronicles of Narnia*, which my mother the former English teacher force-fed me in third grade when I was sick with chicken pox. From there I got into Lloyd Alexander and Ray Bradbury, and even if you're 8 years old, you're going to come away from reading Bradbury for the first time wanting to tell stories of your own.

Which is exactly what happened to me. Mom set me up with a copy of *The Halloween Tree* - it was a really long case of chicken pox - and like that, I had the bug. It took a while to manifest, but that's the earliest moment I can remember thinking I wanted to tell stories. Now, here we are 35 years later and I'm writing games about Sam Fisher and stories about sasquatches who moonlight as private eyes. So I guess whatever sneaky plan my mom had all those years ago, it worked.

  ❖ I believe you said in an interview once that your dad had a big influence on how you view your writing. How so?

My father was and is a huge speculative fiction fan, and he had a huge
in third grade, I just started

minimums. But just talking with my
which he enjoyed strictly as a reader, is a great and constant reminder to me to always keep the audience in mind. It's not about me being clever or getting off a zinger one-liner or anything other than what the audience gets out of it, and I owe that 24/7 awareness to Dad.

  ❖ Which genre do you enjoy more: the noir world of Sam Fisher or the demonic world of horror you have put into original novels like your *Firefly Rain*? Do you miss playing with vampires? (laughs)

I didn't miss playing with vampires. Ghosts, on the other hand, well, that's a whole other story...

One of the great things about the sort of subject matter dichotomy is that they are so diverse, and so they scratch different itches. I'm a total foreign policy geek, so writing in the Clancyverse is a chance to play in one of my favorite sandboxes. And it's so distinct from the horror writing I do for my personal project that switching from one to the other feels like I'm doing two different things, not two variations on one thing. And that makes all the difference in keeping the creativity stoked and pumping.

  ❖ From what I have observed, you really seem to have a passion for Fisher, your Clancy protagonist. Tell us about the character from your perspective.

I love writing Sam Fisher. The way I approach him is based to a certain extent on some guys I knew in high school who just sort of hung out in the quad and smoked and then all of a sudden, graduation hit and they had to pull themselves and their lives together for the next step. And in a lot of ways, that's Sam, and so I always feel like I might have known him.

And of course, I love the fact that he's this force for good who's capable of these astonishing acts of violence as needed. He's this incredible bundle of contradictions, a guy who wants to be a good dad who's always off in strange places risking his life, a moral figure in this vast grey landscape, and having that sort of tension built into a character makes it really fun to write.

And of course, the one-liners don't hurt, either.

> ❖ Can you tell us about the changes Fisher goes through in the *Echoes*, which was designed as a bridge between *Conviction* and *Blacklist*?

There are two, really. One is that we see Sam slowly but inexorably being drawn back into the world he'd walked away from at the end of Conviction. It's his friend Vic Coste who does it, because he recognizes that Sam needs to be doing something with these talents he has, something he can feel good about doing. And that's why he hooks up with Vic's company in the comic, as a way to use his skills and scratch that itch and do some good, on his terms, too. So the positioning of Sam as working with Vic Coste on this sets up their relationship in Blacklist nicely.

And the other thing we see is Sam coming to terms with what he does and how he does it, and how that can still be very useful to the world. Try as he might, Sam's just not the sort of guy who can put on black knee socks and cargo shorts and a plaid shirt and mow the lawn on Sundays - he's just not wired that way. And so Sam coming to grips with the fact that everything else aside, he's good at this and he kind of likes being good at it, well, that's an important thing for Sam to understand about himself. And that helps him transition to becoming the leader of this team in the game that originally, he didn't ask for or really want.

> ❖ Sam has some iconic elements about him, gadgets that harken to James Bond (trifocal goggles, the Stealth suit, etc.). Why do you like these items and which is your favorite?

There's just something about the sound the goggles make when they're activated that says "Splinter Cell" to me in a way that nothing else does. So the goggles have it strictly on the audio, and that's before you get to that iconic glow in the darkness. The other elements like the suit are great, but there's nothing in the world like hearing those goggles go off to make you feel seriously Sam Fisher-style badass.

> ❖ Unlike Bond, Fisher seems to prefer to be discreet. No fancy shoes or tuxes; he seems just a regular guy who would rather blend into a crowd. Correct?

Q: Absolutely. One of the things that always resonated with me about Sam was that he was absolutely pragmatic about how he went about his business. He was never interested in credit or standing out, because let's face it, in his line of work, you stand out, you're likely to get forcibly retired very quickly. So he stays hidden, he doesn't draw attention to himself, he blends into the crowds and he gets the job done, which is the point of the exercise.

I will say that somewhere in Ubi Toronto there's a document detailing everything Sam likes, from his favorite reading material to his favorite beer to the sports teams he roots for. Would you believe the guy's an Orioles fan?

❖ Would you say Fisher is a reluctant hero, and why or why not?

I think to Sam, "hero" is a loaded term and it's one he's very careful of. Sam's very much a pragmatist. He's very good at his job and he understands how important it is, but he's also keenly aware of how much violence he's responsible for along the way. And of course, he knows that one side's hero is another side's villain, and that even the most noble and necessary good deeds have consequences. Or, to put it another way, hired goons and gun-toting mercenaries have families, too, and Sam is ⸱ ⸱ ⸱ ⸱ beyond the immediate.

and he tries hard, but ⸱⸱⸱ ⸱ ⸱ point in his life, and by the time we get to *Blacklist*, he's matured. He's gotten Sarah back into his life, he's lost her and found her again, and he's gotten perspective from inside and outside the system. And I think that helped him involve into someone who was a little more fiercely protective of the people he considers family, which, by the end of Blacklist, encompasses the team. And that's a good thing for Sam, as he's moved from lone wolf to leader of the pack. He needs to get into a place where he can trust other people enough to do things he instinctively wants to do himself to make sure they're "done right". You can't trust people that way without caring about them a bit, too, and as we've learned, Sam's always going to try to protect the people he cares about.

❖ What changes to the man did the apparent death of his daughter Sarah bring?

Ultimately, thinking that he had lost Sarah really focused Sam in some frightening ways. She really was his anchor to the world outside his job, and he'd just started getting to a point where he was comfortable being her dad again when she was "killed". And losing her, once he had time to go through the grieving process, really focused Sam on doing what he did best to find out who'd killed her. Which meant diving into some really murky waters, but that sort of determination to act, without the voice in his ear telling him where to go next and regardless of cost, that was a very interesting side of Sam to write.

❖ What would you like the *Echoes* comic book series achieve for *Blacklist*?

I think the comic did two things. It did a great job of providing context for the opening of Blacklist, where Sam is working directly with his old friend Vic Coste in a way that might be surprising after the way Conviction ended. And it's just a great Splinter Cell story. Getting both of those under one cover was like hitting the jackpot.

♣ What is on the horizon after *Blacklist* for Sam Fisher?

That, I'm afraid, is classified. Though if they ask me to write for Splinter Cell: Cart Racing, I'm in.

♣ And what is on the horizon for writer Richard Dansky?

Within Ubi? All sorts of interesting things. Outside of Ubi? Well, I'm getting back into tabletop RPG design with the 20th anniversary edition of W*raith: The Oblivion*, and I'm continuing to write my own fiction. And there might be a card game about single malt whisky and Bigfoot coming down the pike at some point, but that's a whole other discussion.

♣

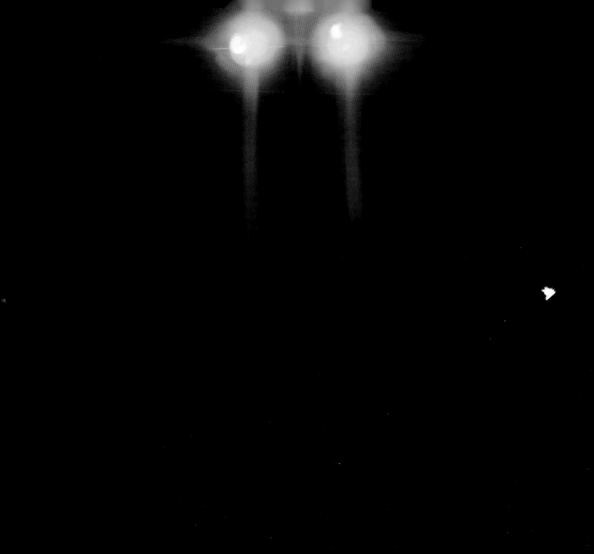

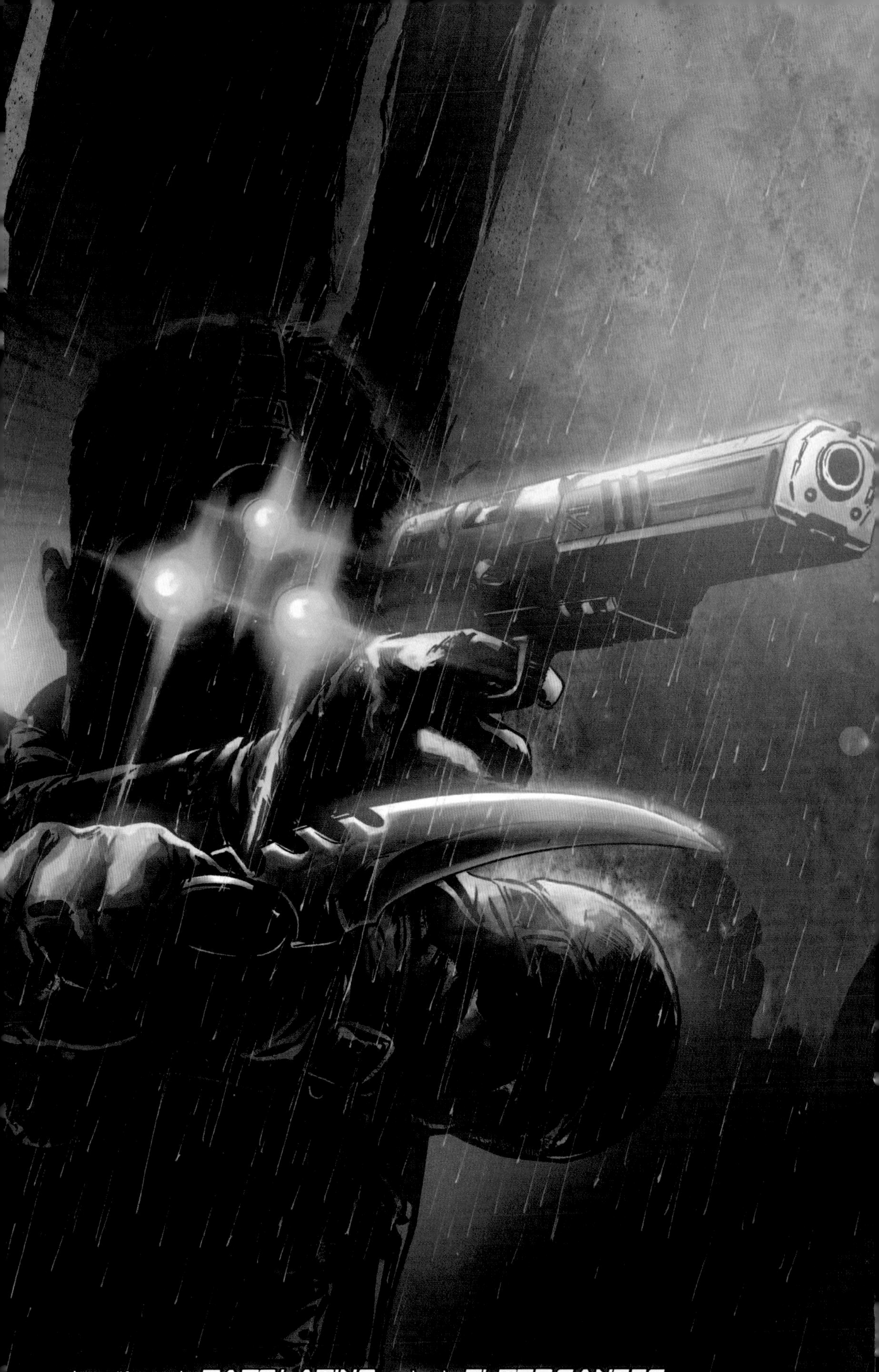

issue #1 cover by MARC LAMING colors by ELMER SANTOS

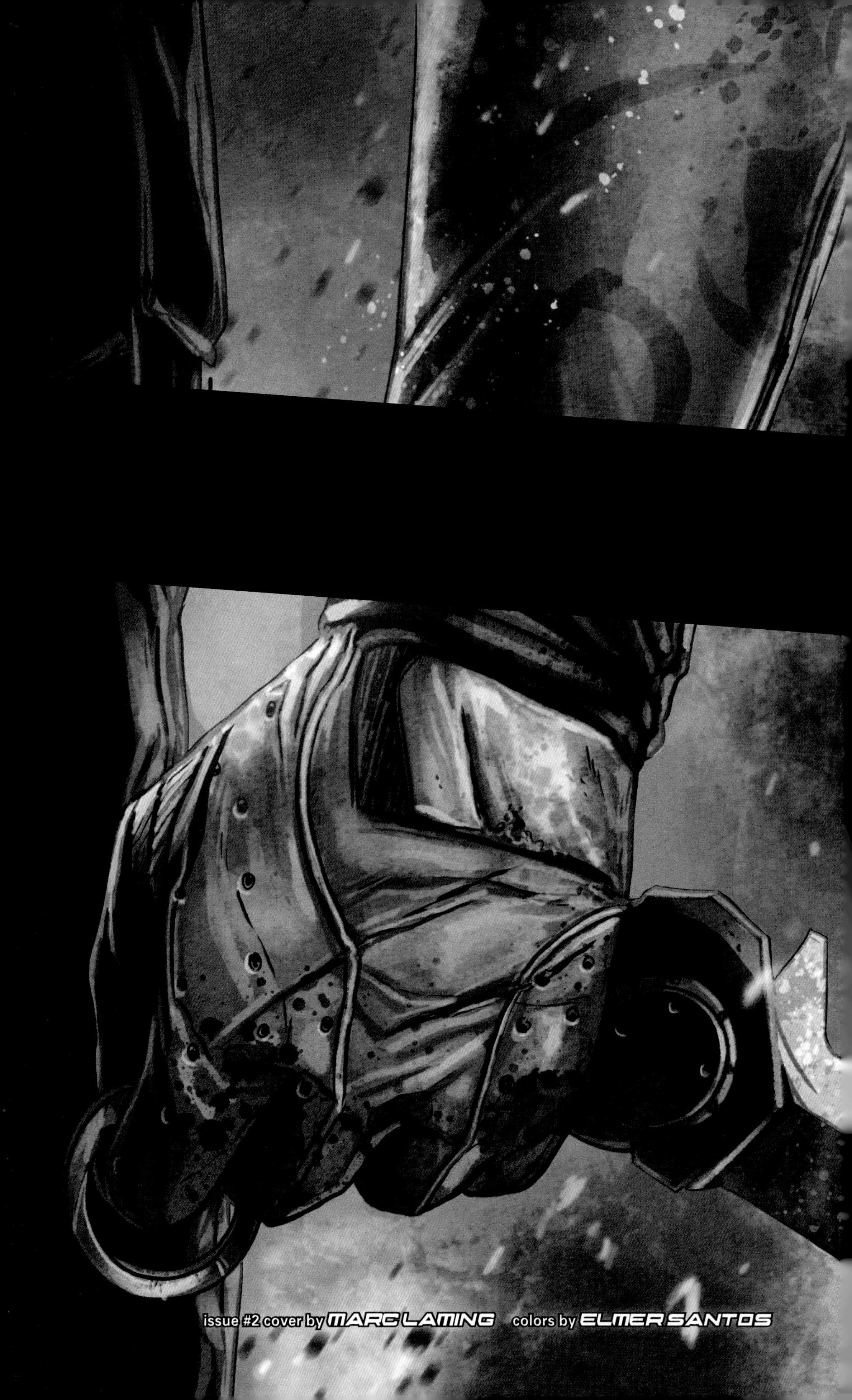

issue #2 cover by MARC LAMING colors by ELMER SANTOS

issue #3 cover by **MARC LAMING**   colors by **ELMER SANTOS**

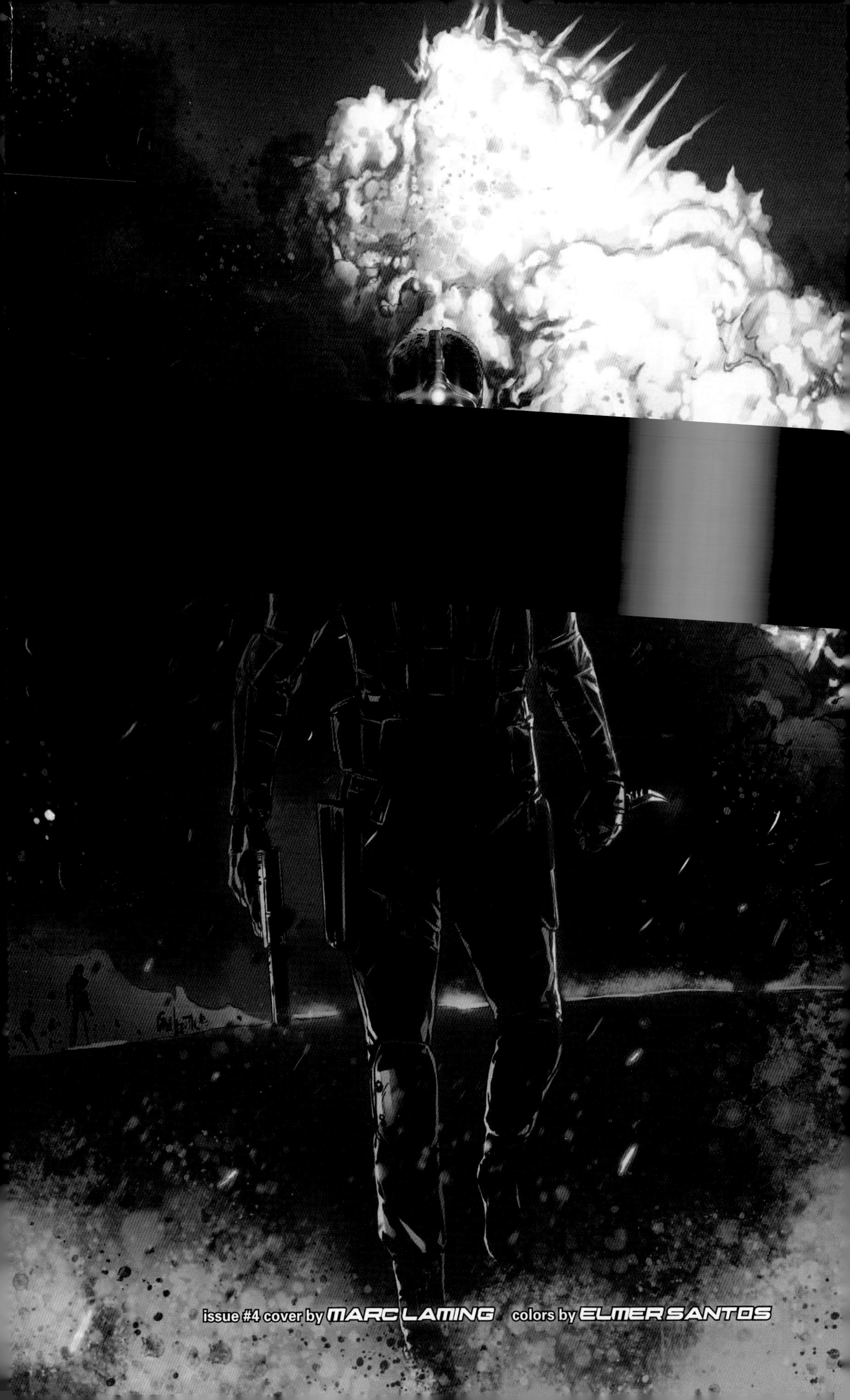

issue #4 cover by MARC LAMING colors by ELMER SANTOS